THE RUSSIAN JOURNALS OF
THE MARQUIS DE CUSTINE

JOURNEY FOR
OUR TIME

THE RUSSIAN JOURNALS OF
THE MARQUIS DE CUSTINE

JOURNEY FOR OUR TIME

Edited and translated by
PHYLLIS PENN KOHLER

INTRODUCTION BY GENERAL
WALTER BEDELL SMITH

GATEWAY EDITIONS
Washington, D.C.

Manufactured in the United States of America
1991 printing

Library of Congress Cataloging-in-Publication Data

Custine, Astolphe, marquis de, 1790–1857.
  [Russie en 1839, English]
  Journey for our time: the Russian journals of
the Marquis de Custine/edited and translated by
Phyllis Penn Kohler; introduction by Walter Bedell
Smith.
      p.   cm.
  Translation is based on the 3rd French ed. of
La Russie en 1839.
      "A Gateway edition."
      1. Soviet Union—Description and travel.
2.Custine, Astolphe, marquis de, 1790–1857—
Journeys—Soviet Union.
I. Kohler, Phyllis Penn.   II. Title.
DK25.C9713   1987
914.7′0473—dc19
ISBN 0-89526-786-1   87-22383

Published in the United States by
Regnery Gateway
1130 17th Streeet, NW
Washington DC 20036

Distributed to the trade by
National Book Network
4720-A Boston Way
Lanham, MD 20706

CONTENTS

v

Contents

vi

Contents

Contents

THE RUSSIAN JOURNALS OF
THE MARQUIS DE CUSTINE

JOURNEY FOR
OUR TIME

NOTE

THE *Marquis de Custine's* Russia in 1839 *was first published in Paris in 1843. In 1844 there was a second edition, and in 1846 a third—reviewed, corrected and augmented by the author. At this period, translations appeared in England and other European countries. D. Appleton and Co. published an abridged translation in the United States in 1854. The work was revived in France in 1946 in the form of an abridgement entitled* Lettres de Russie *published by Les Editions de la Nouvelle France.*

My translation is based on the third French edition of La Russie en 1839 (*Librairie d'Amyot, Editeur, Paris, 1846—4 volumes, approximately 400 pages each) and I wish to acknowledge my appreciation to Admiral Leslie C. Stevens for the use of his copy of this edition. The omitted sections cover principally Custine's review of his family history, stories, anecdotes, and conversations without general interest or present-day consequence, lengthy descriptive passages, and voluminous notes and appendices. Wherever notes seemed essential to a proper understanding of the text, those of the author appear in parentheses and my own in brackets.*

JOURNEY FOR OUR TIME *came out of my Russian experience. My husband and I were assigned to the American Embassy in Moscow from Feb-*

ruary 1947 to July 1949 and it was there that we, along with our embassy colleagues, were introduced to the writings of the Marquis de Custine and deeply impressed by this century-old analysis of our current experiences. We all said repeatedly that the Marquis' journal on Russia should be read by all Westerners and sighed over the fact that it was not available in English. However, the years went by and neither our concerted opinion nor our sighs produced any tangible result—Custine was still a long-closed book to the English-speaking public.

One day last year we were at General Smith's with a few of our old Moscow companions. The conversation, as usual in such gatherings, fell on Russia and, in turn, on Custine. The same old sighs, the same old question—why doesn't someone translate Custine?

A few days later I was writing a letter to a friend. I was trying to answer a question about the Russian people (apparently anyone who has lived in Russia qualifies as an expert and should be able to answer all questions). My ideas wouldn't gel. I turned to Custine for help. I started translating passages here and there. The conversation at General Smith's flashed through my mind—the old question with its frayed edges—why doesn't someone translate Custine? Suddenly a variation occurred to me: Why shouldn't I? I could find the time.

Well, it took more time than I had expected, but my interest grew continually and gradually assumed the proportions of true missionary zeal.

4

Note

My letter is finally finished and ready for publication—with an introduction by General Walter Bedell Smith. I trust it answers my friend's question.

PHYLLIS PENN KOHLER

New York, February 15, 1951

INTRODUCTION

THE READERS of this journal are about to share a most thrilling and enlightening experience—acquaintance with the Marquis de Custine. Here are colorful, dramatic, and accurate accounts of Russia and the Russians. Here is the first "fellow-traveler's" confession of disillusionment with a god that always failed. Here is political observation so penetrating and timeless that it could be called the best work so far produced about the Soviet Union. Here is the measure of the extent to which the Stalinist régime is turning the clock back in Russia.

We "discovered" the Marquis de Custine early in the second year of my tour as American Ambassador in Moscow. We owe this fortunate acquaintance to the existence in Moscow of second-hand bookshops, which even the far-reaching controls of the Soviet Police do not always succeed in ridding of publications lately found unsuitable for the reading public. For the Soviet régime had, itself, discovered the Marquis some seventeen years earlier, and in 1930 had published an abridged edition of his letters under the title of *Nicholas' Russia—La Russie en 1839*. We were unable to ascertain at exactly what point it dawned upon the rulers in the Kremlin that Custine's observations were as revealing with respect to their own despotic régime as to the des-

7

potism of Czar Nicholas I. It was clear, however, that many years before my arrival on the scene the 1930 Russian edition of these letters had been removed from the approved to the black list of publications.

Astolphe de Custine was born into the French aristocracy in 1790, during the period of great civil upheaval in France. His father, François de Custine, and his grandfather, General Phillippe de Custine, were guillotined during the Reign of Terror in the early days of the Revolution. His mother barely escaped the same fate after many months in prison. An established traveler and journalist with an anti-revolutionary background and well-known monarchical ideas, Custine went to Russia in 1839 "to find arguments against representative government." He returned to France, after accomplishing astounding feats of travel and observation, "a partisan of constitutions." He was thus, in a sort of reverse sense, the first of the fellow-travelers to make public confession of his disillusionment.

The parallels which could be drawn between the reactions of Custine and deluded latter-day visitors to the Soviet Union—Gide, Koestler, and Silone—are infinite and would themselves constitute a fascinating study. In general, they demonstrate that Russian despotism, whether viewed from the right or the left, is repugnant to the ideas and ideals of our civilization. Above all, these partisans have uniformly been shocked by the contradiction between the pretense and the reality. "I do not blame the Russians for being what they are," said Custine; "I blame them for pretending to be what we are." A century later his fellow countryman, André Gide, put it this way: "I blame the Soviet Union not for having failed to achieve more . . . what I complain of is the extent of their bluff . . . this from the country of my hopes and trust was painful to me." *

But more than most of his modern successors, the Marquis de Custine was a trained political observer imbued with a broad knowledge and understanding of history and political and cultural developments. His journal is therefore less an account of his personal soul-searching than a thorough and penetrating analysis of the basic character of the society in which he found himself.

Custine's letters were the greatest single contribution in helping us to unravel, in part, the mysteries that seem to envelop Russia and the Russians. For, like Custine, we Americans in Moscow felt ourselves in a profoundly different and strange civilization. His observations, as fresh as yesterday despite their age of a century, served to bring the Soviet Union into perspective better than any of our previous readings, studies, and observations. They underscored the fact that the problem is not something new, not merely the product of a so-called Communist Revolution which took place some thirty years ago, but one of the epochal problems in the development of the history of man. This same service Custine can perform for others who now gain access to his

* *The God That Failed,* pp. 194-5, New York: Harper & Brothers, 1950.

work. And a world-wide understanding of this problem is essential if there is ever to be the development of a Russian nation which will play a constructive rather than a destructive rôle. It is not enough and basically it is not true to say, as so many have said to me, that the Russian people are like people everywhere and only the Government is different.

The people, too, are different. They are different because wholly different social and political conditions have retarded and perverted their development and set them apart from other civilizations. This Custine points up graphically: "Russia alone, belatedly civilized, has been deprived of a profound fermentation and of the benefit of a slow and natural cultural development, because of the impatience of her leaders."

We take for granted the factors which are responsible for the differences between the Russians and ourselves. While the Western world was progressing under the stimuli of the Renaissance, the Reformation, the Age of Exploration and Discovery, and the Industrial Revolution, the Russian peoples were held in a condition of abject ignorance and social and economic slavery under the Czars. Thus, their background lacks many of the ideas and ideals which are basic in the formation of the Western character: the respect for the individual and the concept of the State as his servant, which come to us from classical Greece and Rome; the ethical heritage derived largely from the recorded experience of an ancient and advanced civilization in the Holy Land incorporated

10

Introduction

into the teachings of our dominant religions; and
the traditions of individual initiative and independence, acquired through the exploration and
settlement of the world's frontiers.

Custine vividly describes the resultant society
as well as its physical framework. I could have
taken many pages verbatim from his journal and,
after substituting present-day names and dates for
those of a century ago, have sent them to the State
Department as my own official reports. Washington would have found them in complete harmony
with what I had had to say about my experiences
and observations. It might only have wondered
how I had acquired a more fluid and colorful
style.

My own position and that of my staff as foreign
diplomats in the Soviet Union showed little variation from that of our predecessors accredited to
the Czarist court a century before. In both eras
one finds the same restrictions, the same surveillance, the same suspicion. Custine can say: "The
diplomatic corps and Westerners in general have
always been considered by this Government, with
its Byzantine spirit, and by Russia as a whole, as
malevolent and jealous spies." A century later
Soviet Major General Sarayev, a member of the
wartime Soviet Military Mission in Washington,
admits to us quite frankly that all foreign officials
"are considered potential spies." The handicaps
which this attitude and its corollary practices
place on Western diplomacy could not be better
described than in Custine's words: "If better diplomats are found among the Russians than among

11

highly civilized peoples, it is because our papers warn them of everything that happens and everything that is contemplated in our countries. Instead of disguising our weaknesses with prudence, we reveal them with vehemence every morning; whereas the Russians' Byzantine policy, working in the shadow, carefully conceals from us all that is thought, done, and feared in their country. We proceed in broad daylight; they advance under cover: the game is one-sided."

A change in nomenclature has not altered the character of Russia's rulers or of its institutions. Whether it is Stalin or the Czar, it is still "the little father" of the Russian people and it is still merciless despotism. Here is the Marquis' description: "The Russian Government is the discipline of the camp substituted for the civic order—it is a state of siege become the normal state of society." Even the Czarist *tchin,* that "military order applied to an entire society," has been revived and applied to civilian functions. During the period of my stay in Moscow, entire ministries and entire industries were actually being put into paramilitary uniform, ranging from the employees of the Ministry of Finance to the entire personnel of the mining industry, down to the lowliest miner. The privileged class is today as remote from the mass of citizens as was Nicholas' court. The rank and position of the individual derives from the new Soviet "Czar" as surely as it did in the days of Nicholas I or in the days of Peter the Great. The ruler continues to be the most powerful and least accessible of all the world's sovereigns. Cut off from his own people as well as from foreigners by the forbidding Kremlin walls, the army of police assigned to guard him, and the deep secrecy maintained concerning his personal life, Stalin is to most Russians merely a name and a symbol. But like his Czarist predecessors, he is omnipresent, dominating the lives and thoughts of his subjects in every city, village, and hamlet across one-sixth of the world's surface. In Custine's words: "All must strive scrupulously to obey the thought of the sovereign; his mind alone determines the destiny of all."

The great arranged fêtes which enable the people to participate in the glory of the ruler still take place. One inevitably compares the Fête of Peterhof so vividly described by the Marquis with the colossal mass parades in the Soviet Union today. Twice a year Nicholas opened his court to chosen representatives from all classes who were permitted to pay him homage. Twice a year chosen representatives from all classes are permitted to pay homage to Stalin. As Custine says: "In this language of the oppressed, interpreted by the oppressor, permissions are obligatory." Thus on May Day and on the anniversary of the so-called October Revolution "spontaneous demonstrations" take place in Moscow's Red Square. More than a million souls who have received "permission" and who have stood in line for hours awaiting their turn to demonstrate their zeal for the Little Father, all bedecked in colorful regalia, bearing pennants and flowers, silent and somber, file past Stalin and his suite. This spectacle always evoked

13

in us Custine's sentiment at Peterhof: "I have never seen anything lovelier for the eye or sadder for the mind. . . ." But this magnificent and costly show is open only to those participating and to invited guests, including, as in Custine's day, the foreign diplomats. The streets are cleared for blocks around and heavily policed. This is not a spectacle for the masses as it would be in any other country; it is rather another instrument of absolute and arbitrary rule.

During my assignment to Moscow the history of events as recent as World War II was gradually rewritten under our eyes. When I went to the Soviet Union in 1946 there still remained some of the aura of our wartime alliance. By the time I left in 1949 one would have thought from reading the Soviet press that the Western Powers had been the allies not of the Soviet Union but of Hitler, and that their evil designs had been similarly foiled. Our Marquis waxed indignant over comparable phenomena in Czarist Russia and cogently described the practice: "Russian despotism not only counts ideas and sentiments for nothing but remakes facts; it wages war on evidence and triumphs in the battle."

Another story with numerous modern parallels is Custine's account of the troubles of a French citizen who had been overheard expressing his disapproval of Russian despotism before he had even arrived in Russia. The arrest in the middle of the night, the incommunicado imprisonment, the refusal of any explanation, the final expulsion from the country after the intervention of the am-

14

bassador—how many times have I been involved in such cases. A change of names, a change of dates and Custine's story would have served as a report on the treatment accorded the American journalist, Anna Louise Strong, despite her previous years of service to Communist propaganda.

Finally, how pat from Stalin's lips would come the statement of Czar Nicholas I to our Marquis: "One does not know me very well when one criticizes me for my ambition. Far from seeking to extend our territory, I would like to be able to draw the populations of all of Russia closer around me. It is solely over misery and barbarism that I wish to make conquests: to ameliorate the lot of the Russians, this would be better than to aggrandize myself."

These examples may suffice to demonstrate that the analogy between Russia of 1839 and the Soviet Union today is so striking that one must pinch himself to recall that Custine was writing more than a hundred years ago. The exercise of sovereignty through fear, the omnipresence of the secret police, the operation of the bureaucracy, the absence of personal and public liberty, the uprooting and banishment to Siberia of whole populations, the repression of non-conformist artistic endeavor, the sudden imposition of drastic monetary reforms, the subjugation of the Church, the conquest of foreign lands; above all, the secrecy, deceit and hypocrisy—all these and hundreds of other phenomena are historic as well as actual.

Custine's reflections on this strange society,

combining the science of Europe with the genius of Asia, led him to dire forebodings. The only explanation he could find for "the excessive sacrifices imposed here on the individual by society" was the goal of "the conquest of the world." More specifically, he continued: "Russia sees Europe as a prey which our dissensions will sooner or later deliver up to her; she foments anarchy among us in the hope of profiting by a corruption she promotes because it is favorable to her views." Did we think this was a Communist idea?

A present-day observer is bound to share Custine's apprehensions and to feel with him that as long as the Russians remain enslaved, isolated and deceived by ambitious rulers, they will indeed be a menace to the whole world. But though the Marquis tended to take a dismal view of the eventual outcome, he still saw hope, both in terms of what the West could itself accomplish and in terms of what might eventually develop within Russia. His remarks on the former score read like a text for our time: "If passions calm themselves in the West," he said, "if unity is established between governments and subjects, the avid hope of the conquering Slavs will become an idle fancy. Therein lies the danger of allowing them to interfere in our policy and in the counsels of our neighbors."

As to internal developments, Custine was more pessimistic, though even in this case not without hope. And I think it must be pointed out that encouraging factors which he could scarcely foresee

16

have emerged in the century since he wrote: incredible development in the means of communication and an era of progressive enlightenment in Russia. Like almost all observers who have traveled or lived among them, Custine agreed that the Russian people had not been wholly corrupted by centuries of oppression by arbitrary power—that they had retained, alongside and even in contradiction to their submissiveness, a store of virility, imagination, skepticism and curiosity. He speaks for all of us when he writes: "My discomfort is increased since I have been living among Russians by the fact that everything reveals to me the real worth of this oppressed people. The idea of what they could do if they were free provokes the anger I feel when I see what they are doing today."

Custine sensed an eagerness for enlightenment at the time of his visit and signalled its potential importance. "The Customs has no power over thought," he wrote; "armies cannot exterminate it; ramparts cannot stop it; it goes underground; ideas are in the air; they are everywhere, and ideas change the world." But he could not, of course, foresee the magnificent flowering of Russian culture and political philosophy, then barely beginning. Under the stimulus of Western thought, Russia, in the nineteenth century, produced masters of literature, drama, music and art. Pushkin, Turgenev, Gogol, Dostoievsky, Tolstoy, Gorky, Chekhov, Tchaikovsky, Rimsky-Korsakov, Herzen—none of these great figures had left his impress on Russian society when Custine

17

wrote. The works of these masters continue to be the basic nourishment for the spirit of the Soviet citizen of today. Some have been suppressed, it is true, but their collective force cannot be suppressed by any Russian régime. And these giants of the Russian flowering bring to the Soviet citizen many of the values of Western civilization.

Along with this period of cultural enlightenment, there developed in Russia during the latter part of the past century a really progressive revolutionary movement, the approach of which Custine also anticipated. This movement had its fruition in the Revolutions of 1905, which extracted liberal concessions from a reluctant Czar, and of February 1917, which destroyed the Czarist régime. It is one of the greatest tragedies of history that the subsequent Bolshevik coup d'état —today celebrated as the October Revolution— destroyed all this progress and proved Herzen's penetrating prediction, in 1855, that Communism would be "Russian autocracy turned upside down." It is in fact a measure of the extent to which the Bolshevik régime has turned the clock back to say that Custine's account of his travels in the Russia of Nicholas I is more aptly descriptive of Stalin's Soviet Union than of any intervening rule in that land. But although today's observer is saddened to find that the bulk of the Russian population has again lapsed into that apathetic submissiveness which Custine deplored, he is encouraged to note that Soviet rewriting of history has not completely obliterated the memory of this really progressive revolutionary movement.

Introduction

The influence of the memory of this enlightened era and the fundamental strength of the Russian character which have defied strangulation are on the side of the West in the titanic long-range struggle now facing us for a civilized and peaceful world. These factors are still relatively feeble. They are half smothered, not only by deliberate suppression but by "the inevitable ravages" of centuries of oppressive and arbitrary rule; nevertheless, they provide the basis for a resumption of that "profound fermentation and the benefit of a slow and natural cultural development" essential for the realization in Russia of the kind of civilized society with which the rest of the world can live. This will inevitably be a slow process. Centuries of history cannot be spanned in a matter of years. The change must come primarily through the efforts of the Russian people themselves when their eyes have been opened and when they demand their heritage—the right to live as a free people. We must do what we can to hasten this process; to stimulate these healthy influences and to prevent the complete monopolizing of the minds of the Russian peoples by their Kremlin masters. Meanwhile, we must take measures to prevent those ambitious masters from leading the Russians (and with them all the rest of us) into disaster. The reflections of Custine strikingly illustrate the profundity of the problem. But it is by no means hopeless if we have the requisite determination, patience, and understanding; for we can then appreciate with Custine that: "In general, the education that a people

19

receives determines in a large measure the morality of each individual. From this it follows that a frightening and mysterious responsibility for rights and wrongs has been established by Providence between governments and subjects, and that there comes a moment in the history of societies when the State is judged, condemned, exterminated like an individual man."

WALTER BEDELL SMITH

Washington, D.C.

The Russian Journals of the
Marquis de Custine

AUTHOR'S FOREWORD

THE LETTERS you are about to read were not all intended for publication. Several of the early ones were purely confidential. Tired of writing but not of traveling, it was my intention this time to observe without plan and to keep my descriptions for my friends. Later, for reasons which will become clear in this book, I decided to publish everything.

The principal reason for my decision was that each day I felt my ideas being modified by the scrutiny to which I was subjecting a society that was absolutely new to me. It seemed to me that in telling the truth about Russia I would be doing something useful, new, and daring. Up to the present, fear and self-interest have dictated exaggerated praises, and hatred has caused the publication of calumnies. I have neither fear nor hatred.

I went to Russia in search of arguments against representative government. I returned from Russia a partisan of constitutions. A representative government is not the government best adapted to action; but mature peoples have little need for action, and it is the form of government that stimulates production and provides the greatest wellbeing and the greatest wealth. Above all, representative government permits the greatest mental activity in the sphere of practical ideas. Finally,

23

the representative government creates an independent citizen—not by arousing emotions but by legal action. Certainly these are great compensations for great disadvantages.

To the extent that I have come to know the terrifying and extraordinary government formalized, if not founded, by Peter I, I have better understood the importance of the mission that fell to my lot.

The extreme curiosity that my movements aroused in the Russians, evidently worried by the restraint of my comments, made me think at first that my prestige was greater than I had assumed. I became attentive and cautious, for I soon discovered the danger to which my frankness could expose me. Not daring to send my letters by the post, I saved them and kept them hidden with extreme care, as if they were suspicious papers. By this means, upon my return to France I held in my own hands a complete record of my journey. Nevertheless, I have hesitated for three years to make this account public. That was the time I required to reconcile, in the depths of my conscience, what I believed I owed to gratitude with what I owed to truth. Truth finally triumphed because I deemed it to be in the interest of my country. I cannot forget, above everything else, that I write for France, and I believe it is my duty to reveal grave and instructive facts to my countrymen.

I feel free to judge, even severely if my conscience demands it, a country where I have friends; to analyze, without falling into offensive personalities, the character of political men—be ginning with the principal personage of State; to describe their actions, and to pursue to their logical end the reflections that such analysis may suggest to me; provided always that in following the course of my ideas wherever they may lead I pass on my opinions only for what they are worth in my own eyes: this, it seems to me, is what might be called the integrity of a writer.

But, in yielding to duty, I have respected—I hope, at least—the laws of courtesy. There is an acceptable manner of saying hard truths; this manner consists in speaking only through conviction while avoiding any suggestion of self-complacency. Furthermore, as I admired a great deal in Russia, I have included much praise in my descriptions.

The Russians will not be satisfied. Is *amour-propre* ever satisfied? However, no one has ever been more impressed than I with the grandeur of their nation and its political importance. Throughout my sojourn there, I sensed strongly the great destiny of this people, the last to appear in the ancient theater of the world. Collectively the Russians seemed to me great, even in their most shocking vices. Individually they appeared amiable, and I found them interesting in character. These flattering truths should suffice, I think, to compensate for others less pleasing.

If the contradictions which one cannot help noticing in their society, if the spirit of their government, essentially opposed to my ideas and my traditions, have torn reproaches from me, my

25

praises, as involuntary as my cries of indignation, have only the more value.

But these Oriental people, accustomed as they are to breathe and dispense the grossest incense, considering themselves always convincing when they praise one another, will be sensitive only to blame. They see disapproval as treason. They describe any harsh truth as a lie. They will not see how much subtle admiration underlies my apparent criticism, how much regret—and, in certain respects, sympathy—there is beneath my most severe observations.

If the Russians have not converted me to their religions (they have several and with them political religion is not the least intolerant)—if, on the contrary, they have modified my monarchical ideas toward opposition to despotism in favor of representative government, they will be incensed only by the fact that I am not of their opinion. This I regret, but I prefer regret to remorse.

If I were not resigned to their injustices I would not publish these letters. Furthermore, although they may accuse me in words they will absolve me in their consciences. Any Russian of good faith will acknowledge that, if I have committed errors in detail for lack of time to rectify my illusions, in general I have painted Russia as it is. He will take into account the difficulties I had to overcome, and he will congratulate me on the success and the promptness with which I was able to divine the basic traits of their character under the political mask which has disfigured them for so many centuries.

26

Author's Foreword

The events which I witnessed I have reported as they happened before my eyes; the ones that were recounted to me I have reproduced just as I got them; I have not tried to deceive the reader by substituting myself for people I have consulted. If I have abstained not only from naming but from designating in any fashion the people I have consulted, my discretion, without doubt, will be understood. It is one more guarantee of the degree of confidence deserved by these well-informed minds to whom I thought I could address myself for enlightenment on certain facts that were impossible for me to obtain for myself. It is superfluous to add that I have cited only those facts to which the character and position of the men from whom I learned them give, in my opinion, an incontestable seal of authority.

Thanks to my scrupulous fidelity, the reader will be able to judge for himself the degree of authority he should attribute to these second-hand accounts which comprise only a very small portion of my narrative.

MY FIRST FOREBODINGS

Ems, June 5, 1839

YESTERDAY I started my journey to Russia. The hereditary Grand Duke arrived at Ems, preceded by ten or twelve carriages and followed by a retinue consisting of a great number of persons. The thing that struck me from the first moment, in seeing the Russian courtiers at work, was that they follow their rôle of grandees with an extraordinary obsequiousness. They are a species of exalted slaves. However, as soon as the prince withdrew, they assumed an easy air, resolute manners, and a bold demeanor which produced an unpleasant contrast to the complete self-abnegation they had effected an instant before. In a word, a practice of meniality, from which the masters were no more exempt than the valets, reigned in this entourage of the heir to the imperial throne.

Their behavior was not simply a form of etiquette, like that governing other courts, where official respect, the sentiment that the importance of the trust exceeds that of the person—the *rôle obligé* in short—may lead to lassitude and at times even to ridicule. It was more than that. It was a gratuitous and automatic servility which did not exclude arrogance. I seemed to hear them say, in confronting their situation, "Since it cannot be otherwise, I am very well off." This mixture of arrogance and humiliation offended me and presaged nothing in favor of the country I was going to visit.

Among the crowd of onlookers, I found myself beside the Grand Duke just as he got down from his carriage. Before entering the bath house, he stopped for a long time at the door to talk with a Russian lady, the Countess X, thus providing me with an opportunity to examine him at my leisure. He is twenty years old, and that is the age one would have given him. He is tall, but seemed a little heavy for such a young man. His features would be handsome if it were not for the puffiness of his face which blurs his expression. His round face is more German than Russian. It makes one think about what the Emperor Alexander must have been at the same age—without, however, recalling in any way the Mongolian type. This countenance will pass through many phases before taking on its definite character. The habitual disposition that it denotes today is sweet and well-disposed. However, there is, between the youthful smile of the eyes and the constant contraction of the mouth, a conflict that indicates a lack of sincerity and perhaps some inner suffering. . . . The expression of the eyes of this young prince is benevolent; his bearing is pleasant, easy, and aristocratic—truly that of a prince. He has an air of modesty without timidity for which one is grateful to him—the embarrassment of the great is so annoying to everybody that their ease appears to us as affability, which it is in reality. When they look upon themselves as idols, they are disturbed by the opinion they have of themselves and which they hope to avoid imparting to others.

This foolish anxiety has not attacked the Grand Duke; above all, his demeanor gives the impression of a man of perfect breeding; if he ever reigns, it will be through inherent devotion to the crown that he will make himself obeyed and not through terror—unless the exigencies adhering to the trust of the Emperor of Russia change his character while changing his position.

I LAUGH OFF THE WARNINGS
OF AN INNKEEPER

Travemünde, July 4, 1839

AT LÜBECK this morning the innkeeper, on learning that I was going to Russia, came into my room
with an air of compassion that made me laugh.
This man is shrewder, has a livelier wit, and is
more inclined to raillery than the mournful tone
of his voice and his manner of speaking French
would lead one to believe at first glance.

When he learned I was traveling only for pleasure, he began to lecture me, with German good
nature, in an effort to dissuade me from this project.

"You know Russia?" I asked him.

"No, sir, but I know the Russians. Many of
them pass through Lübeck, and I judge the country by the faces of its inhabitants."

"Then what do you find in the expression of
their faces which should prevent me going to see
them in their native land?"

"Sir, they have two expressions (I am not
speaking of the lackeys who have only one; I am
speaking of the nobles). When they come through
here on their way to Europe they have a gay,
free, happy air. They are like horses turned to
pasture, like birds who have flown the cage—
men, women, young, old, all are as happy as

school children on a holiday. The same people, on their return, have long, gloomy, tormented faces; they have a worried look. Their conversation is brief and their speech abrupt. I have concluded from this difference that a country which one leaves with so much joy and returns to with so much regret is a bad country."

"Perhaps you are right," I replied, "but your observations prove that the Russians are not as deceptive as one paints them. I thought they were more inscrutable."

"They are inscrutable in their own country; but they do not suspect us good Germans," said the innkeeper, withdrawing and smiling in a sly manner.

Laughing to myself, I thought there is a man who is indeed afraid of being taken for a simpleton! One must travel oneself to realize how much the reputation of travelers influences the opinions of various peoples who, through mental laziness, are often superficial in their judgments. Each individual privately strives to protest against the generally established opinion with regard to the people of his country . . .

. . . Tomorrow I embark on a vessel all of whose discomforts I will brave with pleasure, provided that it takes me toward deserts and steppes. Steppes! This oriental name alone presents to my mind an unknown and marvelous nature.

GOD MAKES ONLY THE FUTURE; THE CZAR REMAKES THE PAST

July 8. Aboard the Steamer Nicholas I

HAVING been in ill health for a long time, I was ill in Travemünde, so ill that on the day of departure, I thought of giving up the journey.

Would it not be madness to embark on a long voyage with a fever? But would it not be an even more ridiculous folly to draw back before the last lap and have my carriage returned to shore to everybody's great astonishment? What would I say to the people of Travemünde? How would I explain my belated decision to my friends in Paris?

I really no longer knew what course to take to get out of a situation which was more than painful because it was ridiculous . . . I called my servant, determined to do what he should decide. I asked his advice.

"We must go on," he replied, "we are so near."

. . . Anchor was raised: I lowered my head and covered my eyes with my hand in a fit of stupid despair. Scarcely had the wheels begun to turn when a change took place in me, as sudden and as complete as it was inexplicable. . . . In brief, the pangs, the chills vanished; my head cleared; the sickness evaporated like steam and I was suddenly in perfect health. The sea cured

34

me of seasickness: that is what is called homeopathy on a grand scale.

Actually, since we embarked, the weather has been excellent.

We were ready to leave Travemünde and were just going to lift anchor when, at the peak of my anguish, I saw a very fat old man coming on deck where I had settled myself beforehand. He supported himself with difficulty on his two enormously swollen legs. His head, well-placed between his broad shoulders, appeared to me a noble one. He was the very picture of Louis XVI. I soon learned that he was Russian, a descendant of the conquering Varangians and consequently of the most ancient nobility. He was Prince K.

When I saw him, leaning on his secretary's arm, painfully drag himself to a small table, at first I thought—there is a doleful traveling companion; but when I heard his name I recalled that I had known him by reputation for a long time, and I reproached myself for my incurable habit of judging by appearances. The old man had an open countenance and a shrewd, although noble and sincere, look. Scarcely seated, he addressed me by name although we had never met. Summoned so brusquely, I got up with surprise but did not reply. The prince continued with the air of a great lord whose perfect simplicity excludes all ceremony by virtue of true courtesy.

We reviewed most of the notable events and persons of this world and especially of this century. I collected a store of anecdotes, portraits, definitions, keen perceptions which hurled themselves automatically from the profundity of his understanding and his natural and cultivated wit. This rare and delicate pleasure made me blush for the offhand opinion I had formed of this gouty old man when I saw him come on the ship. Never have hours passed more quickly than those, for my part spent almost entirely in listening. I was instructed as much as I was entertained.

In spite of the reserve of my replies to Prince K, the old diplomat was immediately struck by the direction of my ideas: "You are neither of your country nor of your time," he said to me. "You are an enemy of the word as a political lever . . ."

"That is true . . . I am afraid of lawyers and their echo. I am afraid of the press which is only a word whose echo lasts twenty-four hours. They are the tyrants which threaten us today."

"Come to our country," he said, "you will learn to fear other tyrants."

"You speak in vain, Prince; you will not succeed in giving me a bad opinion of Russia."

"Do not judge Russia either by me or by any Russians who have traveled. With our flexible nature we become cosmopolitans from the moment we leave home, and this trend of mind is already a satire against our government."

At this point, in spite of his habit of speaking frankly on all subjects, the prince became afraid of me, of himself, even more of others, and dropped into rather vague descriptions.

I will not uselessly exhaust my memory to recall for you a dialogue which had become too in-

sincere to add anything to the depth of ideas. . . .
Later the prince availed himself of a moment of
solitude to develop for me his opinions on the
character of the people and institutions of his
country. This is approximately what I remember
of his deductions:

"Russia today is scarcely four hundred years
removed from the invasion of the barbarians,
whereas the West was subjected to the same crisis
fourteen centuries ago. A civilization a thousand
years older puts an immeasurable distance between the morals of nations.

"The Russians have not been molded in that
brilliant school of good faith by which chivalrous
Europe has so well profited that the word 'honor'
has for a long time been a synonym for fidelity to
the word; and 'word of honor' is still a sacred
thing, even in France where so many other things
have been forgotten! The noble influence of the
Knights of the Crusades stopped in Poland along
with that of Catholicism. The Russians are warriors, but for the purpose of conquest; they fight
through obedience and through avarice; the Polish
knights fought through pure love of glory. Thus,
although in origin these two nations being from
the same stock had between them great affinities,
the result of history, which is the education of
peoples, has so profoundly separated them that it
will require more centuries for Russian policy to
reunite them than were required by religion and
society to divide them. . . .

"The complete despotism that rules in Russia
was founded at the moment when serfdom was

being abolished in the rest of Europe. Since the invasion of the Mongolians the Slavs, until that time one of the freest peoples of the world, have become slaves—first of the conquerors and afterwards of their own princes. Serfdom is established then in Russia not only as a fact but as a constitutive law of society. It has degraded the human word in Russia to the point that it is no longer considered there except as a trap: our government lives on lies, for truth frightens the tyrant as well as the slave. However little one speaks in Russia, one always speaks too much; since in this country all discourse is the expression of religious or political hypocrisy.

"Our autocrats formerly served, at their own expense, the apprenticeship of tyranny. The *great princes,* forced to overtax their people for the profit of the Tartars, often themselves drawn in bondage to the remotest part of Asia, relegated to the horde for a whim, ruling only on the condition that they serve as docile instruments of oppression, dethroned the moment they ceased to obey, instructed in despotism by servitude, have familiarized their people with the violences of the conquest to which they personally submitted. That is how, in the course of time, the princes and the nation were mutually perverted.

"Thus, note the difference; this took place in Russia in the era during which the kings of the Occident and their great vassals were magnanimously fighting to free the populations.

"The Poles find themselves today vis-à-vis the Russians in exactly the same position the Russians were in, vis-à-vis the Mongolians, under the successors of Batu [grandson of Genghis Khan and founder of the Golden Horde in the south-eastern steppes of Russia in the 13th century]. The yoke that one has worn does not always serve to make the one that he imposes less heavy. Princes and peoples, like simple individuals, sometimes avenge themselves on innocents; they consider themselves strong because they have created victims."

"Prince," I replied after listening attentively to this long series of deductions, "I cannot believe you. To raise oneself above national prejudice and to do, as you have done, the honors of one's country to a foreigner is an admirable manifesta-tion of tact, but I have no more confidence in your apologia than in the pretentions of others."

"In three months you will do more justice to the government of the word and to me. Mean-while, and since we are still alone," he looked around on all sides when he said this, "I wish to fix your attention on a capital point: I am going to give you a key that will serve to explain every-thing in the country you are entering. Think at each step you take in this land of Asiatic people that the influence of chivalry and Catholicism has been missed by the Russians; not only have they not received it, they have reacted against it with animosity during their long wars against Lithu-ania, Poland, and against the Teutonic Order and the Teutonic Knights."

"You make me proud of my perspicacity. I re-cently wrote to one of my friends that, according

39

to what I had glimpsed, religious intolerance was the secret strength of Russian policy."

"You have perfectly divined what you are going to see. It would not be possible for you to form a correct idea for yourself of the profound intolerance of the Russians. Those who are educated and who have relations with western Europe exercise the greatest art in hiding their dominant thought, which is the triumph of Greek Orthodoxy—a synonym in their minds for Russian policy.

"Without this thought, nothing is explained either in our morals or in our policy. You do not believe, for example, that the persecution of Poland is the result of the personal resentment of the Czar. It is the result of cold and deep calculation. These acts of cruelty are praiseworthy in the eyes of true believers, for it is the Holy Spirit that enlightens the sovereign to the point of raising his soul above all human sentiment; and God blesses the executor of His high purposes: in accordance with this point of view, the more barbarous the judges and executioners the more saintly. Your legitimist journals do not know what they want when they look for allies among the schismatics. We shall see a European revolution before seeing the Emperor of Russia serve a Catholic party in good faith. The Protestants will be reunited to the Pope more easily than the chief of the Russian autocracy; for the Protestants, having seen all their beliefs degenerate into systems and their religious faith change into philosophical doubt, have no more than their pride of sects to

40

sacrifice to Rome; whereas the Czar possesses a very real and very positive spiritual power which he will never voluntarily relinquish. Rome and all that is tied up with the Roman Church has no more dangerous enemy than the autocrat of Moscow, the visible chief of his church, and I am astonished that Italian perspicacity has not yet discovered the danger which threatens Catholicism from this side. Following this very honest picture, judge the illusion which lulls a party of legitimists in Paris! . . ."

The above conversation gives you an idea of all the others. Each time the subject became distressing for Muscovite self-esteem, Prince K stopped, at least until he was perfectly sure that no one could hear us.

These confidences made me reflect and my reflections made me fear.

There is as much future and perhaps more in this country long counted for nothing by our modern thinkers—so backward it seems to them—than there is in the English society planted on the soil of America and excessively extolled by philosophers whose systems have brought forth our present democracy with all its abuses.

If the military spirit which rules in Russia has produced nothing resembling our religion of honor, that does not mean that the nation has less strength because its soldiers are less illustrious than ours. Honor is a human divinity; but in practical life duty is worth as much as honor and even more than honor; it is less magnificent, but it is more sustained and stronger. Heroes of Tasso or

41

of Ariosto will not come out of this; but personages worthy to inspire another Homer, another Dante, can be reborn from the ruins of a second Ilium attacked by another Achilles, by a man who, as a warrior, is worth by himself all the heroes of the Iliad.

My opinion is that the empire of the world is vested, henceforth, not in turbulent peoples but in patient peoples. Europe, enlightened as she is, can no longer be subjugated except by actual force. Thus the real strength of nations is obedience to the power which commands them, just as that of armies is discipline.

When our cosmopolitan democracy, bearing its last fruits, will have made war a thing odious to entire populations, when the nations, so-called the most civilized on earth, will have succeeded in enervating themselves by their political debauches and step by step will have fallen into slumber within their own boundaries and into contempt for the outside world—all alliance being recognized as impossible with these societies, senseless in egoism—the floodgates of the North will again be raised upon us; then we will undergo a last invasion, no longer of ignorant barbarians but of masters—cunning and canny, more canny than we for they will have learned from our own excesses how one can and how one should govern us.

It is not for nothing that Providence amasses so many inactive forces in the East of Europe. One day the sleeping giant will arouse himself and violence will put an end to the reign of speech.

July 8: Aboard the Nicholas I

. . . Society will perish through being entrusted to empty or contradictory words; then the deceptive echoes of opinion, the newspapers, wishing at any price to keep their readers, will push on to destruction, be it only to have something to recount for one more month. They will kill society in order to live on its corpse. . . .

My curiosity to see Russia and my admiration for the spirit of order which must prevail in the administration of this vast state do not prevent my judging the policy of its government with impartiality. A Russian domination that limited itself to diplomatic demands without going to the point of conquest appears to me to be the greatest menace to the world. We deceive ourselves on the rôle that Russia wants to play in Europe: according to its constitutive principle, it would represent order; but according to the character of its men, it would propagate tyranny under the pretext of correcting anarchy—as if despotism corrected any evil! The moral element is lacking in this nation; with its military traditions and its memories of invasions, Russia is still waging wars of conquest, the most brutal wars of all; whereas the battles of France and of the other nations of the West will henceforth be wars of propaganda.

Prince K took my arm to help himself up and asked me to assist him to his cabin, where he made me sit down and said to me almost in a whisper: "As we are alone and you are interested in history, here is an impressive episode. I am telling it to you alone, for in front of Russians one cannot speak of history!

43

"You know," began Prince K, "that Peter the Great, after much hesitation, destroyed the Patriarchate of Moscow in order to unite the tiara with the crown on his own head. Thus the political autocracy openly usurped the spiritual omnipotence it had coveted and challenged for many years: a monstrous union, an aberration unique among the nations of modern Europe. The idle dream of the Popes of the Middle Ages is today realized in an empire of sixty million people, part of them Asiatics who are surprised at nothing and who are by no means disgruntled to find a great Lama in their Czar.

"The Emperor Peter wished to marry Catherine the washerwoman. In order to accomplish this imperial vow, first a family had to be found for the future empress. An obscure gentleman was found in Lithuania, I believe, or in Poland, who was first declared to be of high nobility *by origin* and later christened with the title of brother of the Empress Elect.

"Russian despotism not only counts ideas and sentiments for nothing but remakes facts; it wages war on evidence and triumphs in the battle . . . for evidence has no defender in our country, no more than justice, when they embarrass the power."

I began to be frightened by the strong language of Prince K.

What an extraordinary country this must be to produce only slaves receiving on bended knee opinion that has been made for them, spies who have no opinion—the better to grasp that of

44

others, or scoffers who exaggerate the evil—another shrewd way of avoiding the observant eye of foreigners; but even this finesse becomes a confession, for what other people has ever believed it necessary to have recourse to this? The practice of mystifying foreigners is unknown except in Russia, and it serves to make us divine and understand the condition of society in this extraordinary land. While these thoughts were passing through my mind, the prince pursued the course of his philosophic deductions:

"The people and even the nobility, resigned spectators in this war against truth, support the shame because the lie of the despot, however gross the pretense, always looks like flattery to the slave. The Russians who tolerate so many things would not tolerate tyranny if the tyrant did not humbly pretend to believe them duped by his policy. Human dignity, crushed under absolute government, clings to any straw it can grasp in the wreckage. Mankind is very willing to allow itself to be disdained, sneered at, but is not willing to let itself be told, in explicit terms, that it is disdained and sneered at. Outraged by actions, it takes refuge in words. Falsehood is so degrading that to force the tyrant to hypocrisy is a vengeance which consoles the victim. A miserable and final illusion of wretchedness that must, however, be respected for fear of making the serf even more abject and the despot even more insane!

"There was an ancient custom according to which in solemn processions the Patriarch of Moscow had the two greatest lords of the Empire walk

45

at his side. At the time of the marriage, the Czar-Pontiff decided to choose as acolytes in the ceremonial procession on one side a famous boyar and on the other the new brother-in-law he had just created; for in Russia the sovereign power makes more than nobles, it creates relatives for those who had none; it treats families like trees that a gardener can prune, pull up by the roots, or on which he can graft anything he wishes. In our country despotism is stronger than Nature; the Emperor is not only the representative of God, he is the creative power itself—power more far-reaching than that of our God, for God makes only the future, while the Czar remakes the past! The law has no retroactive effect—the caprice of a despot has.

"The man Peter wished to appoint along with the new brother of the Empress was the highest nobleman of Moscow, and, after the Czar, the principal personage of the Empire—Prince Romodanovsky. . . . Peter had his prime minister inform Prince Romodanovsky that he should betake himself to the ceremony and walk in the procession at the side of the Czar, an honor which the boyar would share with the new brother of the new Czarina.

" 'Very well,' replied the prince, 'but on which side does the Czar want me to place myself?'

" 'My dear Prince,' replied the court minister, 'how can you ask? The brother-in-law of His Majesty—should he not be on the right?'

" 'I will not go,' responded the proud boyar.

"This response, reported to the Czar, provoked

a second message: 'You will come,' the tyrant, in a moment of unguarded anger, had him told. 'You will come, or I will have you hanged!'

" 'Tell the Czar,' replied the indomitable Muscovite, 'that I beg him to begin with my only son who is only fifteen years old; it is possible that this child, after having seen me perish, would consent, through fear, to walk at the left of the sovereign; whereas, I am sure enough of myself never to shame the blood of the Romodanovsky, either before or after the execution of my child.'

"The Czar, I will say in his favor, ceded; but out of revenge against the independent spirit of the Muscovite aristocracy, he made of Petersburg, not a simple port of the Baltic Sea, but the city that we see.

"Nicholas," added Prince K, "would not have ceded; he would have sent the boyar and his son to the mines and *declared* by a ukase [official decree], *couched in legal terms,* that neither the father nor the son could have children. Perhaps he would have decreed that the father had never even been married: such things still happen in Russia rather frequently, and the fact that one is forbidden to talk about them proves that they are still permissible."

In any event, the pride of the noble Muscovite perfectly conveys the idea of the singular combination that has brought about present-day Russian society. This unnatural composite of the minutiae of Byzantium and the ferocity of the horde, this struggle between the etiquette of the Byzantine Empire and the uncivilized virtues of Asia has produced the prodigious State that Europe sees rising today and whose influence she will perhaps feel tomorrow without the power to understand its source. . . .

The thing that has most amused me during this short crossing is that I have constantly found myself in the position of being obliged to justify Russia against Prince K. This side, which I have taken without any calculation, solely to obey my instinct for balance, has won the good will of all the Russians who hear us talk. The sincerity of the opinions this amiable Prince K expresses on his country proves to me that in Russia there is someone who can say what he thinks. When I say this to him, he replies that he is not Russian! A strange pretension! Russian or foreign, he says what he thinks; he is allowed to talk because he has held important offices, dissipated two fortunes and his poverty detracts from the weight of what he says; because he has enjoyed the favor of several rulers; because he is old and sick and privately protected by a member of the imperial family. Furthermore, in order to escape Siberia, he claims to be writing his memoirs and as each volume is completed he deposits it in France. The Emperor fears such publicity as much as the Russians fear the Emperor.

I am struck by the excessive uneasiness of the Russians concerning the opinion that a foreigner might form of them; it would not be possible to show less independence. The impression that their country must make on the mind of a traveler dis-

turbs them endlessly. If Prince K's quips shock
his compatriots, they do so much less because of
their offense to any real patriotism than because
of their possible influence on me—an important
man in the eyes of these people who have been
told that I write about my travels.

"Do not let yourself be prejudiced against Russia by this bad Russian; do not write under the
influence of his lies. He talks this way because he
is trying to make French jests at our expense; but,
at heart, he does not believe a word he says to
you."

That is what was whispered to me ten times a
day. My opinion is like a treasury from which
each believes he has the right to draw for his own
profit; consequently, I feel my poor ideas becoming so confused that at the end of the day I am in
doubt myself as to my opinion. This pleases the
Russians; when we no longer know what to say
or what to think of them and of their country, they
are triumphant. It seems to me that they resign
themselves to appearing worse and more barbaric
than they are so that one will think them better
and more civilized than they are. I do not like beings who are disposed to make so light of the
truth; civilization is not a fashion, a ruse; it is a
force which has its effect, a root which pushes its
stalk, produces its flower, and bears its fruit.

"At least you will not call us the barbarians of
the North as your compatriots do. . . ." That is
what they say every time they see me amused or
touched by some interesting account, by some

49

national melody, some beautiful trait of patriotism, some noble and poetic sentiment attributed
to a Russian.

I reply to all these fears with insignificant compliments; but I think to myself that I should prefer
them as barbarians of the North rather than apers
of the South.

There are remedies for primitive savagery,
but there are none for the mania of appearing to
be what one is not.

A sort of Russian scholar, a grammarian, a
translator of several German works, a professor at
I do not know what college, approached me as
often as possible during the voyage. He has just
traversed Europe and is returning to Russia full
of zeal, he says, to propagate there any good there
is in the modern ideas of the people of the West.
The freedom of his conversation appeared suspicious to me; it was not the luxury of independence
of Prince K; it was a studied liberalism calculated
to make others talk. I reflected that one must always meet some scholar of this nature on the way
to Russia—in the inns of Lübeck, on the steam-
ers, or even at Havre, which, thanks to the navigation of the North and Baltic Seas, is becoming the
Muscovite frontier.

This man got little from me. He wanted, above
all, to know whether I was going to write about
my journey and obligingly offered me the benefit
of his knowledge. I barely questioned him; my
reticence served only to provoke a certain astonishment mixed with satisfaction, and I left him
convinced that "I am traveling only for pleasure,

this time, with no intention of publishing an account of a trip which will be so quick that I would not be able to amass sufficient detail to interest the public."

He seemed relieved by this assurance, which I gave him in every possible form—directly and indirectly. But his uneasiness, which I was able to assuage, aroused my own. If I wish to write about this journey, I must expect to arouse the suspicion of a government which is the shrewdest and the best served by its spies of any in the world. That is always unpleasant; I will hide my notes, I will keep quiet, but I will affect nothing; as a mask, an open face is still the most deceptive.

My next letter will be dated from Petersburg.

MY FIRST VIEW OF RUSSIA

Petersburg, July 10, 1839

ON APPROACHING Kronstadt, a submersed fortress of which the Russians are justly proud, one sees the Gulf of Finland suddenly come to life. The imposing ships of the Imperial Navy cover it in every direction—the Emperor's fleet. It is ice-bound in port during more than six months of the year, and during the three months of summer the Navy cadets do their maneuvers between St. Petersburg and the Baltic Sea. Thus, they make use of the time during which the sun permits navigation in these latitudes for the instruction of youth.

The Baltic Sea with its somber shades and its little traveled waters proclaims the proximity of a continent deprived of inhabitants by the rigors of the climate. There the barren shores harmonize with the cold and empty sea. The dreariness of the earth, of the sky, and the cold tinge of the waters, chill the heart of a traveler. Almost before he touches this uninviting shore he would like to leave it. With a sigh he remembers the words of one of the favorites of the Empress Catherine when she was complaining of the effects of the Petersburg climate on her health: "It is not God's fault, Madam, if men are so obstinate as to build the capital of a great empire in a land destined by

52

Nature to be the habitation of bears and wolves!"

My traveling companions proudly explained the recent progress of the Russian Navy. I expressed admiration for this marvel without appreciating it as they do. It is a creation, or more correctly a recreation, of the Emperor Nicholas, who enjoys realizing the dominant desire of Peter I. But however powerful a man may be, he is forced, sooner or later, to admit that Nature is stronger than man. As long as Russia does not exceed her natural limits, the Russian Navy will be the plaything of emperors—nothing more!

In spite of the courtly pride with which the Russians vaunted the miracles of the will of the master who wishes to have, and who does have, an imperial navy, from the moment I knew that the ships I saw were there solely for the instruction of students, a secret disinterest smothered my curiosity.

This activity, which does not have its compulsion in events, which is neither the result of war nor of commerce, seemed to me just a parade. But heaven and the Russians know what a pleasure a parade is! The taste for reviews is pushed in Russia to the point of madness: and behold, even before entering this empire of military maneuvers I must attend a review on the water! . . . I am not moved to laughter; puerility on a grand scale is to me an appalling thing; it is a monstrosity which is possible only under tyranny, of which it is perhaps the most terrible revelation!

Everywhere, except under absolute despotism, when men put forth great effort it is to achieve a

53

great goal; it is only with blindly submissive peoples that a ruler can demand immense sacrifices to produce trifles.

Far from inducing the admiration expected from me here, this despotic improvisation evokes a sort of fear—not fear of war, but fear of tyranny. This useless navy of Nicholas I brings back to me all the cruelty in the heart of Peter the Great, the model of all Russian sovereigns, ancient and modern, and I ask myself where I am going? What is Russia? Russia is the country where one can do the greatest things for the most insignificant result. Don't go there!

Nothing is as sad as nature on the approach to Petersburg. As one sinks into the Gulf, the marshy Ingermanland, which steadily becomes lower, dwindles in the end to a quivering little line drawn between the sky and the sea; that line is Russia. . . . In other words, a low, humid land strewn as far as the eye can see with poor, miserable birch trees. This landscape—flat, empty, regular, without color, without bounds but even so without grandeur—is barely lighted enough to be visible. Here the gray earth is indeed worthy of the pale sun which lights it, not from above but from the sides, almost from below, as its oblique rays form such a sharp angle with the surface of the earth—stepchild of the Creator. In Russia the nights have a clarity which is astonishing, but the days have an obscurity which is depressing. The best of the days have a bluish tint.

Kronstadt with its forests of masts, its substructures, and its granite walls nobly interrupts the

54

monotonous revery of the pilgrim who comes like me asking for pictures from this ungrateful land. I have never seen anything in the neighborhood of any big city as sad as the shores of the Neva.

Before arriving at Petersburg you cross a desert of water framed by a desert of peat bog: seas, shores, sky, everything mingles; it is like a mirror, but so muddy, so dull you would say that the glass has not been foiled, for it reflects nothing.

Such is the approach to Petersburg. In choosing this site, did all the drawbacks from the point of view of nature and the obvious needs of a great people pass through the mind of Peter the Great without impressing him? The sea at any price— that is what he said! . . . What a weird idea for a Russian to found the capital of the Empire of the Slavs on Finnish territory opposite the Swedes! It was useless for Peter the Great to say that he wished only to give Russia a port. If he was the genius he is reputed to be, he should have foreseen the full consequence of his choice; and, as for me, I do not doubt that he did foresee it. Policy and, I very much fear, the vengeance of the Czar's *amour-propre,* irritated by the independence of the old Muscovites, decided the destiny of modern Russia. The Russians in vain applaud with words the fate that has befallen them; secretly they think, just as I do, that the contrary would have been better.

Russia is like a man, full of vigor, suffocating. She lacks outlets. Peter the Great promised them to her; he opened to her the Gulf of Finland without perceiving that a sea necessarily closed eight

55

months out of the year is not the same thing as other seas. But labels are everything for the Russians. The efforts of Peter I, of his subjects, and of his successors, astonishing as they are, have produced only a city which is difficult to inhabit, where the Neva disputes her ground with every puff of wind that leaves the Gulf and where men think of flight at every step war permits them to take toward the south. For a bivouac, wharves of granite were superfluous.

Kronstadt is a very flat island in the middle of the Gulf of Finland. This aquatic fortress rises above the sea only just enough to prevent the navigation of enemy vessels attempting an attack on Petersburg. Its dungeons, its foundations, its strength are largely under water. The artillery with which it is armed is placed, the Russians say, with great art—in a single volley each shell would tell, and the entire sea would be plowed up like earth crumbled by the plow and the harrow. Thanks to this hail of bullets that an order from the Czar can make rain at will upon the enemy, the place is considered impregnable. I do not know if these cannons can close the two passes of the Gulf; the Russians who would be able to enlighten me would not wish to do so. To answer this question, it would be necessary to calculate the carriage and the direction of the missiles and sound the depth of these two straits. My experience, however recent of date, has already taught me to distrust the empty blusterings and the exaggerations of Russians inspired by an excess of zeal for the service of their master. This national conceit would seem tolerable to me only in a free people. So much vainglory is only from fear, I tell myself; such haughtiness only a meanness ingeniously disguised. This discovery makes me hostile.

In France, as in Russia, I have met two kinds of parlor Russians: those whose discretion conspires with their vanity to praise their country beyond measure, and those who, wishing to give themselves a more elegant, a more civilized air, affect either a profound disdain or an excessive modesty every time they speak of Russia. Up to the present I have not been duped by either the one or the other; but I should like to find a third type—the completely natural Russian. I am looking for it.

We arrived at Kronstadt toward dawn on one of those fine days without beginning and without end that I am tired of describing but not tired of admiring—that is to say, about midnight. The season of these long days is short and already nearing its end.

We dropped anchor in front of the silent fortress, but we had to wait a long time for the arousing of an army of employees who came on board one after another—police commissars, directors, assistant directors of the Customs, and finally the Governor of the Customs himself. This important personage felt himself obliged to pay us a visit in honor of the illustrious Russian passengers aboard the *Nicholas I*. He talked at length with the princes and princesses who were returning to Petersburg. They spoke Russian, probably because the subject of conversation was Western

European politics; but when the conversation turned to the difficulties of landing and to the necessity of abandoning one's carriage and changing ships, they spoke French.

The Russian princes were obliged, like me, a simple foreigner, to submit to the customs laws. This equality pleased me at first, but upon arriving at Petersburg, I saw them cleared in three minutes while I had to struggle for three hours against annoyances of all kinds. Privilege, for a moment poorly disguised under the leveling process of despotism, reappeared, and I did not like this resurrection.

The profusion of small, superfluous precautions creates here a population of clerks. Each one of these men discharges his duty with a pedantry, a rigor, an air of importance uniquely designed to give prominence to the most obscure employment. He does not permit himself to say so, but you can see him thinking approximately this: "Make way for me, I am one of the members of the great machine of the State."

This member of the machine, functioning according to a will which is not his own, lives as much as the movement of a clock; however, in Russia this is called a man! The sight of these voluntary automatons frightens me. There is something supernatural in an individual reduced to the state of pure machine. If, in countries where machines abound, wood and metal seem to have a soul, under despotism men seem to be of wood. One asks oneself what they can do with their excess of thought and you feel uncomfortable at the idea of the force that had to be exerted against intelligent beings to succeed in making them only things. In Russia I pity persons as in England I feared machines. In England the creations of man lack only speech; in Russia speech is too much for the creatures of the State.

These machines inconvenienced with a soul are, however, appallingly polite; you can see that from the cradle they have been forced to civility just as much as to the handling of arms. But what value can the forms of politeness have when respect is by command? Whatever despotism may do, the free will of man will always be a necessary consecration to every human act if that act is to have significance; the ability to choose his own master can alone give value to fidelity. Since in Russia an inferior chooses nothing, nothing that he does or says has either meaning or value.

At the sight of all these categories of spies who examined and questioned us, I was seized by a desire to yawn, which could easily have turned into a desire to weep, not for myself but for this people. So many precautions, considered indispensable here but completely dispensed with elsewhere, warned me that I was on the verge of entering an empire of fear; and fear like sadness is contagious. Thus I was afraid and I was sad . . . through politeness . . . to put myself in tune with everybody else.

I was asked to go to the saloon of our ship, where I had to appear before a tribunal of clerks assembled to question the passengers. All the members of this tribunal, more dreadful than imposing, were seated in front of a large table. Several of them leafed through registers with sinister attention. They appeared to be too absorbed not to have some secret duty to perform—their acknowledged function was not sufficient to motivate such gravity.

Some, pen in hand, listened to the responses of the travelers, or, it would be more accurate to say, of the accused, for all foreigners are treated as criminals upon arrival at the Russian frontier. Others dictated in a loud voice to copyists words to which we attached no importance; these words were translated from language to language, from French to German and finally to Russian, at which point the last of the scribes entered them irrevocably and perhaps arbitrarily in his book. They copied the names inscribed on the passports; each date, each visa was examined with minute care; but the passenger, persecuted by this mental torture, was never questioned except in phrases of which the extremely polite form seemed to me calculated to console one in the dock.

The result of the long interrogation, to which I, like the others, was subjected, was that they took my passport after making me sign a card which would enable me, I was told, to reclaim my passport at St. Petersburg.

Everybody seemed to have satisfied the formalities prescribed by the police. The trunks and the passengers were already on the new boat. For four hours by the clock we had been languishing in front of Kronstadt and, as yet, nothing had been said about leaving.

Petersburg, July 10, 1839

Every minute new black skiffs came out of the city and rowed sadly toward us. Although we had anchored very near the walls of the city, there was a deep silence. Not a sound came out of this tomb. The shadows one saw sailing around it were as mute as the stones they had just left. One would have said like a convoy prepared for a corpse that was keeping it waiting. The men who managed these lugubrious, dirty little boats were clad in heavy gray woolen storm-coats and their faces lacked expression; their eyes were lifeless and their complexion of a jaundiced yellow. I was told that they were the sailors attached to the garrison, and they looked like soldiers. It had long been broad day, but there was scarcely more light than at dawn, and the sun, still not high but reflecting on the water, bothered me. Sometimes small boats turned around us in silence without anyone coming on board; other times six or twelve ragged seamen, half covered with inverted sheepskin— the wool inside and the filthy leather outside— brought us a new police agent, or an officer of the garrison, or a tardy customs officer. These goings and comings, which did not further our business, at least gave me leisure for sad reflections on the kind of filth particular to men of the North. People of the South spend their lives in the open air, half-naked, or in the water; whereas, people of the North are nearly always shut up and have a deep, oily dirtiness that seems to me much more repulsive than the negligence of the peoples destined to live under the sky and born to warm themselves under the sun.

61

The tiresomeness to which the Russian minutiae condemned us also gave us occasion to note that the grandees of the land are not very long-suffering with regard to the inconveniences of the public order when this order weighs on them.

"Russia is the land of useless formalities," they murmured among themselves, but in French lest they be understood by subordinate employees. I have remembered this observation as my own experience has already proven the justice of it only too well. From what I have been able to find out up to now, a book entitled *Russians Judged by Themselves* would be severe—love of their country is for them only a means of flattering the ruler. As soon as they think the ruler cannot hear them, they speak of everything with a frankness which is all the more dreadful because those who listen share the responsibility. The reason for so much delay was finally revealed to us. The chief of chiefs, the superior of superiors, the director of directors of the customs officers appeared. Instead of confining himself to wearing a uniform, this supreme functionary appeared in a dress coat like a private individual. It seems that his rôle is to play the man of the world. Our drawing-room customs officer, all the while giving himself airs of the court, politely confiscated a parasol, took away a dressing-case, took custody of a trunk, and renewed, with an imperturbable *sang-froid,* the searches already conscientiously made by his subordinates.

In the Russian administration the minutiae do not eliminate disorder. They take a great deal of trouble to achieve a small end, and they believe they can never do enough to prove their ardor. The result of this emulation of clerks is that one formality does not insure the traveler against another. It is like pillage—the fact that the traveler has escaped from the hands of one band is no reason to say he will not encounter a second and a third; and all these gangs, spaced along his route, pester him to their hearts' content.

The more or less scrupulous conscience of these employees of all grades with whom the traveler can have to do decides his fate. It is useless to speak if one has a complaint against an employee, for a complaint will never be in order. And this is a country, thus administered, which wishes to be considered civilized in the same sense as the states of the Occident.

The supreme chief of the jailers of the Empire proceeded slowly to examine the ship. He took a long time, a very long time, to fulfill his duty. The necessity of keeping up a conversation is a burden which complicates the functions of this musky guardian—musky in the literal sense, for one can smell the musk a mile away. At last we finished with the customs ceremonies, the courtesies of the police, were rid of the military salutes and a spectacle of the most profound misery which can mar the human race, for the oarsmen of the gentlemen of the Russian Customs are creatures of a kind apart. As I could do nothing for them, their presence was odious to me, and each time these miserable wretches brought to the ship officials of all grades employed by the Customs Service

63

and by the Maritime Police—the most severe police of the Empire—I turned my eyes. These ragged seamen are a disgrace to their country; they are a species of greasy galley slaves who spend their lives transporting the clerks and officials of Kronstadt aboard foreign vessels. In seeing their faces and in thinking about what is called existence for these poor devils, I asked myself what man has done to God that sixty million of the human race should be condemned to live in Russia.

THE "SIMPLE FORMALITIES" OF
THE RUSSIAN POLICE
AND CUSTOMS

Petersburg, July 11, 1839—Evening

To the eyes of a Frenchman, the streets of Petersburg have a strange appearance. I shall try to describe them to you, but I wish first to speak about the entry into the city by way of the Neva. It is famous, and the Russians are justly proud of it; however, I found that it did not live up to its reputation. When from a great distance one begins to make out a few spires, what one can distinguish produces an effect more strange than imposing. The thin line of earth that one perceives from a distance between the sky and the sea becomes a little more uneven in some places than in others— that is all. These imperceptible irregularities are the gigantic structures of the new capital of Russia. It is like a line traced by the unsteady hand of a child drawing some mathematical figure. Coming closer, one begins to recognize the Greek campaniles, the gilded cupolas of convents, then modern monuments, public buildings—the façade of the Bank, the white columns of the schools, the museums, the barracks, the palaces which border granite quays. Once in Petersburg, you pass before sphinxes also in granite; they are of colossal dimensions and imposing in appearance. A city

65

of palaces—it is majestic! Yet, the imitation of classical monuments shocks you when you think of the climate under which these models have maladroitly been transplanted. But soon you are struck by the form and the quantity of shafts, of turrets, metallic needles which rise from all sides —this, at least, is national architecture. Petersburg is flanked by vast and numerous steepled edifices, the religious communities, and these sacred cities serve as ramparts to the profane city. These Russian churches have conserved their primitive originality; not that the Russians originated this heavy and capricious style called Byzantine, but they are of the Greek religion, and their character, their belief, their instruction, and their history justify the loans they have taken from the Byzantine Empire. One can permit them to look to Constantinople for their architectural models, but not to Athens. Seen from the Neva, the parapets of the Petersburg wharves are impressive and magnificent; but from the first step on land you discover that these same wharves are paved with inferior stones, inconvenient, uneven —as disagreeable to the eye as they are painful to pedestrians and treacherous to carriages. Gilded shafts, fine as lightning rods; porticos whose foundations almost disappear under the water; squares adorned with columns which are lost in the vastness of the ground that surrounds them; statues copied from the antique, whose lines, style, and arrangements clash to such an extent with the nature of the soil, the color of the sky, and the climate, as well as with the faces, dress, and customs of the people, that they resemble heroes imprisoned in the land of their enemies; expatriated edifices, temples fallen from the summit of the mountains of Greece into the marshes of Lapland —consequently, they appear much too low for the site to which, for no apparent reason, they have been transplanted. Such were my first impressions.

Here nature demands from men exactly the contrary of what the Russians have imagined—instead of imitating pagan temples, they should surround themselves with structures bold in form, with vertical lines to pierce the fogs of an Arctic sky and to break the monotonous surface of the damp gray steppes which form, beyond the reach of the eye or the imagination, the territory of Petersburg. The suitable architecture for such a country is not the colonnade of the Parthenon, the dome of the Pantheon; it is the tower of Peking. Man must build his own mountains in a land where nature has denied any undulation of terrain. I begin to understand why the Russians bid us with such insistence to visit them during the winter—six feet of snow would hide all I have just described, whereas one sees the country in summer.

Traverse the territory of Petersburg and the neighboring provinces and you will find, I am told, for hundreds of leagues nothing but pools of water, stunted pines, and birches with their somber foliage. Certainly, the white shroud of winter is better than the gray vegetation of summer. Always the same lowlands, adorned with the same shrubs for scenery, unless you are headed toward Sweden or Finland. In that direction you will see a succession of small granite crags bristled with pines which change the aspect of the ground without changing the landscape very much. You can well imagine that the mournfulness of such a country is scarcely cheered by the lines of little columns that men have thought they should erect on this flat, barren land. Greek peristyles must have mountains for pedestals. Here there is absolutely no relation between the inventions of man and the gifts of Nature, and this lack of harmony shocks me at every turn. The portico and the airy ornamentation is here another cross added to that of the climate. In short, the taste for structures without taste prevailed at the founding and the aggrandizement of Petersburg. Contradiction seems to me the outstanding characteristic in the architecture of this huge city; it produces, in my opinion, the effect of a factory of bad style in a park. But the park is a third of the world and the architect was Peter the Great.

However shocked one may be by the stupid imitations that ruin the appearance of Petersburg, one cannot contemplate it without a sort of admiration for this city raised from the sea at the command of a man, which, in order to survive must fight against periodic inundation by ice and permanent inundation by water. It is the result of an immense force of will, and, if one does not admire it, one fears it—which is almost to respect it.

The Kronstadt boat anchored inside Petersburg in front of a granite quay. The English Quay in front of the Customs Bureau is not far from the famous square where the statue of Peter the Great rises on its rock. Once anchored there one stayed a long time; you will see why.

I should like to spare you the details of the new persecutions to which I was subjected, under the generic term of *simple* formalities, by the Police and its faithful associate the Customs; however, I must give you an idea of the difficulties that await a foreigner at the maritime frontier of Russia— entry by land is said to be easier.

We had to present ourselves before a new court which was assembled, like the one in Kronstadt, in the saloon of the ship. The same questions were asked with the same politeness and my replies translated with the same formalities.

"What are you going to do in Russia?"

"See the country."

"That is not a motive for traveling." (Do you not admire the humility of the objection?)

"I have no other."

"Whom do you intend to see in Petersburg?"

"Any persons who will allow me to make their acquaintance."

"How long do you expect to stay in Russia?"

"I do not know."

"Say approximately."

"Several months."

"Do you have a public diplomatic mission?"

"No."

"Secret?"

"No."

"Some scientific purpose?"

"No."

"Have you been sent by your government to observe social and political conditions in this country?"

"No."

"By a commercial company?"

"No."

"You are then traveling freely and entirely through curiosity?"

"Yes."

"Why did you head toward Russia?"

"I do not know. . . ." etc., etc., etc.

"Do you have letters of recommendation to anyone in this country?"

As I had been forewarned of the inadvisability of replying too frankly to this question, I mentioned only my banker.

Upon leaving this session of the court of assizes, I saw ahead of me several of my accomplices. The Russian Police practise a fine art of chicanery on foreigners. These bloodhounds have a keen sense of smell; they are difficult or easy with passports according to the individual. It was apparent to me that their method of treating travelers was one of great inequality. An Italian merchant, who went ahead of me, was searched pitilessly—I almost said searched to the bone—on leaving the ship. They made him open everything, down to his pocketbook; they looked inside the clothes he was wearing. If they had done the same to me, I thought, they would have found me very suspect.

I had my pockets full of letters of recommendation which had been given to me in Paris, in part by the Russian ambassador himself, as well as by other equally well-known persons; but as they were sealed I had been afraid to leave them in my portfolio; consequently, I buttoned my coat when I saw the police approaching. They let me pass without searching my person, but when I had to unpack all my trunks before the customs officers, these new enemies undertook the most minute examination of my effects, particularly the books. After being subjected to an interminable examination, all of my books were confiscated—always with the most extreme politeness, but with no regard for my protests. They also took from me two sets of traveler's pistols and an old travel clock. I tried in vain to understand and explain to myself why this latter object should have been subject to confiscation. Everything taken from me was later returned, as they had assured me it would be, but not without a great deal of annoyance and lengthy discussions. Accordingly, I repeat what the Russian gentlemen said: Russia is the country of useless formalities.

Between nine and ten o'clock I found myself released from the clutches of the Customs and permitted to enter Petersburg, where I was able to profit from the assistance of a German traveler whom I met by chance on the dock. If he was a spy he was none the less useful. He spoke Russian and French and was good enough to have a droshky found for me, while with a cart he himself helped my valet transport the small part of my baggage that had just been released to me to the

Coulon Inn. I had recommended to my servant
that he express no dissatisfaction.

Coulon is a Frenchman who is reputed to have
the best inn in Petersburg, which does not necessarily mean that I shall be comfortable there. In
Russia, foreigners soon lose all trace of their na-
tionality—without ever being assimilated, however. The helpful foreigner even found me a
guide who spoke German and who got in the
droshky behind me, in order to answer all my
questions. This guide told me the names of all
the monuments we had to pass on the way from
the Customs to the inn, a journey which could not
help but be long as distances are great in Petersburg.

The highly overrated, famous statue of Peter
the Great was the first thing to attract my attention; it seemed to me to have a singularly disagreeable effect; placed on its rock by Catherine, with
this inscription—rather conceited in its apparent
simplicity—"To Peter I Catherine II." This figure of a man on a horse is neither ancient nor
modern; it is a Roman of the time of Louis XV.

I stopped for a moment in front of the scaffolding of a building already famous in Europe, in
spite of the fact that it is not finished. This will be
the Church of Saint Isaac. Finally, I saw the
façade of the new Winter Palace, another prodigious product of the will of a man applied to align-
ing the strength of men against the laws of nature.
The goal was attained, for in one year this palace
rose up out of its ashes. I believe it is the largest

palace in existence. It is the equivalent of the Louvre and the Tuileries combined.

In order to finish the work in the period specified by the Emperor, unprecedented efforts were required. The interior construction was continued during the bitterest cold of winter. Six thousand laborers were continually at work; a considerable number died each day, but, as the victims were instantly replaced by other champions who filled their places, to perish in their turn in this inglorious gap, the losses were not apparent. And the only purpose of so much sacrifice was to satisfy the caprice of a man! With naturally civilized people, that is to say of an old civilization, men's lives are risked only for common interests whose gravity is recognized by the majority. But how many generations of sovereigns have been corrupted by the example of Peter I!

During freezes of fifteen to twenty degrees below zero, six thousand obscure martyrs, martyrs without merit, martyrs of an involuntary obedience—for this virtue is innate and forced in the Russians—were shut up in rooms heated to eighty-six degrees in order to dry the walls more quickly. Thus these wretches on entering and leaving this abode of death—now become, thanks to their sacrifice, the home of vanity, magnificence and pleasure—underwent a difference in temperature of 100 to 108 degrees.

Work in the mines of the Urals is less injurious to life; however, the laborers employed in Petersburg were not malefactors. I have been told that the unfortunate ones who painted the interior of the hottest rooms were obliged to put a kind of ice cap on their heads in order to keep their senses under the boiling temperature they were condemned to endure while they were working.

If one wished to disgust us with art, gilt, luxury, and with all the pomp of courts, one could not choose a more efficacious means. Nevertheless, the sovereign was called "Father" by men sacrificed in such great numbers under his eyes and for the satisfaction of sheer imperial vanity.

I feel ill at ease in Petersburg since I have seen this palace and heard what it cost in human lives. I guarantee the authenticity of the details; they were given to me by people who are neither spies nor scornful Russians.

The millions spent on Versailles fed as many French workers' families as these twelve months of the Winter Palace killed Slav serfs; but, by means of this sacrifice, the command of the Emperor accomplished miracles and the completed palace, to the general satisfaction, is to be inaugurated by the festivals of a marriage. A prince can be popular without attaching a high price to human life. Nothing colossal is obtained without pain; but when a man is himself both the nation and the government he should impose upon himself the law of employing the great resources of the machine he operates only for the attainment of an end worthy of the effort.

It seems to me that even in the interest of his own power, if properly understood, he could have allowed another year for his artisans to repair the disasters of the fire.

An absolute sovereign is wrong to say that he is in a hurry; he should, above all, fear the zeal of his subjects who can use the word of the master, innocent in appearance, like a sword to bring about miracles, but at the cost of an army of slaves! It is great, it is too great; God and mankind will finish by taking vengeance for these inhuman wonders. It is imprudent, to say the least, for a prince to rate satisfaction of vanity at so high a price; but the renown that they gain abroad is more important to the Russian princes than anything else—more important than the reality of power—for in that they are acting in the sense of public opinion; furthermore, nothing can discredit authority with a people for whom obedience has become a condition of life. Some peoples have worshiped light; the Russians worship eclipse. How can their eyes ever be opened?

I do not say that their political system produces nothing good; I say only that it produces at too high a cost.

It is not only now that foreigners are astonished by the love of these people for slavery; you are about to read an excerpt from the correspondence of the Baron von Herberstein, Ambassador of the Emperor Maximilian, father of Charles V, to the Czar Vassili Ivanovitch. It is fresh in my memory, for I found this passage in Karamsin [Russian historian, 1766-1826], which I was reading yesterday on the steamer. The volume which contained this passage escaped the vigilance of the police as it was in the pocket of my steamer coat. The keenest spies are never enough—I told you they did not search my person.

If the Russians knew all that even slightly attentive readers can learn from this flattering historian whom they glorify and whom foreigners consult only with extreme distrust because of his obsequious partiality, they would hate him and repent having ceded to the folly of the open minds by which modern Europe is possessed; they would beg the Emperor to suppress the works of all Russian historians, Karamsin at their head, and thus leave the past in an obscurity equally favorable to the peace of mind of the despot and the happiness of his subjects, who never have so much to complain of as when they are criticized. These poor people believe themselves happy if we foreigners do not indiscreetly describe them as victims. Good order and obedience—the two divinities of the Russian Police and the Russian Nation—demand, it seems to me, this final sacrifice.

Here, then, is what von Herberstein has written in decrying the despotism of the Russian monarch: "He (the Czar) speaks and everything is done: the life, the fortune of the laity and of the clergy, of the nobility and of the citizens, all depend on his supreme will. He has no opposition, and everything in him appears just—as in the Divinity—for the Russians are persuaded that the Great Prince is the executor of celestial decrees. Thus, God and the Prince willed it; God and the Prince know best, such are the ordinary

76

expressions among them; nothing equals their zeal for his service.

"I do not know whether it is the character of the Russian nation which has formed such autocrats or whether the autocrats themselves have given this character to the nation."

This letter written more than three centuries ago paints the Russians of that time absolutely as I see the Russians of today. Like Maximilian's ambassador, I still ask myself whether it is the character of the nation that has made the autocrat or the autocrat who has made the Russian character, and I cannot answer the question any more than the German diplomat.

It seems to me, however, that the influence is reciprocal—the Russian government would never have been established anywhere other than in Russia, nor would the Russians have become what they are under a different government.

Today you will hear, in Paris or in Russia, any number of Russians become ecstatic over the miraculous effects of the word of the Emperor; and, while they are priding themselves on the results, not one will be moved to pity by the means employed. The word of the Czar has the power to create, they say. Yes, it brings stones to life, but in doing so it kills men. Despite this small reservation, all Russians are proud of the ability to say to us: "You see, in your country one deliberates three years over the means of rebuilding a theater, whereas our Emperor builds the biggest palace in the world in one year." This childish triumph does not seem to them too dearly paid for by the death of some paltry thousands of workers sacrificed to this regal impatience, to this imperial fantasy, which becomes, to use a fashionable plural, one of the national glories. As for me, however, being French, I see in this only inhuman pedantry. But from one end of this vast Empire to the other, not a single protest is raised against these orgies of absolute sovereignty.

People and government—here all is harmony. The Russians would not give up the miracles of will of which they are witnesses, accomplices, and victims, if it were a question of bringing back to life all the slaves they have cost. All the same, the thing that surprises me is not that a man, steeped in self-idolatry, a man ascribed as all-powerful by sixty million men, or so-called men, undertakes and brings to conclusion such things; it is that among the voices which recount these accomplishments to the glory of this one man, not one separates itself from the chorus to protest in the name of humanity against the miracles of autocracy. It can be said of the Russians, great and small—they are intoxicated with slavery.

THE DEAD SEEMED FREER
THAN THE LIVING

Petersburg, July 12, 1839

IT WAS the day before yesterday, between nine
and ten o'clock, that I obtained free entry to
Petersburg. Petersburg is not an early-rising city;
at that time of day it gave me the impression of a
vast solitude. From time to time I met a few
droshkies. . . .

The movements of the people I met seemed to
me stiff and constrained; each gesture expresses a
will which is not the will of the man who makes it.
All those I saw passing were carrying orders. The
morning is the time for commissions. Not a person
seemed to be working for himself, and the sight
of this constraint aroused in me an involuntary
sadness. I observed few women in the streets—
which were not enlivened by a single pretty face
or by the voice of a single young girl; everything
was dismal, regulated as in a barracks or a camp;
it was like war—but with less enthusiasm and less
life. Military discipline dominates Russia. The atmosphere of this country makes me wish for Spain
as if I had been born Andalusian; it is not the heat
of Spain that one misses here—that is stifling—
but the light and the joy.

Occasionally one sees an officer on horseback
galloping at a great pace to take an order to some

79

troop commander; sometimes it is a courier who is "taking the order" to some provincial governor, perhaps at the other end of the Empire, where he goes in a *kibitka;* a kibitka is a little Russian wagonette without springs and without padding. This cart, driven by an old bearded coachman, rapidly bears away the courier whose rank would prevent his using a more comfortable rig even if such had been at his disposal. Farther off, some infantrymen are coming back from drill and presenting themselves at their quarters to take orders from their captain—nothing but superior officers who command inferior officers. This population of automatons is like half a game of checkers, for a single man makes all the plays and the invisible adversary is humanity. One does not die, one does not breathe here except by permission or by imperial order; therefore, everything is gloomy and constrained. Silence presides over life and paralyzes it. Officers, coachmen, Cossacks, serfs, courtiers, all are servants, of different rank, of the same master and blindly obeying an idea that they do not understand. It is a masterpiece of military mechanics; but the sight of this beautiful order does not satisfy me at all, as so much regularity cannot be obtained except through the complete absence of independence. I seem to see the shadow of death hovering over this part of the globe.

Among these people deprived of leisure and of will one sees only bodies without souls, and one trembles in thinking that for such a great multitude of arms and legs there is only one head.

Despotism is a composite of impatience and laziness; with a little more forbearance on the part of the power and activity on the part of the people, the same result could be obtained at a very much lower price; but what would become of the tyranny? . . . It would be recognized as useless. Tyranny is the imaginary ailment of peoples; the tyrant, disguised as the doctor, has persuaded them that health is not the natural state of the civilized man and that the greater the danger the more violent must be the remedy—thus he preserves the illness under the pretext of curing it. The social order in Russia is too costly for me to admire it.

When Peter the Great established what is called here the *tchin,* that is to say, when he applied military hierarchy to the entire administration of the Empire, he changed this nation into a regiment of mutes and declared himself the colonel with the right to pass this rank on to his heirs.

The Russian government is the discipline of the camp substituted for the civil order—it is a state of siege become the normal state of society.

The morning hours over, the city wakes up little by little, but it becomes noisier without—it seems to me—becoming gayer. One sees only carriages, not very elegant, which transport, with all the speed of their two, four, or six horses, people who are always in a hurry because their entire life is spent in making their way up in the world. Pleasure without end, so-called pleasure for here real pleasure is a thing unknown.

The Hotel Coulon (where I am stopping) faces

81

a sort of square which is reasonably cheerful for this country. This square is bounded on one side by the new Michael Palace—the pompous residence of the Grand Duke Michael, brother of the Czar. I could not go out without passing in front of the gate of this palace which attracted my attention at once. The other three sides of the square are closed in by beautiful rows of houses intersected by beautiful streets. Rare luck! I had scarcely left the new Michael Palace when I found myself in front of the old one. The old Michael Palace is a vast square building, somber and in every way different from the elegant and modern residence of the same name.

Although men may be silent in Russia, the stones speak and speak with a mournful voice. I am not surprised that the Russians fear and neglect their old monuments, for they are witnesses to history they would usually like to forget. When I discovered the dark steps, the deep canals, the massive bridges, the desolate peristyles of this sinister palace, I asked its name, and the name recalled to me, in spite of myself, the catastrophe which placed Alexander on the throne. Immediately all the circumstances of the lugubrious scene which terminated the reign of Paul I were depicted in my imagination.

That is not all; through a cruel irony, before the main door of this sinister edifice there had been placed, before the death of its occupant and in accordance with his order, the equestrian statue of his father, Peter III—another victim whose deplorable memory the Emperor Paul took pleasure in honoring in order to dishonor the triumphant memory of his mother. How many tragedies are coldly played in this land where ambition, even hatred, are calm in appearance! Among peoples of the South passion reconciles me to some extent to their cruelty; but the calculated reserve, the coldness of the men of the North adds a varnish of hypocrisy to crime—the snow is a mask. Here man appears gentle because he is impassive; but murder without hate is more horrible to me than vindictive assassination. Is not the religion of vengeance more natural than betrayal through self-interest? The more I recognize an involuntary impulse in crime, the more I am consoled. Unfortunately, it was calculation and not anger—it was caution which reigned at the murder of Paul. Good Russians pretend that the conspirators intended only to put him in prison. I saw the secret door which led, by way of a hidden stairway, to the apartment of the Czar; this door opens on a part of the garden near a large moat. Pahlen [one of the leaders of the palace conspiracy] had assassins stationed there lest the victim think of escaping by this passage.

This is what he is supposed to have said to the conspirators the preceding evening: "Either you will have killed the Emperor by five o'clock tomorrow morning, or at half-past five I will denounce you to the Emperor as conspirators." There was no doubt as to the result of his eloquent and laconic oration.

Thereupon, for fear of last-minute repentance, he left his house, not to return that night; and

83

in order to be absolutely certain that none of the conspirators would find him before the execution, he visited the various barracks of the city: he wanted to know the temper of the troops.

The next day at five o'clock Alexander was Emperor and reputed to be a parricide, although he had consented (this circumstance is true I believe) only to imprison his father in order to save his mother from prison—perhaps from death —to save himself from a similar fate and to save the country from the furies and caprices of a mad autocrat.

Today Russians pass before the old Michael Palace without daring to look at it. It is forbidden to recount, in the schools or elsewhere, the story of the death of the Emperor Paul, or even to believe this event which has been relegated to the realm of fables.

I am astonished that they have not torn down this palace with its disturbing memories. But for the traveler it is good fortune to find one building remarkable for its air of antiquity in a country where despotism makes everything uniform, everything new—where the dominant idea erases each day the traces of the past. For that matter, it is this mobility which explains why the old Michael Palace is standing; it has been forgotten. Its square mass, its deep moats, its tragic history, its hidden stairs, its secret doors so favorable to crime, its height—unusual in a country where all the buildings seem flat—give it an imposing style: a rare quality in Petersburg. I am amazed at every turn to see the confusion that has

84

been made continuously here between two arts as different as architecture and decoration. Peter the Great and his successors have mistaken their capital for a theater.

I was struck by my guide's frightened look when I questioned him, as naturally as I could, about what had happened in the old Michael Palace. His expression said: "It is easy to see that you are a new arrival."

Everyone here, you see, thinks about what no one says. The astonishment, the terror, the defiance, the affected innocence, the feigned ignorance, the experience of an old cunning difficult to fool, expressed alternately, made of this face, agitated in spite of itself, a book as instructive as it was amusing to study.

When your spy is foiled by your apparent sincerity, he makes a truly grotesque face, for he believes himself compromised by you since he sees you have no fear of being compromised by him. The spy believes only in espionage, and if you escape his snares he figures that he is about to fall into yours.

A walk through the streets of Petersburg under the custody of a local guide is, I assure you, most interesting and scarcely resembles a tour in the capitals of other countries of the civilized world. Everything is constrained in a state governed with a logic as tightly drawn as that directing Russian policy.

On leaving the old and tragic Michael Palace, I crossed a big square which looks like the Champs de Mars in Paris in that it is so big and so empty.

On one side a public garden, on the other a few houses, sand in the middle and dust everywhere —there you have this square. Its shape is undefined, its size immense—ending at the Neva near a bronze statue of Suvorov.

The Neva, its bridges and its wharves, are the real glory of Petersburg, a picture so vast that all the rest seems insignificant. The Neva is a vase full to the brim which disappears under the water on the verge of overflowing on all sides. Venice and Amsterdam seem to me better protected against the sea than Petersburg.

I do not like a city which is not dominated by anything, and certainly the vicinity of a river, which is as wide as a lake and flows on a level with the ground in a swampy plain lost between the fog of the sky and the mists of the sea, was of all the sites in the world the one least advantageous for the founding of a capital. Here, sooner or later, the water will settle accounts with the arrogance of man. Even the granite is not secure against the ravages of winter in the damp ice-well where the citadel built by Peter the Great has already twice worn out its walls and foundations of rock. They have been rebuilt and they will be rebuilt again in order to preserve this masterpiece of conceit and of will which is less than a hundred and forty years old. What a battle! Here the stones suffer violence just as the people do.

I wanted to cross the bridge that very instant to see this famous citadel at close range; first, my guide took me opposite the fortress to the house of Peter the Great which is separated from the fortress by a road and a strip of land. It is a cottage preserved, it is said, in the state in which it was left by the Czar. In the citadel today the Czars are buried and the prisoners of state are confined— a strange way to honor the dead! If one thinks of all the tears shed under the tombs of the sovereigns of Russia, one believes himself at the funeral of some king of Asia. Even a tomb sprinkled with blood would seem to me less impious; tears flow longer and perhaps more painfully. While the Emperor-Worker was living in the cottage, his future capital was built under his eyes. It must be said to his praise that at that time his palace concerned him less than the city. One of the rooms of this illustrious hut—the one that served as the workshop of the Czar-Carpenter—has now been transformed into a chapel, and one enters it with as much meditation as one enters the most revered churches of the Empire. The Russians make saints of their heroes at will. They like to mix the terrible virtues of their masters with the beneficent power of their patrons, and force themselves to bury the cruelties of history under the cover of faith.

But let us return to the cottage of the Czar. There I was shown a boat, constructed by the Czar himself, and other religiously preserved objects; they are now guarded by a veteran. In Russia, the churches, the palaces, and many public as well as private buildings are guarded by disabled soldiers. These unfortunates, always old when they leave the barracks, are transformed into porters—their only resort.

My guide did not spare me a single image or a single piece of wood in the imperial hut. The veteran who guards it, after having lighted several tapers in the chapel which is no more than a celebrated hole-in-the-wall, showed me the bedroom of Peter the Great, Czar of All the Russias. A carpenter in our time would not lodge his apprentice in such a place.

This glorious austerity paints the period and the country as much as the man. In Russia at that time everything was sacrificed to the future; they were building monuments, magnificent to excess, for the following generations. The constructors of so many superb public buildings, without feeling the need of luxury for themselves, were content with the rôle of the scouts of civilization, far ahead of the unknown potentates for whom they were proud to build the city, while expecting that their successors would come to inhabit and embellish it. Certainly there is grandeur of soul in this solicitude of a chief and his people for the power and even for the vanity of generations yet to be born. This confidence of living men in the glory of their remotest descendants holds something noble and original. It is a disinterested and poetic sentiment far above the ordinary respect of men and of nations for their forefathers.

However, the history of Russia does not date, as ignorant and frivolous Europe seems to think, from the reign of Peter I—Moscow explains St. Petersburg, and the Ivans prepared the way for Peter the Great.

The deliverance of Muscovy after long centuries of invasion, later the siege and capture of Kazan by Ivan the Terrible, the fierce battles against Sweden and so many other brilliant and patient feats of arms justify the proud attitude of Peter I and the humble confidence of his nation. Faith in the unknown is always impressive. This man of iron had a right to lean on the future; characters like his accomplish what others hope for. I see him in the simplicity of a truly great lord, even of a great man, seated on the doorstep of this cabin from where he prepared against Europe, all at the same time, a city, a nation, and a history. The grandeur of Petersburg is not empty and this powerful city, dominating its ice and its swamps in order to dominate the world is magnificent —still less magnificent to the eye than to the mind. It is true, this marvel has cost a hundred thousand men, swallowed up through obedience in the pestilential marshes which are today a capital.

On leaving the house of Peter the Great, I again crossed in front of the bridge over the Neva which leads to the islands and entered the fortress.

I was not allowed to see the prisons: there are dungeons under the water; there are cells under the roof; all are full of men. I was taken only to the church where the tombs of the reigning family are enclosed.

In this funereal citadel the dead seemed to me freer than the living. During the time that I remained in its depths I breathed only with difficulty. If it had been a philosophic idea which made them shut up in the same tomb the prisoners of the

89

Czar and the prisoners of death, the conspirators and the sovereigns against whom they conspired, I would respect it; but I see in it only the cynicism of absolute power, the brutal confidence of an assured despotism. With this supernatural force, one can raise oneself above the little human delicacies, good for the common run of governments; an Emperor of Russia is so full of what he owes to himself that his justice is not eclipsed before that of God. We, men of the Occident . . . see in a prisoner of state at Petersburg only an innocent victim of despotism—the Russians see a reprobate. That is what political idolatry leads to. Russia is a country where misfortune defames, without exception, everyone that it touches.

I have seen fortified castles elsewhere, but the words do not mean the same thing they mean in Petersburg. I shivered in thinking that the most scrupulous fidelity and the most complete integrity do not insure any man against the subterranean prisons of the citadel of Petersburg, and my heart expanded when I recrossed the moats that guard this sad enclosure and separate it from the rest of the world.

TO THINK, TO DISCERN, IS TO
BECOME SUSPECT . . .

Petersburg, the same day, July 12, 1839

O THAT this capital without roots either in history or in the soil would be forgotten by its sovereign for a single day, that a new policy would carry the thoughts of the ruler elsewhere, that the granite hidden under the water would crumble, that the low flooded lands would return to their natural state and the denizens of solitude would retake possession of their natural habitat!

These ideas occupy the mind of every foreigner who walks amid the superficial décor of Petersburg; no one believes this wondrous capital can endure. If one meditates ever so little (and where is the traveler worthy of his profession who does not meditate?) one foresees such a war, such a revision of policy, that would make this creation of Peter I disappear like a soap bubble in a breeze. I have been no place that is more penetrated with the instability of human things. Often in Paris, in London, I have said to myself—a time will come when this noisy abode will be more silent than Athens, than Rome, Syracuse, or Carthage; but it is not given to any man to foresee the hour or the immediate cause of this destruction; whereas the disappearance of Petersburg can be foreseen; it can happen tomorrow in the middle of the triumphant shouts of its victorious people. The decline of other capitals follows the extermination of their inhabitants; but this one will perish at the very moment when the Russians see their power extending. I believe the duration of Petersburg will be that of a political system, or that of the constancy of a man. This is something which cannot be said of any other city in the world.

In contemplating Petersburg and in reflecting upon the terrible life of the inhabitants of this camp of stone, one can have doubts about the mercifulness of God; one can groan, blaspheme, but it is impossible to become bored. There is in this city an incomprehensible mystery, but at the same time a prodigious grandeur. Despotism organized as it is here becomes an inexhaustible subject for observation and musing. This colossal Empire that I see suddenly rise before me in the East of Europe, that Europe in which societies are suffering from the impoverishment of all recognized authority, produces on me the effect of a resurrection. I believe myself in a nation of the Old Testament, and I stop in fear mingled with curiosity at the feet of this antediluvian giant.

On entering the country of the Russians, one sees at a glance that the social order as arranged by them can serve only for their use. One must be Russian to live in Russia, although on the surface everything proceeds there as elsewhere. The difference is in fundamentals. . . .

I was told this evening of several peculiar characteristics relative to what we call the slavery of the Russian peasants.

It is difficult for us to form a correct idea of the real position of this class of men who have no acknowledged rights but who, nevertheless, are the nation itself. Deprived of everything by law, they are not as morally degraded as they are socially debased. They have intelligence 'and sometimes pride; but the thing that dominates their character and the conduct of their entire life is cunning. No one has the right to reproach them for this most natural consequence of their situation. These people, always on guard against their masters whose shameless bad faith they experience at every instant, make up for the lack of integrity on the part of the lords toward their serfs by means of artifice.

The relations of the peasant with the owner of the land, as with the fatherland—that is to say the Emperor who represents the State—would be a subject for study worthy of a long sojourn in the interior of Russia.

In many parts of the Empire the peasants believe they belong to the land—a condition of life which seems natural to them, whereas they have trouble understanding how men can be the property of a man. In many other parts the peasants think the land belongs to them, and these are the happiest, if not the most submissive of slaves.

There are those who, when they are put up for sale, send afar to beg a master, whose reputation for kindness has reached them, to buy them—them, their land, their children, and their livestock—and if this landlord, famous among them for his gentleness (I do not say justice, for the sentiment

93

of justice is unknown in Russia even among men
stripped of all power), if this desirable landlord
does not have money they will give themselves to
him in order to be sure that they belong only to
him. So the good landlord, in order to satisfy his
new peasants, buys them with their own funds and
accepts them as serfs. Afterwards, he exempts
them from levies for a number of years, thus in-
demnifying them for the price of their persons
which they have paid in advance in paying off for
him the value of the domain on which they depend and of which they have, so to speak, forced
him to become the proprietor. That is how the
opulent serf puts the poor landlord in the position
of owning, in perpetuity, him and his descendants
—happy to belong to him and to his posterity, to
escape in this manner the yoke of an unknown
master, or of a landowner reputed to be bad. You
see the sphere of their ambition is not very exten-
sive.

The greatest misfortune that can happen to
these human plants is to see their native soil sold.
They are always sold with the land to which they
are permanently bound. The only real advantage
they have drawn up to now from the relaxation in
the modern laws is that a man cannot be sold
without the land. Yet even this protection is
eluded by means known to everyone; thus, instead of selling the land in its entirety with its
peasants, one sells a few arpents (several acres)
with one or two hundred men to the arpent. If the
authorities learn of this shuffling, they are very
severe; but they rarely have occasion to intervene,

for between the offense and the supreme justice, that is to say the Emperor, there is a whole world of people interested in perpetuating and concealing these abuses.

The proprietors suffer as much as the serfs from this state of affairs, particularly those whose affairs are not in order. Land is hard to sell, so hard that a man who has debts and who wishes to pay them finishes by borrowing the sum that he needs at the Imperial Bank, and the bank takes a mortgage on the possessions of the borrower. The result of this is that the Emperor becomes the treasurer and the creditor of all the Russian nobility, and the Russian nobility, thus curbed by the supreme power, has no possibility of fulfilling its obligations toward the people.

One day a landowner wished to sell a piece of land. The news of this project put the region in a state of alarm; the proprietor's peasants sent him a deputation of village elders who threw themselves at his feet and with tears told him they did not wish to be sold.

"It has to be done," replied the landlord, "since it is against my principles to increase the levy my peasants pay and I am not rich enough to hold land that brings me nothing."

"Is it only that?" cried the deputies of the landlord's domains. "We are rich enough ourselves to enable you to keep us."

Of their own free will, they immediately fixed their rents at twice what they had paid from time immemorial.

Other peasants with less kindness and more indirect shrewdness revolted against their masters, solely in the hope of becoming serfs of the crown —which is the ultimate ambition of all Russian peasants.

Suddenly emancipate such men and you will set fire to the country. From the moment that the serfs, separated from the land, see that the land is sold, that it is rented, or that it is cultivated without them, they would rise up as a body, shouting that they had been robbed of their property.

Recently, in a distant village which had caught fire, the peasants, who complained of their master because of his tyranny, profited from the disorder, which they themselves had probably brought about, to seize their enemy, that is to say their master, take him aside, impale him, and roast him in the very fire that was burning the village. They believed they justified themselves sufficiently for this crime by taking oaths that the victim had intended to burn their houses and that they had done nothing more than protect themselves.

On such occasions the Czar usually orders the deportation of the entire village to Siberia; that is what in Petersburg is called "populating Asia."

If, as is said, Russia should become an industrial country, the relations between the serfs and the landowners would not be slow in changing, as a population of merchants and independent artisans would grow up between the nobles and the peasants. However, at present this new class has hardly begun to form and its recruits are almost solely from among foreigners. The manufacturers, the businessmen, the merchants are nearly all Germans.

It is only too easy in Petersburg to let yourself be taken in by the appearances of civilization. When you see the Court and the people who crowd it, you think you are in a country advanced in culture and political economy. But when you think about the relations that exist between the various classes of society; when you see how many classes are still insignificant in size; finally, when you study the basis of customs and events, you perceive a real barbarism barely disguised under a revolting magnificence.

I do not blame the Russians for being what they are; I blame them for pretending to be what we are. They are still uneducated—this condition, at least, leaves the field open for hope. But I see them endlessly possessed with a mania for imitating other nations, and they imitate them in the manner of monkeys, making what they copy ridiculous. Then, I tell myself: these are men lost for the savage state and deficient for civilization, and the terrible words of Voltaire or of Diderot, forgotten in France, come back to my mind: "The Russians have rotted before they are ripe."

In Petersburg everything has an air of opulence, grandeur, magnificence; but, if you judge the reality by this appearance, you will find yourself strangely deceived. Ordinarily the first effect of civilization is to make material life easy; here everything is difficult; crafty indifference is the secret of the life of the great majority.

Would you like to find out exactly what one

97

should see in this great city? No bookshop sells a complete index of the sights of Petersburg; furthermore, the educated people whom you question have an interest in not telling you anything, or they have something to do other than reply to you. The Emperor, the place where he lives, the problem with which he is ostensibly occupied— these are the only subjects worthy of absorbing the mind of a Russian who thinks. This catechism of the Court is enough for life. Everybody wishes to please his master by contributing toward the concealment of some corner of the truth from foreigners. No one dreams of assisting the curious— on the contrary, they like to deceive them with false documents. One needs the perspicacity of an experienced observer to travel successfully in Russia. Under despotism curiosity is a synonym for indiscretion; the reigning Emperor is the Empire; if he is well you are relieved of any worry, and your heart and your mind have their daily bread. Provided that you know where and how this cause for all thought, this author of all will and of all action, lives, then, whether a foreigner or a Russian subject, you have nothing to ask from Russia, not even your way, for on the Russian map of the city of Petersburg you find only the names of the principal streets.

Moreover, this frightening degree of power was not sufficient for the Czar Peter; this man was not satisfied with being the mind of his people; he wished also to be their conscience. He dared to arrange the destiny of the Russians in eternity just as he controlled their steps in this world. This

98

power which follows a man beyond the tomb seems to me monstrous. The sovereign who did not recoil before such a responsibility, and who, despite long hesitations, apparent or real, in the end made himself guilty of such an exorbitant usurpation has done more harm to the world by this lone assault against the prerogatives of the priest and the religious freedom of man than he has done good for Russia by all his martial and administrative qualities and by his industrious genius. This Emperor, pattern and model of the Empire and of the present Emperors, is a strange composite of grandeur and of minutiae. Overbearing in spirit like the cruelest tyrants of all centuries and of all countries, worker sufficiently ingenious to rival the best engineers of his time, a scrupulously terrible ruler, eagle and insect, lion and beaver—this master, pitiless during his life, still imposes himself as a sort of saint upon posterity whose judgment he wishes to tyrannize after having passed his days in tyrannizing the acts of his subjects. To judge this man, to describe him with impartiality, is still today a sacrilege which is not without danger even for a foreigner obliged to live in Russia. I brave this peril every instant of the day, for of all yokes the most insupportable for me is that of expedient admiration.

In Russia, the ruling power, unlimited as it is, has an extreme fear of censure, or of mere frankness.

All Russians and all who wish to live in Russia impose on themselves unconditional silence. Here, nothing is said, but everything is known. Secret conversations should be very interesting; but who permits himself to indulge in them? To think, to discern, is to become suspect.

M. de Repnin governed the Empire and the Emperor. M. de Repnin has been in disfavor for two years and for two years Russia has not heard this name spoken—this name which not long ago was on every tongue. He fell, in one day, from the highest power to the darkest obscurity. No one dares to remember him or even to believe in his existence—either his present existence or his past existence. In Russia, the day a minister falls, his friends become deaf and blind. A man is buried as soon as he appears to be in disfavor. I say appears, because no one ever goes so far as to say that a man is out of favor, although he may appear to be. To avow disgrace is to kill. That is why Russia does not know today if the minister who governed yesterday exists. Under Louis XV, the exile of M. de Choiseul was a triumph; in Russia the retirement of M. de Repnin is death.

To whom will the people appeal one day against the silence of the great? What explosion of vengeance is being prepared against the autocracy by the abdication of such a cowardly aristocracy? What is the Russian nobility doing? It adores the Czar and makes itself an accomplice in all the abuses of the sovereign power in order to continue, itself, to oppress the people, whom it will flog as long as the god it serves leaves the whip in its hand (note that it is the nobility that created this god). Was this then the rôle Providence reserved for the nobility in the economy of this vast

Empire? The nobles hold the posts of honor. What do they do to deserve them? The exorbitant and ever-increasing power of the master is an all too just punishment for the weakness of the aristocracy. In the history of Russia, no one except the Emperor has fulfilled his rôle; the nobility, the clergy, all the classes of society have been found wanting. An oppressed people has always merited its suffering; tyranny is the work of nations. Either the civilized world will, before fifty years have passed, fall again under the yoke of the barbarians, or Russia will undergo a revolution more terrible than the revolution whose effects are still felt in Western Europe.

On returning to my room this evening, I found a letter which gave me the most agreeable surprise. Thanks to the protection of our ambassador, I shall be admitted tomorrow to the Imperial Chapel where I shall see the marriage of the Grand Duchess.

THE IMPERIAL WHIRLWIND

July 14, 1839

I AM BACK from the court where I attended, in the Imperial Chapel, the Greek Orthodox rites of the marriage of the Grand Duchess Marie to the Duke of Leuchtenberg. Shortly, I shall do my best to describe the ceremonies to you in detail, but before anything else I want to tell you about the Emperor.

In the first place, the dominant characteristic of his countenance is a worried severity—not a very agreeable expression, it must be said, despite the regularity of his features. The physiognomists pretend, and justly so, that the hardening of the heart can mar the beauty of the face. However, in the case of Czar Nicholas, this unpleasant expression appears to be the result of experience rather than the work of nature. Would it not be necessary for a man to have been tortured by a long and cruel suffering for his countenance to make us afraid in spite of the spontaneous confidence that a noble face usually inspires?

One who is all-powerful, who does all, is accused of all. Subjecting the world to his supreme commands, he sees in the most insignificant events a shadow of revolt; persuaded that his rights are sacred, he recognizes no limits to his power other than those of his own intelligence and strength, and he is indignant about these limits. He is called upon as a god, little short of adored, and the prayers that are addressed to him serve only to expose his weakness. A fly that buzzes unseasonably in the chapel during the ceremony humiliates the Czar. The independence of nature seems to him a bad example; any being he cannot subject to his arbitrary laws becomes in his eyes a soldier who revolts against his commanding officer in the middle of the battle—the shame is reflected on the army and even on the general. The Czar of Russia is a military chief, and each of his days is a day of battle.

However, at rare intervals, lights of kindness temper the imperious or imperial look of the master; then an expression of affability suddenly brings back the native beauty of this classic head. . . .

He always expects to be looked at and does not forget for an instant that he is being looked at; you would even say that he wishes to be the object of all eyes. People have too often repeated to him or made him suppose that he is handsome to look upon and good to show both to the friends and to the enemies of Russia.

In studying the beautiful face of this man whose will decides the life of so many men, I noticed with an involuntary pity that he cannot smile with his eyes and his mouth at the same time—a discord which denotes perpetual constraint and makes me regret all the shades of natural grace that one admires in the face, less regular perhaps but more agreeable, of his brother, the Czar Alexander. The latter, always charming, sometimes had a deceptive appearance. Czar Nicholas is more sincere, but habitually has an expression of severity; sometimes this severity even goes so far as to give him a hard and inexorable look. If Nicholas is less captivating than his brother, he has more force—but then he is much more often obliged to make use of force. Charm guarantees authority by preventing resistance. This skillful economy in the use of power is a secret unknown to Czar Nicholas. He is always the man who wishes to be obeyed: others have wished to be loved.

The Czarina is a most elegant figure and, in spite of her extreme thinness, I find in her entire person an indefinable grace. Her attitude, far from being arrogant as I had been told, expressed the habit of resignation in a proud soul. On entering the chapel she was strongly moved; she appeared to me to be a dying person . . . her eyes —sunken, blue, and gentle—betrayed profound suffering borne with angelic calm.

Everybody sees the Czarina's condition; no one speaks of it . . . in Russia, all must follow the Imperial whirlwind, smiling until death.

All must strive scrupulously to obey the thought of the sovereign; his mind alone determines the destiny of all; the closer a person is placed to this mental sun, the more he is the slave of the glory attached to his rank—the Czarina is dying of it.

That is what everyone knows here and no one talks about, for the general rule is that no one ever proffers a word which could actively interest anyone—neither the man who speaks nor the man who listens should admit that the subject of any conversation is worthy of sustained attention or arouses any real feeling. All the resources of language are exhausted to strike ideas and emotions out of conversation, without, at the same time, having the appearance of concealing them, since that would be awkward. The profound difficulty resulting from this prodigious work, prodigious above all because of the art with which it is hidden, poisons the life of the Russians. Such labor serves as atonement for men who willingly strip themselves of the two greatest gifts of God—the soul and the speech which communicates it; in other words, feeling and freedom.

The more I see of Russia, the more I agree with the Emperor when he forbids Russians to travel and makes access to his own country difficult for foreigners. The political system of Russia could not withstand twenty years of free communication with Western Europe. Do not listen to the boasts of Russians; they take pomp for elegance, luxury for politeness, police and fear for the foundations of society. In their minds, to be disciplined is to be civilized. They forget that there are savages with gentle manners who are very cruel soldiers. In spite of all their pretensions to good manners, in spite of their superficial education and their profound and premature corruption, in spite of their facility in recognizing and understanding the realities of life, the Russians are not yet civilized. They are regimented Tartars, nothing more.

So far as civilization is concerned, they are up to the present content with the appearance of it; but if they are ever able to avenge their real inferiority, they will make us cruelly atone for our advantages.

This morning, after hastily dressing to go to the Imperial Chapel, alone in my carriage, I followed the French Ambassador across the squares and streets which led to the palace, and I watched everything along my route with keen interest. I noticed, along the passages leading to the palace, troops which did not appear to me sufficiently magnificent to merit their reputation; however, the horses were superb. The immense square which separates the residence of the sovereign from the rest of the city was crossed in all directions by court carriages, by men in livery and by soldiers in uniforms of all colors. The Cossacks are the most outstanding. In spite of this influx, the square is so vast it was not crowded.

In new States there is space everywhere, especially when their government is absolute; absence of freedom creates solitudes and spreads sadness. Only free countries are populous.

The rites of the Greek Orthodox marriage are long and majestic. Everything is symbolic in this church of the East. It seemed to me that the religious splendors set off the lustre of the court solemnities.

The walls, the ceilings of the chapel, the robes of the priests and their acolytes, all glittered with gold and gems—a richness to astonish the least poetic imagination. This spectacle is worthy of the most fantastic descriptions in *A Thousand and One Nights*; it is poetry like Lalla Rookh, like Aladdin's marvelous lamp—oriental poetry where sensation sways the mind and soul.

The Imperial Chapel is not large; it was filled by the representatives of all the sovereigns of Europe and of almost all of Asia, a few foreigners such as myself, permitted to enter along with the diplomatic corps, the wives of the ambassadors, and lastly by the high officials of the court. A balustrade separated us from the circular interior where the altar stood.

I have seen few things to compare with the magnificence and the solemnity of the entrance of the Emperor into this chapel brilliant with gold leaf. He appeared, advancing with the Empress and followed by the entire court. Immediately my eyes and those of the audience were fixed on him; afterwards we admired his family. The bridal couple shone in the midst of all. A marriage of inclination, with embroidered attire and in such pompous surroundings, is a rarity which climaxed the interest of the scene. That is what everyone was saying around me; but, as for myself, I do not believe in this miracle and I could not help seeing political intent in all that was done and said. The Czar is, perhaps, deceiving himself; he believes he is performing an act of paternal tenderness, whereas, at the bottom of his mind, the hope of some advantage to come determined his choice. In this choice there is ambition as well as avarice; greed is always calculating, even when it thinks it is yielding to disinterested sentiments.

Although the court was numerous and the chapel small, there was no confusion. I was standing in the midst of the diplomatic corps, near the balustrade which separated us from the sanctuary. We were not too crowded to be able to distinguish the features and the movements of each of the personages that either duty or curiosity had gathered together there. The silence of respect was not disturbed by any disorder. A brilliant sun illuminated the interior of the chapel, where the temperature mounted, I was told, to eighty-six degrees. In the Czar's suite there was a Tartar khan, half tributary, half independent of Russia; he was clad in a long robe, overlaid with gold, and a pointed hat, also decorated with gold embroidery. This little sovereign-slave thought, in conformity with the equivocal position in which he had been placed by the conquering policies of his protectors, that it would be fitting to come to beg the Emperor of All the Russias to admit *among his pages* the twelve-year-old son he had brought to Petersburg in order to assure this child of a suitable existence. The picture of this fallen power in contrast with its conqueror reminded me of the splendor of Rome.

The first ladies of the court of Russia and the wives of the ambassadors of all the courts adorned the periphery of the chapel; at the rear, terminated by a rotunda brilliant with paintings, all the imperial family was arrayed. The gold of the canopy caressed by the fiery rays of the sun formed a sort of halo on the heads of the sovereigns and their children. The finery and the diamonds of the

108

women shone with a magic brilliance against a
background of all the treasures of Asia displayed
on the walls of the sanctuary. Here the royal magnificence seemed to defy the majesty of the God
it honored without forgetting itself. All of this was
beautiful; above all it is astonishing for us if we
remember the time, still not long ago, when the
marriage of the daughter of a Czar would have
been practically ignored in Europe, and when
Peter I declared his right to leave the crown to
whomever he wished. What progress in a few
years!

When one considers the diplomatic and other
conquests of this power, but lately counted of little importance in the affairs of the civilized world,
one asks himself if what he sees is not a dream.
The Emperor himself did not seem very accustomed to what was happening before him, for
every instant he was leaving his prayer stool and
stepping from one side to the other to correct his
children's or his clergy's faults of etiquette. He
showed me that in Russia the court itself is still in
a formative stage. His son-in-law was not in the
right place; he made him draw back or advance a
couple of steps; the Grand Duchess, the priests as
well, the court officials, all seemed subjected to his
direction—minute although supreme. I should
have found it more dignified to let things go as
they would, and I should have preferred that,
once in the chapel, he think only of God, leaving
each man to acquit himself of his functions without scrupulously correcting the minutest fault of
religious discipline or court ceremony. But in this

strange country the absence of freedom reveals itself everywhere; it is found even at the foot of the altar. Here the spirit of Peter the Great dominates all spirits.

There comes a time in the long ceremony when everyone must kneel. The Czar, before prostrating himself like the others, first cast an ungracious look of inspection over the assembly. He seemed to wish to assure himself that nobody remained standing—a superfluous precaution for, although there were Catholics and Protestants present, certainly it had not entered the mind of any of these foreigners not to conform outwardly to all the rites of the Orthodox Church.

The possibility of doubt in this respect justifies what I have said above and authorizes me to repeat that uneasy severity has become the habitual expression of the Emperor's face.

Today, when revolt, so to speak, is in the air, the autocracy itself stands in dread of some blow at its power. This fear creates a disagreeable and even a frightening contrast to the idea that it holds of its rights. Absolute power becomes too dreadful when it is afraid.

I have told you that everybody had knelt and the Emperor after everyone else. The bridal couple are married. The imperial family, then the audience stand up. At this moment the priests and the choir chant the *Te Deum,* while outside an artillery salute announces to the city the consecration of the marriage. The effect of the celestial music accompanied by the shots of cannon, by the tinkling of bells and by the distant acclamations of the people is inexpressible. All musical instruments are banished in the Orthodox Church, and only male voices celebrate the praises of the Lord. This severity of the Eastern rite is favorable to an art which conserves all the simplicity, and produces the effect, of a truly celestial chant. It seemed to me that I heard, in the distance, the beating of the hearts of sixty million subjects, the living orchestra which followed, without covering, the triumphal chant of the priests. I was moved— music can make one forget everything for a moment, even despotism.

For an amateur of the arts the music of the Imperial Chapel is in itself worth a trip to Petersburg. The *piano,* the *forte,* the finest nuances of expression are observed with a deep sentiment, a marvelous skill, and an admirable ensemble. The Russian people are musical; one cannot doubt this when one has heard the chants of the church.

At a given moment during the *Te Deum* two choirs respond, the tabernacle opens and one sees the priests with their tiaras sparkling with jewels, with their long golden robes, over which their silver beards fall majestically—some of them to the waist. The audience is as brilliant as those officiating. This court is magnificent and the military uniform shines here with all its brilliance. With admiration, I saw the world bring to God the homage of all its pomp and all its richness.

The officiating archbishop did not mar the majesty of this scene. Although not handsome, he is venerable. His little face is that of a miserable weasel, but his head is white with age. He has a tired, sick appearance—a priest, old and feeble, cannot be ignoble. At the end of the ceremony, the Czar approached, bowed before him and kissed his hand with respect.

The autocrat never misses an occasion to give an example of submission when this example can be of profit to him. I admired this poor archbishop, who appeared to be dying in the midst of his glory, this Emperor, of great stature and noble face, who humbled himself before the religious power; and farther away, the bridal couple, the family, the crowd, finally the entire court which filled and animated the chapel.

The religious ceremony accomplished in the Orthodox chapel had to be followed by a second nuptial benediction, performed by a Catholic priest in one of the halls of the palace consecrated, for today only, to this pious use. After these two marriages, the bridal couple and their family had to dine together; I, not having permission to attend either the Catholic marriage or the banquet, followed the bulk of the court and went out to breathe less stifling air.

Upon leaving the palace, I found my carriage without difficulty; I repeat to you, there are no great throngs in Russia. Space is always too vast for them to form. That is the advantage of a country where there is no nation. The first time there is a crowd in Petersburg, the city will be crushed. In a society organized as this one is, a crowd would mean a revolution.

The emptiness that reigns everywhere here makes the edifices appear too small for their

sites; they are lost in the vastness. The column of
Alexander is considered higher than that of the
Place Vendôme in Paris because of the dimensions of its pedestal. This pedestal is made of a
single piece of granite, the largest that has ever
been worked by the hand of man. This huge column, which is erected between the Winter Palace
and the arc of buildings which terminates one of
the extremities of the square, looks like a post,
and the houses that border this square look so flat
and low they have the appearance of a palisade.
Imagine a square that still seems practically empty
with a hundred thousand people circulating in it.
Obviously nothing can seem big in such a place.
This square, or rather this Russian Champs de
Mars, is enclosed by the Winter Palace, whose
façades have just been rebuilt on the plan of the
old Palace of the Empress Elizabeth. This at least
rests the eyes from the stiff and paltry imitation
of so many monuments of Athens and Rome. It
is in the style of the Regency, degenerated Louis
XIV, but very grand. The side of the square opposite the Winter Palace ends in a semi-circle and
is enclosed by buildings where several ministries
are established. These buildings are, for the most
part, constructed in the ancient Greek style. A
strange taste—temples erected to clerks! The
buildings of the Admiralty, which are picturesque,
are along the same square. Their little columns,
their gilded spires, their chapels give a pleasing
effect. A passage of trees bedecks the square in
this spot and makes it less monotonous. Toward
one end of this immense space, on the side oppo-

site the column of Alexander, stands the Church
of Saint Isaac, with its colossal peristyle, and its
copper cupola half hidden under the architect's
scaffolding. Farther on, you see the Palace of the
Senate and other buildings, always in the form of
pagan temples even though they serve to house
the Ministry of War. Then in the forward angle
which forms this long square, at the end toward
the Neva, you see, or at least you try to see, the
statue of Peter the Great, supported by its rock of
granite which disappears in the vastness like a
pebble on the beach. The statue of the hero has
been made too famous by the empirical conceit of
the woman who had it erected and falls far short
of its reputation. With all these edifices I have just
enumerated there would be enough material to
build an entire city, and even so, they are insufficient for the Great Square of Petersburg—it is a
field, not of wheat but of columns. . . .

I had just time to reach my hotel before a storm
broke. Coming at this time, the storm, through its
more or less significant portents, was frightening
to all the superstitious people of the city. Darkness in broad day, a stifling temperature, claps
of thunder which reverberated without bringing
rain, a wind strong enough to blow away houses,
a dry tempest—such was the spectacle the sky
presented during the nuptial banquet. The Russians reassured themselves by saying the storm
was brief and the air already purer than before
the outbreak. I relate only what I see without taking part; I bring here no other interest than that
of an inquisitive and attentive person but a stran-

114

ger at heart to what is happening under his eyes. Between France and Russia there is a Wall of China—the Slavic language and character. In spite of the pretensions inspired in the Russians by Peter the Great, Siberia begins at the Vistula.

A PERMANENT CONSPIRACY
OF SMILES

July 15, 1839

YESTERDAY EVENING at seven o'clock I returned to the palace, along with several other foreigners. We were to be presented to the Czar and the Czarina.

One sees that the Czar cannot forget for a single instant who he is or the constant attention he excites. He poses incessantly, with the result that he is never natural, even when he is sincere.

With a height that surpasses that of ordinary men as his throne towers above other seats, he would accuse himself of weakness if he were for a moment just human, and if he let it be seen that he lives, thinks, and feels as a mere mortal. Without appearing to share any of our feelings, he is always chief, judge, general, admiral—prince in sum, nothing more and nothing less. He will find himself very weary toward the end of his life; but he will have a high place in the minds of his people and perhaps of the world, for the mob loves efforts which astonish it and is proud in seeing the trouble one takes to dazzle it.

To abdicate a disputed power is sometimes a vengeance; to abdicate an absolute power would be cowardice.

Whatever it may be, the singular destiny of an

116

Emperor of Russia inspires in me a lively interest, curiosity at first, charity later—how is it possible not to have compassion for the troubles of this glorious exile!

The more one sees what court life is, the more one sympathizes with the lot of the man who is obliged to direct it—especially the court of Russia. It produces the effect of a theater where the actors spend their lives in dress rehearsals. Not one knows his rôle and the day of the presentation never arrives as the director is never satisfied with the performance of his subjects. Actors and directors thus waste their lives preparing, correcting, endlessly perfecting their interminable comedy of society which is called "Of the Civilization of the North." If this is tiring to watch, think what it must exact from the players! . . . I prefer Asia; there is more harmony. At every turn in Russia, one is struck by the consequences that innovation in things and institutions and the inexperience of man must have. All this is hidden with great care; but a little attention suffices for the traveler to sense what they do not wish to show him.

I was presented this evening, not by the French Ambassador, but by the Grand Master of Ceremonies of the court.

The Emperor received us with studied and delicate courtesy. One immediately recognized a man obliged, and accustomed, to consider the *amour-propre* of others. Each felt himself classified with a word, a look, in the royal mind and, consequently, in the mind of all.

To let me know he would not be displeased to have me travel in his country, the Czar did me the favor of telling me I should go at least as far as Moscow and Nizhni to get a fair idea of the country. "Petersburg is Russian," he added, "but not Russia."

These few words were pronounced in a tone of voice that one cannot forget—so much authority it has, so grave and firm it is. Everybody has spoken to me of his imposing appearance, the nobility of his features, and his great height; no one had warned me of the power of his voice. His voice is indeed that of a man born to command. In it there is neither effort nor study. It is a gift developed by habitual use.

The fête which followed our presentation was one of the most magnificent I have ever seen. It was like a fairyland, and the admiration and astonishment that was inspired in all the court by each room of this palace, renovated in one year, added a dramatic interest to the rather cold pomp of the usual solemnities. Each room, each painting, was a subject of surprise for the Russians, themselves, who had witnessed the catastrophe and had not seen this marvelous abode since, at the word of the god, the temple had risen again from its cinders. What an effort of will! I thought at each gallery, each statue, each painting I saw. The style of these ornaments, although they were remade only yesterday, recalled the century when the palace was founded; what I saw seemed already antique. They copy everything in Russia, even time. These wonders inspired a contagious admiration in the crowd; while seeing the triumph of the will of a man and while listening to the exclamations of the other people, I, myself, began to be less indignant at the price this miracle had cost. If I feel this influence at the end of two days' stay, how much indulgence do we not owe to men who are born and who spend their lives in the atmosphere of this court! . . . that is to say in Russia, for the air of the court is breathed from one end of the Empire to the other. I am not speaking of serfs: still, even they, through their association with the owner, feel the effect of the sovereign thought which animates the Empire. The courtier, who is their master, is for them the image of the supreme master. Thus the Emperor and the court appear before the Russians everywhere there is a man who obeys a man who commands.

Ambassadors from all of Europe had been invited to the palace to admire the marvelous accomplishments of this government—the more it is envied and admired by political men, essentially practical men who must be impressed at first by the simplicity of the machinery of despotism, the more bitterly it is criticized by the common people. A palace, one of the biggest in the world, rebuilt in a year—what a subject for admiration for men accustomed to breathe the air of courts!

Great things are never achieved without great sacrifices—unity of command, force, authority, military power, are bought here by the absence of freedom; whereas, political liberty and indus-

119

trial wealth have cost France its old chivalrous spirit and the old sensibility of feeling that one formerly called national honor.

The hall where supper was served seemed to me even more spectacular than the ballroom, completely gilded as it was. The banquet table was brilliant; at this fête everything seemed colossal and countless; I did not know which should be most admired, the effect of the ensemble or the grandeur and the quantity of the objects considered separately. A thousand persons were seated at this one table in the banquet hall.

Being a complete stranger both to the people and to the objects that surrounded me, I hardly expected to enjoy this ball. I should like to speak of the impression made on me by a great natural phenomenon. The heat of the day had risen to 86 degrees and, in spite of the freshness of the evening, the atmosphere of the palace was stifling. On leaving the table, I took refuge as quickly as possible in the recess of an open window. There, completely unmindful of what went on around me, I was all of a sudden struck with wonder at the sight of the light effects which one experiences only in the North and during the magic clarity of the Arctic nights. Several tiers of very heavy, black storm clouds divided the sky into zones; it was half-past midnight—the nights which are beginning again for Petersburg are still so short one scarcely has time to notice them; at this hour dawn was already appearing in the direction of Archangel. The land wind had fallen, and in the spaces which separated the bands of motionless

120

clouds one saw the base of the sky—its whiteness was so alive and so shining it resembled swords of silver separated by massive garlands of embroidery. This light was reflected on the motionless Neva—the Gulf, still agitated by the storm of the day, pushed the water back into the bed of the river and gave to this vast sheet of sleeping river the appearance of a sea of milk or a lake of mother-of-pearl.

Most of Petersburg, with its quays, and the spires of its chapels, stretched before my eyes; it was a veritable composition of Breughel. The tints of this picture cannot be put into words. The Church of St. Nicholas with its bell tower stood out in lapis blue against a white sky; lights, dimmed by the dawn, still gleamed under the portico of the Bourse, a Greek building which terminates, with theatrical pomp, one of the islands of the Neva where the river divides into two main branches; the open columns of the edifice, whose bad style was not apparent at this hour and at this distance, were reflected in the water of the white river on which they sketched a reversed fronton and peristyle of gold. The remainder of the city was of a deep blue like the colored roof of the Church of St. Nicholas and like the background of the landscapes of old painters. This fantastic picture, painted on a foundation of ultramarine and framed by a golden window, contrasted in an entirely supernatural manner with the light of the chandeliers and the pomp of the interior of the palace. One would have said that the city, the sky, the sea, that all of nature wished to join with

121

the splendors of the court and solemnize the fête given by the ruler of these vast regions for his daughter. The appearance of the sky had something so astonishing about it that, with a little imagination, one could have believed that from the deserts of Lapland to the Crimea, from the Caucasus and the Vistula to Kamchatka, the king of the sky was responding by some sign to the call of the king of the earth. The sky of the North is rich in omens. All this was extraordinary and even beautiful.

Upon leaving the banquet hall on my way to the ballroom I approached another window. It opened on the interior court of the palace. There I had a spectacle of a completely different sort but as little expected and as amazing, in its way, as the daybreak in the beautiful Petersburg sky. This was the view of the great courtyard of the Winter Palace which is square like that of the Louvre. During the ball, little by little, all this enclosure had filled with people. The glimmers of the dawn had become more distinct and day was appearing. On seeing this crowd speechless with admiration, this motionless people, silent, and, so to speak, fascinated by the splendors of the palace of its master, inhaling with a timid respect, with a sort of animal joy, the emanations of the royal festival, I experienced a sensation of pleasure. Finally I had found a crowd in Russia; I saw nothing below but people; so great was the crush that not an inch of ground was visible. However, in despotic countries all the amusements of the people seem to me suspect when they coincide with those of the prince—the fear and the flattery of the little people, the vanity and the hypocritical generosity of the great are the only sentiments which I believe to be real among people who live under an autocratic régime.

In the midst of the fêtes of Petersburg, I could not forget the progress of the Empress Catherine to the Crimea and the façades of villages set up at spaced intervals along the way. These façades made of wood and painted canvas were placed a quarter of a league from the route to make the triumphant sovereign believe that the desert had been peopled under her reign. Russian minds are still obsessed by similar preoccupations. Everyone hides the bad and presents the good to the eyes of the master. It is a permanent conspiracy of smiles plotting against truth for the satisfaction of the one person who is reputed to wish and act for the good of all. The Emperor is the only man of the Empire who lives, for only to eat is not to live!

It must be admitted, however, that these people remained in the courtyard almost voluntarily; nothing seemed to me to force them to appear under the windows of the Emperor and to seem to be amused; then they were enjoying themselves, but for the sole pleasure of their masters. The coiffures of the women of the people, the beautiful cloth robes and the brilliant belts of wool or silk of the men dressed in Russian style—that is to say in Persian style—the diversity of colors, the stillness of the people gave me the illusion of a huge Turkish carpet thrown from one end of the courtyard to the other by order of the magician who presides here at all miracles. A floor of heads—the most beautiful ornament of the Czar's palace on the night of his daughter's wedding. The Emperor felt about this as I did, for he complacently brought the attention of the foreign guests to this crowd who, without acclamations and by its presence alone, bore witness to the rôle it plays in the good fortune of its masters. It was the shadow of a people kneeling before invisible gods. . . .

A WORLD OF ILLUSION

Petersburg, July 19, 1839

ONE MUST BE Russian and even Czar to stand up under the fatigue of life in Petersburg at this moment: in the evening, fêtes such as one sees only in Russia; in the morning, court felicitations, ceremonies, receptions, or perhaps public solemnities, parades on land and sea—for example, a vessel of 120 cannons launched on the Neva in the presence of the court reënforced by the entire city. Such are the things that absorb my energy and engage my curiosity.

Scarcely rested from the court ball, we had another fête yesterday at the Michael Palace, home of the Grand Duchess Helen, sister-in-law of the Emperor.

The interior of the great hall where they were dancing was decorated with an astounding richness; fifteen hundred boxes and pots of the rarest flowers formed a fragrant grove. At the end of the hall, in the thickest part of a copse of exotic plants, one saw a fountain of fresh clear water where a sheaflike cluster of jets spouted continuously. These jets of water, lighted by clusters of candles, shone like a spray of diamonds. They cooled the air, which was kept in motion by enormous palm branches and banana plants, glistening with dew, from which the breeze of the waltz shook pearls of moisture onto the moss of

125

the balmy grove. One would have said that all
these foreign plants whose roots were hidden under a carpet of greenery grew there in their own
soil, and that the cortège of dancers of the North
was moving in a magic spell through tropical forests. I thought I was dreaming. It was not only
luxury, it was poetry. The brilliance of this magic
hall was increased a hundredfold by such a profusion of mirrors as I have never seen elsewhere.
One did not know where one was; boundaries had
disappeared; everything became space, light,
gold, flowers, reflection, illusion—the movement
of the crowd and the crowd itself were multiplied
to infinity.

Before the supper hour, the Czarina, seated under her dais of exotic greenery, beckoned me to
her. I had scarcely obeyed when the Czar approached the magic fountain whose jets of spout-
ing water lighted us with its diamonds and
refreshed us with its fragrant emanations. He took
my hand and led me a few steps from his wife's
chair. There he chatted with me for more than a
quarter of an hour on some very interesting subjects. This prince does not talk with you, as do
many other princes, only so that it will be seen
that he is speaking to you.

He first said a few words about the beautiful
arrangement of the ball. I replied that with a life
as active as his I was surprised that he could find
time for everything, even participation in the
pleasures of the crowd.

"Happily," he replied, "the administrative machine is very simple in my country. The distances

126

make everything difficult and if the form of government were complicated the shoulders of one man could not support the burden."

I was surprised and flattered by his tone of frankness. The Emperor, who understands what is not said to him better than anyone, responding to my thoughts continued, "If I speak to you in this manner, it is because I know that you can understand me—we are continuing the work of Peter the Great."

"He is not dead, Sire; his genius and his will still govern Russia . . ."

The Czar went on, "This will is very difficult to have carried out; submission in Russia makes you believe there is uniformity; correct this idea. Nowhere is there a country where there is such diversity of races, of customs, of religion, or mentality as in Russia. The differences are basic; the uniformity superficial, and unity is only apparent. There near us you see twenty officers: only the first two are Russians; the next three are reconciled Poles; some of the others are German; there is everything, even to Kirghiz khans who bring me their sons to be reared among my cadets. There is one of them," he said, pointing out a little Chinese puppet in his bizarre costume of velvet all braided with gold.

"Two hundred thousand children are reared and instructed along with this child at my expense."

"Sire, everything is done on a large scale in Russia; everything is colossal."

"Too colossal for one man."

127

"What man has ever been closer to his people?"

"You speak of Peter the Great?"

"No, Sire."

"I hope you will not limit yourself to seeing Petersburg. What is your plan of travel in my country?"

"Sire, I wish to leave immediately after the Fête of Peterhof."

"To go?"

"To Moscow and Nizhni."

"Good. But you are going too soon; you will leave Moscow before my arrival, and I should have liked to see you there."

"Sire, this word from Your Majesty will make me alter my plan."

"So much the better. We will show you the new work we are doing on the Kremlin. My aim is to make the architecture of these old edifices conform more with the use that is made of them today. The palace, which is too small, was becoming uncomfortable for me. You will also attend an interesting ceremony in the plain of Borodino [site of Napoleon's Pyrrhic victory near Moscow, Sept. 7, 1812]—I must lay the cornerstone of a monument I am having erected in memory of that battle."

I remained silent and no doubt my expression became grave. The Czar fixed his eyes on me, then went on in a gentle tone with a shade of delicateness and even of sensibility which touched me, "The spectacle of the maneuvers *at least* will interest you . . ."

"Sire, everything in Russia interests me."

128

Petersburg, July 19, 1839

I left the Michael Palace ball at a very early hour. In leaving I stopped on the stairway where I should have liked to stay; it was a forest of orange trees in bloom. I have never seen anything so magnificent or better arranged than this fête; but I know of nothing so fatiguing as prolonged admiration when it bears neither on natural phenomena nor on works of art.

I leave you now to dine at the home of a Russian officer, the young Count who took me this morning to the Bureau of Mineralogy, the most beautiful, I believe, in Europe as the mines of the Urals are of an incomparable richness. Here one can see nothing alone; a native of the country is always with you to do the honors of the public establishments. Also there are few days in the year favorable to seeing anything well. In the summer, they replaster the buildings deteriorated by the cold; in the winter, they are occupied with social events—one dances when one is not freezing. You will believe that I exaggerate if I tell you that one sees Russia scarcely better in Petersburg than in France. Detach this observation from its paradoxical form and you will see the pure truth. Certainly it is not sufficient to come into a country to know it. Without protection, you would not get an idea of anything, and often the protection tyrannizes you and exposes you to accepting false ideas—which is what the Russians want.

IF I HAD A SECRET TO HIDE
I WOULD BEGIN BY CONFIDING
IT TO THE CZAR

Petersburg, July 21, 1839

AT THE Opera I saw what is called a gala performance. The magnificently lighted hall was large and beautiful in form. Neither galleries nor balconies are known here. In Petersburg, there is no placing of the bourgeoisie to hinder the architects in their plans; thus the auditorium can be built on simple and regular lines like the theaters of Italy, where the women who are not of high society go to the parterre.

As a particular favor, I had obtained a seat in the first row of the parterre for this performance. On the days of gala performances these places are reserved for the highest nobility, that is to say the most important officials of the court. No one is admitted except in uniform, in the dress of his rank and station.

I did not particularly like the spectacle; I was more interested in the spectators. Finally the court arrived. The imperial loge is a brilliant salon which occupies the back of the hall; this salon is even more brilliantly illuminated than the rest of the theater, which is itself very light.

The Czar's entry was impressive. When he approached the front of his loge. accompanied by the Czarina and followed by their family and the court, the entire audience rose. The Czar, in dress uniform of bright red, was particularly handsome. The uniform of the Cossacks is becoming only to very young men; so this one is better suited to a man the age of His Majesty; it enhanced both the nobility of his features and his height. . . .

Seen from the point where I was sitting, which was approximately in the center between the two theaters, the stage and the court, the Czar appeared to me worthy to command men; he had such an air of greatness, such a noble and majestic face. Immediately, I recalled his conduct at the time he mounted the throne, and this fine page in history distracted my attention from the performance I was attending.

What you are about to read was told to me only a few days ago by the Czar himself. If I did not recount this conversation to you in my last letter, it is because papers which contain such details cannot be trusted to the Russian post or even to any traveler.

The day when Nicholas came to the throne was the day the rebellion broke out in the guard; at the first news of the revolt of the troops, the Czar and the Czarina came down to their chapel alone and there, falling to their knees on the steps of the altar, they swore to each other and before God to die as sovereigns if they could not quell the riot.

The Czar deemed the trouble serious, as he had just learned that the Archbishop had already tried in vain to appease the soldiers. In Russia, when the religious power fails, the disorder is formidable.

After making the Sign of the Cross, the Czar went out to master the rebels solely by his presence and by the force of his calm countenance. He, himself, described this scene to me in more modest terms than those I have just used. Unfortunately, I have forgotten the first part of his recital because at the very beginning I was a little troubled by the unexpected turn our conversation had taken. I will begin at the point from which I remember.

"Sire, Your Majesty had drawn his strength at the true source."

"I did not know what I was going to do and say; I had been inspired."

"To have such inspirations, one must deserve them."

"I did nothing extraordinary; I said to the soldiers: 'Return to your ranks.' And at the moment the regiment passed in review I cried: 'Kneel!' They all obeyed. The thing that made me strong was that a moment before I had resigned myself to death. I am grateful for the success—I am not proud of it for in it I had no merit."

Such were the noble expressions the Czar used to relate this contemporary tragedy.

Eye witnesses have assured me that one saw him grow with each step he took in advancing before the mutineers. His attitude before the rebellious guard was so imposing, they said, that four times while he was haranguing the troops one of the conspirators approached him to kill him, and four times courage failed this wretch. Well-informed people attribute this uprising to the influence of the secret societies by which Russia has been afflicted since the campaigns of the allies in France and the frequent trips of Russian officers to Germany.

I repeat to you only what I have heard—these are obscure facts, and it is impossible for me to verify them.

The means the conspirators employed to arouse the army was a ridiculous lie. They spread the rumor that Nicholas was usurping the crown, opposing his brother, Constantine, who was advancing toward Petersburg to defend his rights—arms in hand. Such were the means they took to persuade the rebels to cry under the windows of the palace: Long live the constitution! The leaders had led them to believe that this word *constitution* was the name of the wife of Constantine and their supposed Empress. You see that an idea of duty was in the hearts of the soldiers, as they could not have been led to rebellion except by fraud.

The fact is that Constantine refused the throne only through weakness—he was afraid of being poisoned; therein consisted his philosophy. God knows, and perhaps some men know, whether his abdication saved him from the danger he believed he was avoiding.

It was, therefore, in the interest of legitimacy that the deceived soldiers revolted against their legitimate sovereign.

It was observed that, during all the time the

133

Czar remained before the troops, he was so calm he did not once put his horse to a gallop; but he was very pale. He was making a test of his power and the success of the proof assured him of the obedience of his nation.

Here is what I still remember of the remainder of our conversation.

"The riot quelled, Sire, Your Majesty must have returned to the palace in a frame of mind very different from that you had before going out, for you had just won the assurance, along with the throne, of the admiration of the world and the sympathy of all high-minded men."

"I was not thinking that; what I did at that time has been too much praised."

"One thing that is certain, Sire, is that one of the principal motives of my interest in coming to Russia was the desire to know a prince who exercises such power over men."

"The Russians are good, but one must make oneself worthy to govern such a people."

"Your Majesty has sensed what is fitting for Russia better than any of his predecessors."

"Despotism still exists in Russia, since it is the essence of my government; but it is in keeping with the character of the nation."

"Sire, you are stopping Russia on the road of imitation and bringing her back to herself."

"I love my country and I believe I understand it; I assure you that when I am very tired of all the miseries of the times, I try to forget the rest of Europe in withdrawing to the interior of Russia."

134

"In order to restore your strength?"

"Precisely! No one is more Russian at heart than I am. I am going to say something to you I would not say to anyone else, but I feel that you will understand me."

Here the Czar interrupted himself and looked at me attentively; I continued to listen without replying; he went on.

"I can understand the republic—it is an open and sincere government, or at least it can be; I can understand the absolute monarchy, since I am the head of such a government; but I cannot comprehend the representative monarchy—it is a government of lies, of fraud and corruption, and I would withdraw as far as China rather than ever adopt it."

"Sire, I have always regarded the representative form of government as an inevitable compromise in certain societies at certain epochs; but, just as all compromises, it resolves nothing; it only postpones the difficulties."

The Emperor seemed to say to me, "Speak." I continued.

"It is a truce signed between democracy and monarchy under the auspices of two very depraved tyrannies—fear and self-interest—and prolonged by the pride of spirit which completes itself in loquacity and by popular egotism which pays with words. Finally, it is the aristocracy of the word substituted for that of birth, for it is the government of lawyers."

"Sir, you speak with truth," the Emperor said, shaking my hand; "I have been a representative

135

sovereign [in Poland until 1832 when the kingdom was deprived of its constitution and reduced to a province of the Russian Empire], and the world knows what it has cost me not to wish to submit myself to the exigencies of this *infamous* government (I quote literally). To buy voices, corrupt consciences, seduce some in order to deceive others: all these means I have disdained as degrading for those who obey as much as for those who command, and I have paid a high price for the trouble of my frankness. But, may God be praised, I have finished forever with this odious political machine. I will never again be a constitutional king. I have too much need to say what I think ever to consent to reign over any people by ruse and intrigue."

The name of Poland, although constantly in our minds, was never pronounced during this strange interview.

The effect he produced on me was great. I felt myself overpowered. The nobility of the sentiments the Czar had just shown me, the frankness of his words seemed to make his all-powerfulness stand out in relief. I was overcome and I admit it! It is not in my nature to doubt the human word at the moment I hear it. A man who speaks is for me the instrument of God—it is only by power of reflection and experience that I recognize the possibility of calculation and feint. You will call that naïveté, and perhaps it is; but I take delight in this weakness of mind because it holds strength of soul. My good faith makes me believe in the sincerity of others—even in that of an Emperor of Russia.

He again took up the conversation.

"What is your definite plan of travel?" he asked me.

"Sire, after the Fête of Peterhof, I intend to leave for Moscow; from there I shall go to the Nizhni Fair, but in time to be back in Moscow before Your Majesty's arrival."

"Good. I should be very happy to have you examine my works on the Kremlin in detail. My quarters there were too small; I am having more commodious ones constructed, and I shall explain to you, myself, all my plans for the embellishment of that part of Moscow which we regard as the cradle of the Empire. But you have no time to lose. You have a lot of territory to cover; distances are the scourge of Russia."

"Sire, do not complain; these distances are frames to be filled; elsewhere people lack space; this will never happen to you."

"I lack time."

"You have the future."

"One does not know me very well when one criticizes me for my ambition. Far from seeking to extend our territory, I would like to be able to draw the populations of all of Russia closer around me. It is solely over misery and barbarism that I wish to make conquests: to ameliorate the lot of the Russians, this would be better than to aggrandize myself. If you knew what good people the Russians are! How gentle, how innately lov-

137

able and courteous! You will see this at Peterhof; but I would particularly like to show it to you here on the first of January."

Then, returning to his favorite theme: "But it is not easy to make oneself worthy of governing such a nation."

"Your Majesty has already done much for Russia."

"I fear sometimes that I have not done all I could have done."

This human cry, coming out of a soul to which everything should have contributed to make proud, moved me unexpectedly. We were in public and I tried to disguise my emotion; but the Czar, who responds more to what one thinks than to what one says (and it was primarily in this powerful sagacity that the charm of his conversation and the efficaciousness of his will lie), perceived both the impression he had produced and the effort I was making to conceal it. Drawing nearer to me at the moment of parting, with an air of good will he shook my hand while saying: "Until we meet again."

The Czar is the only man in the Empire with whom one can talk without fear of informers. He is also the only one, up to the present, in whom I have discovered any natural emotion or sincere language. If I lived in this country and I had a secret to hide, I would begin by confiding it to him.

Before this journey, my ideas on despotism were suggested by the study I had made of Austrian and Prussian society. I did not realize that these states are despotic only in name, and that ethics there serve as a corrective to the institutions. I did not yet know what it is to meet an absolute government and a nation of slaves.

One has to come to Russia to see the result of this terrible combination of the intelligence and the science of Europe with the genius of Asia. I have found it all the more terrible because it can last; ambition and fear, passions which elsewhere men exhaust in talking too much about them, here engender silence. This excessive silence produces a forced calm, an apparent order, stronger and more dreadful than anarchy, because, I repeat to you, the uneasiness that it causes seems permanent.

I admit very few fundamental ideas in political theory, since in actual government I believe more in the efficaciousness of circumstances than in the efficaciousness of principles; but my indifference does not go so far as tolerating institutions which seem to me necessarily to exclude dignity of character.

Perhaps an independent justice and a strong aristocracy would instill calm in Russian minds, dignity in their souls, happiness in their country; but I do not believe the Emperor dreams of this means of ameliorating the condition of his peoples. However superior a man may be, he would not voluntarily give up his rôle as the source of the welfare of others.

Furthermore, what right have we to criticize

139

the Emperor of Russia for his love of authority?
Was not the revolution as tyrannical in Paris as his
despotism is in St. Petersburg?

However, we should make a distinction for
ourselves here in order to establish the difference
between the social state of the two countries. In
France, revolutionary tyranny is an evil of transi-
tion; in Russia, the tyranny of despotism is a permanent revolution.

THE CUSTOMS OF THE NOMADIC RACES WILL PREVAIL FOR A LONG TIME AMONG THE SLAVS

Petersburg, July 22, 1839

THE POPULATION of Petersburg is four hundred thousand souls not counting the troops, according to what the Russians—good patriots—say; but people who are well-informed and who, consequently, pass for ill-intentioned assure me that it has not reached four hundred thousand, including the garrison. The thing that is certain is that this city of palaces, with its great empty spaces called squares, resembles sections of fields fenced off with boards. Little wooden houses hold sway in the quarters outside the center.

The Russians, coming from an agglomeration of tribes—nomadic for a long time and always warlike—have not yet completely forgotten the life of the bivouac. Petersburg is the general staff headquarters of an army; not the capital of a nation. As magnificent as this military city is, it appears naked to the eyes of a man from the West.

Distances are the scourge of Russia, the Czar said to me. One can verify the justice of this remark in the streets of Petersburg itself.

However little you withdraw from the center of the city, you find yourself lost in unlimited territories bordered by barracks which look as if they were intended to lodge workers gathered together temporarily for some big construction project. These are storehouses for fodder, hangars filled with clothing and all sorts of provisions for the soldiers—one thinks oneself on the verge of a review or on the eve of a fair which never takes place. Grass grows in these so-called streets, always deserted because they are too spacious for the population which uses them.

So many peristyles have been added to the houses, so many porticos ornament the barracks which imitate palaces, such a profusion of borrowed decorations prevailed at the construction of this provisional capital that I count fewer men than columns on the squares of Petersburg—these squares that are always silent and sad because of their grandeur and particularly because of their imperturbable regularity. The square and the chalk-line accord so well with the point of view of absolute sovereigns that right angles become one of the attributes of despotic architecture. Living architecture, if you will allow me the expression, does not appear on command; it is born, so to speak, of itself, and evolves as if automatically from the genius and the needs of a people. To create a great nation is unfailingly to create an architecture; I should not be surprised to find that there have been as many original architectures as there have been mother tongues.

The principal street of Petersburg is the Nevski Prospect, one of the three avenues which lead from the Palace to the Admiralty.

Abominable cobblestones are used to pave this

142

boulevard. But here, at least, as in some of the other principal streets, blocks of wood which make paths for the carriage wheels have been incrusted in the midst of the stones. These beautiful paths on the pavement are formed by an inlaid work of square, or sometimes octagonal, blocks of pine deeply imbedded. Two of these paths run the length of Nevski Prospect, one at the right and the other at the left of the street, without reaching the houses from which they are separated by flagstone walks for pedestrians. These beautiful promenades are very different from the miserable boardwalks which still disgrace some of the side streets. There are, in all, four lines of flagstones on this beautiful and spacious avenue which extends, with an almost imperceptibly sparser population and increasing ugliness and sadness, to the ill-defined borders of the habitable city—that is to say toward the boundaries of the Asiatic barbarism which surrounds Petersburg on all sides.

The superb city, created by Peter the Great, embellished by Catherine II, which succeeding sovereigns extended by rule and line across a spongy land nearly always submerged, finally is lost in a horrible mixture of stalls and workshops, confused piles of nondescript buildings, vast spaces without purpose, and all kinds of trash and debris which, thanks to the natural disorder and innate filthiness of the people of this country, have accumulated for a hundred years. This rubbish piles up year after year in Russian cities as though to protest against the pretension of the German princes who pride themselves on civilizing the

143

Slav nations. The original character of these people, however restrained by the yoke that is imposed on them, comes to light at least in some corners of their cities of despots and houses of slaves;
and even if they have things which they call cities
and houses, it is not because they like them or
feel the need of them; it is because they have been
told they must have them, or rather submit to
them, in order to overtake the old races of the
civilized West. Above all, they have them because, if they took it into their heads to argue
against the men who lead them and instruct them
militarily, these men, being at the same time their
corporals and their teachers, would drive them
back with lashes into their native Asia. These
poor exotic birds, caged by European civilization,
are the victims of the folly, or better to say of the
deeply calculated ambition, of the Czars, conquerors of the world to come, who know that before subjugating us they must imitate us.

A horde of Kalmucks who camp in barracks
surrounding a pile of ancient temples, a Greek
city improvised for the Tartars as a theater set—
a décor, magnificent though without taste, prepared to serve as the scene of a real and terrible
drama—this is what one perceives at first glance
in Petersburg.

In the afternoon, Nevski Prospect, the great
palace square, the wharves, and the bridges are
traversed by a considerable number of carriages
of various kinds and strange shapes; this movement slightly enlivens the customary sadness of

this city, the most monotonous of the capitals of Europe.

The interior of the dwellings is equally doleful because, in spite of the magnificence of the furnishings heaped up in English fashion in certain rooms intended for the reception of guests, one sees in the shadow a domestic filth, a natural and deep-rooted disorder which is reminiscent of Asia.

The piece of furniture least used in the Russian household is the bed. The women servants sleep in garrets similar to those of the porters' lodges in France; whereas the men curl up on the stairway, in the halls, and even, it is said, in the reception rooms on pillows which they throw on the floor for the night.

Sometimes one has a bed for show, an object of luxury which is on display, out of deference to the European fashion, but which is not used.

In Russia, existence is painful for everyone; the Czar is scarcely less broken by fatigue than the least of his serfs. I was shown his bed; the hardness of this couch would shock our laborers. Here, all men are forced to repeat to themselves a hard truth—the goal of life is not on this earth and the means of achieving life's goal is not pleasure.

The inexorable specter of duty and submission appears before you constantly and does not allow you to forget the hard conditions of human existence—work and grief! One is not permitted to subsist in Russia except by sacrificing all to the love of the fatherland, sanctified by faith in heaven.

145

If there are times in the middle of a public promenade when idlers give me the illusion that in Russia, as elsewhere, there can be men who amuse themselves for the pure sake of amusement, men for whom pleasure is a business, I am promptly disabused by the sight of a courier who silently and at full speed passes in his kibitka. The messenger is a man of power; he is the word of the master, a living telegraph; he is on his way to deliver an order to another man as ignorant as himself of the thought behind his actions—this other automaton awaits him at a hundred, a thousand, fifteen hundred leagues away in the country. The kibitka in which this man of iron travels is, of all the means of travel, the most uncomfortable. Imagine a little cart with two benches of leather, without springs and without backs; no other equipment can be used on the crooked trails in which all roads, however big at the beginning, across this vast and savage Empire end even to this day. The front bench is reserved for the postilion or the coachman who changes at each relay; the second for the courier who travels until death, which comes soon for men committed to this arduous profession.

Those I see rapidly traversing the beautiful streets of the city in all directions immediately present to my mind the solitudes into which they are plunging. I follow them in my imagination and, at the end of their trail, there appears before me Siberia, Kamchatka, the salt desert, the Wall of China, Lapland, the Glacial Sea, Novaya Zemlya, Persia, the Caucasus; these almost fabulous

146

historic names produce on my mind the effect of a hazy background in a great landscape. You can imagine how this kind of reverie depresses my soul! Nevertheless, the vision of these couriers, deaf and dumb, is a poetic nourishment furnished endlessly to the mind of the foreigner. This man, born to live and to die on his cart, always carrying the destinies of the world in his portfolio, alone gives a melancholy interest to the most insignificant scenes of life. It must be admitted that if despotism makes the peoples it oppresses unhappy, it has been devised for the pleasure of travelers, whom it throws into continuously recurring astonishment. Under a free government everything is published and forgotten, for it is seen at a glance; under an absolute government everything is hidden but is divined and, consequently, evokes a lively interest. I think a little too much about what I do not see to be completely satisfied with what I do see. But for all that, the spectacle, while distressing me, intrigues me.

The amateurs of antiquity say Russia has no past. This is true, but the future and the space there serve as pasture for the most ardent imaginations.

Nature must have put a deep poetic feeling into the soul of the Russians—contemptuous and melancholy people—for them to have found the means of giving an original and picturesque appearance to cities built by men, entirely lacking in imagination, in the dreariest, most monotonous, most barren country on earth. Endless plains, somber and flat solitudes—such is Russia. Nev-

147

ertheless, if I could show you Petersburg, its
streets, its inhabitants, as I see them, I would
show you a picture of life in every line, so strongly
has the genius of the Slav nation reacted against
the sterile madness of its government. This anti-
national government advances only by military
evolutions; it reminds one of Prussia under its first
king.

I have described to you a city without character, more pompous than imposing, more vast
than beautiful, filled with buildings without style,
without taste, and without historical significance.
But in order to give you a complete picture, that is
to say a fair one, I must at the same time make
you see, in this pretentious and ridiculous frame,
a naturally engaging people who, with their oriental genius have been able to adapt themselves to a
city built for a people who do not exist anywhere;
for Petersburg was built by rich men whose ideas
were formed by comparing, without making a profound study, the various countries of Europe.
This legion of travelers, more or less refined,
more experienced than learned, was an artificial
nation, a selection of intelligent and active minds
recruited from all the nations of the world—it was
not the Russian people.

The Russian people are mocking, like the slave
who consoles himself for his yoke by quietly making fun of it; they are superstitious, boastful,
brave, and lazy, like the soldier; they are poetic,
musical, and thoughtful, like the shepherd; for the
customs of the nomadic races will prevail for a
long time among the Slavs. All of this is in keep-

148

ing neither with the style of the buildings nor with the plan of the streets in Petersburg; there is obvious dissension between the architect and the inhabitant. European engineers came to tell the Muscovites how they should build and embellish a capital worthy of the admiration of Europe; and they, with their military submission, ceded to the force of command. Peter the Great built Petersburg against the Swedes much more than for the Russians. But the nature of the people came to light in spite of their respect for the caprices of the master and in spite of their distrust of themselves, and it is to this involuntary disobedience that Russia owes its seal of originality. Nothing has been able to efface the basic character of the inhabitants; this triumph of innate faculties over badly directed education is an interesting spectacle for any traveler capable of appreciating it.

Happily for the painter and for the poet, the Russians are essentially religious—their churches, at least, are their own. The unvarying form of pious edifices is part of the cult, and superstition protects these religious fortresses against the mania for geometrical figures in limestone—rectangles, plane surfaces, and straight lines; if short, against the military, rather than the classic, architecture which gives the air of a camp designed to last a few weeks during the grand maneuvers to all the cities of this country.

The mark of a nomadic people is equally apparent in the Russian chariots, carriages, trappings, and teams. Imagine swarms, hosts of droshkies hugging the earth while rolling between very

low houses, above which one sees the spires of a
multitude of churches and a few celebrated monuments; if this ensemble is not beautiful, it is at
least astonishing. These gilded or painted spires
break the monotonous lines of the roofs of the
city; they pierce the air with such sharp darts that
the eye can scarcely distinguish the point at which
their gold fades into the fog of a polar sky. The
spire of the citadel, root and cradle of Petersburg, and that of the Admiralty, adorned with
gold from the ducats of Holland given to the Czar
Peter by the Republic of the United Provinces,
are the most outstanding. These monumental
clusters, copied from the Asiatic headdresses with
which, it is said, the buildings of Moscow are
adorned, are really extraordinary in height and
boldness. One can understand neither how they
are sustained in the air nor how they were placed
there—this is truly a Russian creation. Imagine,
then, a huge assemblage of domes accompanied
by the four campaniles required, according to the
modern Greeks, to make a church. Imagine a multitude of cupolas—silvered, gilded, tinted blue,
studded with stars—and the roofs of the palaces
painted emerald green or sky-blue, the squares
decorated with statues of bronze in honor of the
Czars and the principal historic personages of
Russia. Frame this picture with an immense river
which on calm days serves to reflect and on stormy
days to set off the ensemble. Add to this the pon-
toon bridge of Troitza thrown across the widest
part of the Neva, between the Champs de Mars
where the statue of Suvorov is lost in space and

the citadel where Peter the Great and his family sleep in their tombs bare of ornamentation (the Greek rite forbids sculptured images in the churches). Finally, remember that the sheet of water of the ever-full Neva runs on a level with the ground and in the center of the city hardly respects an island completely bordered by buildings with Greek columns, supported by foundations of granite and built along the designs of pagan temples. If you grasp this ensemble clearly, you will understand why Petersburg is an infinitely picturesque city in spite of the bad taste of its borrowed architecture, in spite of the marshy tints of the country which surrounds it, in spite of the total absence of contours in the terrain and the pallor of the summer days under the dull climate of the North.

Do not reproach me for my contradictions. I perceived them before you without wishing to avoid them, for they exist in the things that I describe—let this be said once and for all. How can I give you a true idea of what I am describing without contradicting myself at every word? If I were less sincere I would appear more consistent. Consider that in the physical, as in the moral order, the truth here is only an assemblage of such crying contrasts that one would say nature and society were created only to hold together elements which otherwise would despise and exclude each other.

The Russian people are supremely adroit: it is contrary to the intent of Nature that this race of men has been pushed almost to the Pole by hu-

man revolutions and held there by political neces-
sities. Whoever could penetrate further into the
designs of Providence would probably discover
that struggle against the elements is the harsh test
to which God wished to subject this nation
marked by him to dominate, one day, many others. Struggle is the school of Providence.

In general the Russians manifest their intelligence rather by the manner in which they use
poor tools than by the care they put into perfecting these tools. Endowed with little ingenuity, they
usually lack machinery suitable for the end they
wish to achieve. This people, which has so much
grace and facility, lacks creative genius. Once
again, the Russians are the Romans of the North.
Both have taken their sciences and their arts from
foreign lands. They have intelligence but theirs is
an imitative mind and, consequently, more ironic
than fertile—it copies everything and creates
nothing.

Mockery is the dominant characteristic of tyrants and of slaves. Any oppressed nation has its
mind turned toward disparagement, satire, cari-
cature; it avenges its inaction and its humiliation
by sarcasm. It remains to estimate and formulate
the relationship that exists between nations and
the constitutions which they are given or to which
they submit. My opinion is that every civilized
nation has for government the only one it could
have.

A FABULOUS FESTIVAL AND AN UNMENTIONABLE STORM

Peterhof, July 23, 1839

THE FÊTE of Peterhof must be considered from two points of view—the material and the moral —as in these two respects the same spectacle produces different impressions.

I have never seen anything lovelier for the eye or sadder for the mind than this so-called national assembly of courtiers and peasants who meet physically in the same rooms without drawing together in heart.

When the Emperor ostensibly opens his palace freely to the privileged peasants and the chosen bourgeoisie whom he permits the honor of paying him court twice a year, he does not say to the laborer, to the merchant: "You are a man like me," but he does say to the grandee: "You are a slave like them, and I, your god, soar above all of you equally."

To seek a semblance of popularity in the equality of others is a cruel game, the joke of a despot who could dazzle the people of another century but would not be able to deceive peoples come of age through experience and reflection. The Emperor Nicholas was not the first to resort to such a fraud; but since he did not originate this childish policy, it would be fitting for him to abolish it. It is true that nothing is abolished in Russia without danger; peoples who lack any guarantee lean only on their customs. Stubborn attachment to customs, protected by riot and poison, is one of the pillars of the social order, and the periodic assassination of rulers proves to the Russians that this *order* can command respect. The equilibrium of such a machine is a deep and grievous mystery to me.

As to the décor, the picturesque assemblage of men of all stations, the display of magnificent and extraordinary costumes, it would be impossible to say enough in praise of the Fête of Peterhof. Nothing that I had read about it or had been told about it could have given me the idea of such a fairyland; my imagination would not have been up to the reality.

Imagine a palace built on a terrace whose height is the equivalent of a mountain in a land of plains stretching beyond reach of the eye; a country so flat that from an elevation of sixty feet you enjoy a vast horizon. Below this imposing structure begins an immense park which extends all the way to the sea, where you perceive a line of war vessels illuminated for the evening of the fête. It is like magic: the fire is lighted; it shines and spreads like a conflagration from the groves and terraces of the palace to the waves of the Gulf of Finland. In the park, the lanterns create the effect of day. There you see trees diversely lighted by suns of all colors; it is not by thousands but by tens of thousands that one counts the lights of these gardens of Armide, it is even by hundreds of thousands; and you behold all this through the

windows of a castle invaded by a people as respectful as if they had spent all their life at court.

The halls of the old palace, filled with people,
are an ocean of heads with oily hair—all dominated by the noble head of the Czar whose height,
voice, and will soar above his people. At Peterhof,
as on parade, as in war, as in the entire Empire,
as in every minute of his life, you see in him the
man who rules.

This perpetual and perpetually adored rule
would be a true comedy if the existence of sixty
million people, who live only because the man you
see there before you in the rôle of Emperor grants
them the permission to breathe and dictates the
manner in which they shall use this permission,
did not depend on this permanent performance.
This is divine right applied to the mechanism of
social life—such is the serious side of the performance, and from it spring such grave results that
one's fear stifles the desire to laugh.

There does not exist on the earth today another
man who enjoys and exercises such power—not
in Turkey, nor even in China. Picture to yourself
the skill of our governments, proven by centuries
of practice, put at the service of a society still
young and cruel; the methods of the administra-
tions of the Occident, with all their modern experience, aiding the despotism of the Orient; European discipline supporting Asiatic tyranny;
organization applied to hiding and perpetuating
barbarism instead of throttling it; brutality, disciplined cruelty, the tactics of the armies of Europe serving to fortify the policy of the courts of

the Orient—in short, form for yourself the conception of a half-savage people who have been regimented without being civilized and you will understand the moral and social condition of the Russian people.

How to profit from the administrative progress of the European nations in governing sixty million men in the oriental manner—such is the problem which the men who govern Russia have endeavored to solve since Peter I.

The reigns of Catherine the Great and Alexander did nothing but prolong the systematic infancy of this nation which still exists in name only.

Catherine instituted schools to satisfy the French philosophers from whom her vanity sought praise. The Governor of Moscow, one of her former favorites rewarded by a pompous exile in the ancient capital of the Empire, wrote her one day that no one there was sending his children to school. The Empress replied approximately in these terms:

"My dear prince, do not complain that the Russians have no desire to be instructed; if I institute schools, it is not for us but for Europe *where we have to maintain our place in opinion.* But, from the day when our peasants wish to become enlightened, neither you nor I will remain in our places."

This letter was read by a person worthy of all my confidence. The Russians deny the authenticity of the anecdote, in accord with their usual tactics; but if I am not sure of the exactitude of the words, I can affirm that they express the true

156

thoughts of the sovereign. This should be enough for you and me.

In this connection, you can see the spirit of pride which governs and torments the Russians and which perverts to its very source the power established over them.

This unfortunate European opinion is a phantom which pursues them in their innermost thoughts. It reduces civilization for them to a sleight-of-hand trick, more or less skillfully executed.

The present Emperor, with his sound judgment, his clear intellect, has seen the danger, but will he be able to avert it? More than the force of Peter the Great is needed to remedy the evil caused by this foremost corrupter of the Russians.

The evil is so ingrown that it even strikes the eye of fairly inattentive foreigners, although Russia is a country where everybody conspires to deceive the traveler.

Do you know what it is to travel in Russia? For a superficial mind, it is to be fed on illusions; but for one who has his eyes open and, added to a little power of observation, an independent turn of mind, it is continuous and obstinate work, which consists in laboriously distinguishing, at every turn, between two nations in conflict. These two nations are Russia as it is and Russia as it would like to show itself to Europe.

The diplomatic corps and Westerners in general have always been considered by this government, with its Byzantine spirit, and by Russia as a whole, as malevolent and jealous spies. There is this similarity between the Russians and the Chinese—both always believe that foreigners envy them; they judge us by themselves.

The most highly esteemed travelers are those who, the most meekly and for the longest time, allow themselves to be taken in. Here politeness is only the art of reciprocally disguising a twofold fear—the fear one feels and the fear one inspires. I sense a hypocritical violence at the base of everything, worse than the tyranny of Batu from which modern Russia is less far removed than the Russians would like to make us believe. Everywhere I hear the language of philosophy, and everywhere I see oppression as the order of the day. The Russians say: "We should like to dispense with despotism as we would be richer and stronger; but we have to deal with peoples of Asia." At the same time they are thinking: "We should like to be able to stop talking about liberalism and philanthropy; we would be happier and stronger; but we have to deal with the governments of Europe." These governments are hated, feared, and flattered by the Russians.

It must be said that the Russians of all classes conspire with miraculous harmony to make duplicity prevail in their country. They have a dexterity in lying, a naturalness in falsehood, the success of which is as revolting to my candor as it is appalling to me. . . . Everything that gives a meaning and a goal to political institutions reduces itself here to one lone sentiment—fear. In Russia, fear replaces, that is to say paralyzes, thought; this sentiment, when it alone reigns, can produce

158

only the appearance of civilization; though not shunned by shortsighted legislators, fear can never be the soul of a well-organized society; it is not order—it is only the veil over chaos. Where liberty is lacking, soul and truth are lacking. Russia is a body without life—a colossus which subsists through its head, but whose limbs, all equally deprived of strength, languish. Out of this arises a profound anxiety, an inexpressible uneasiness, and this uneasiness is the expression of a positive suffering—the sign of an organic illness.

I believe that of all the parts of the world Russia is the one where people have the least real happiness. We are not happy in our country, but we believe that happiness depends on us; in Russia happiness is impossible. Imagine republican passions (for once again I repeat that under the Emperor of Russia a fictitious equality reigns) boiling in the silence of despotism—this is a terrifying combination, above all for the future it presages for the world. Russia is a pot of boiling water tightly closed but sitting on a fire which is growing steadily hotter—I fear an explosion, and I am not reassured by the fact that several times in the course of his laborious reign the Czar has felt the same fear. This Czar's reign is laborious in peace as in war; for in our time empires are like machines that wear out though not in use—anxiety in inaction devours them.

It is then this head without a body, this sovereign without a people, who gives popular festivals. It seems to me that before creating popularity it would be necessary to create a people.

Actually, this country lends itself marvelously to all kinds of fraud. Russia is always governed by deceit—here admitted tyranny would be a step forward.

On this point, as on many others, foreigners who have described Russia have united with the Russians to deceive the world. Either Russia has as yet been described only by men whose position or character would not permit independence, or the most honest minds lose their freedom of judgment from the moment they enter Russia.

As for me, the aversion I have for pretense protects me from this influence.

I hate only one evil and, if I hate it, it is because I believe it engenders and presupposes all other evils—that is falsehood. I force myself to expose it wherever I meet it. It is the horror that I have of falsehood which gives me the desire and the courage to write about this journey. I undertook the journey through curiosity; I will tell about it through a sense of duty.

Yesterday, as the people of the court passed close to me, I heard them praising the good behavior of their serfs. "Try to give a festival like this in France," they said. I was indeed tempted to reply to them, "To compare our two peoples, wait until yours exists."

The merchants, who would form a middle class, are so few in number they cannot count in the State; furthermore, nearly all of them are foreigners. Writers are counted by ones or twos in each generation; the artists are like the writers—their small number brings them esteem but, while

their rarity serves their personal fortune, it hurts
their social influence. Lawyers do not exist in a
country where there is no justice. Where, then,
can one find that middle class which forms the
might of States and without which a people is only
a herd led by a few skillfully trained bloodhounds?

I have not mentioned a class of men who should
be reckoned neither among the great nor among
the small—these are the sons of the priests. Most
of them become minor clerks and this population
of clerks is the curse of Russia. It forms a sort of
corps of obscure nobility which is very hostile to
the great nobles, a nobility whose spirit is anti-
aristocratic in the true political significance of the
word and which is, none the less, heavy-handed
with the serfs. It is these men—troublesome to the
State, fruits of the schism which permits the priest
to marry—who will start the next revolution in
Russia.

This corps of secondary nobility also draws recruits from administrators, artists, employees of
all kinds brought from abroad and from their ennobled children. Do you see in all this the element
of a truly Russian people, worthy and capable of
substantiating and appreciating the popularity of
the ruler?

Once again I say, everything is deception in
Russia and the gracious hospitality of the Czar,
gathering together in his palace his serfs and the
serfs of his courtiers, is only one more mockery.

The death penalty does not exist in this country except for high treason. However, there are

certain criminals whom they wish to execute. Here is how they arrange to conciliate the gentleness of the codes with the fierceness of their morals. When a criminal is condemned to more than a hundred blows of the lash, the executioner, who knows what this sentence means, out of humaneness kills the condemned man by striking him in a mortal spot on the third blow. But the death penalty is abolished! Is it not worse to lie thus in the very law than to proclaim the most audacious tyranny?

Among the six or seven thousand representatives of this sham Russian nation amassed yesterday evening in the Peterhof Palace, I looked in vain for a cheerful face; one does not laugh when one lies.

You can believe what I say about the effects of absolute government, for when I came to this country, it was in the hope of finding a remedy for the evils which threaten our country. If you think that I judge Russia too severely, blame only the involuntary impressions of things and persons I experience every day, and that any friend of humanity would experience in my place if he had made himself look, as I do, beyond what is shown to him.

This Empire, vast as it is, is only a prison to which the Emperor holds the key; and in this State, which can live only by conquests, nothing in time of peace approaches the misery of the subjects if it is not the misery of the ruler. The life of a jailer has always seemed to me so like that of the prisoner that I can never tire of admiring the power of imagination that enables one of these two men to believe he has infinitely less to complain of than the other.

Here, man knows neither the real social delights of cultured beings, the absolute and brutal liberty of the savage, nor the independence of action of the half-savage—the barbarian. I see as compensation for the misfortune of being born under this régime only dreams of arrogance and the hope of domination: it is to this passion for domination that I return each time I try to analyze the moral life of the inhabitants of Russia. The Russian thinks and lives as a soldier . . . a conquering soldier.

A real soldier, whatever his country may be, is scarcely a citizen. He is even less so here than in other places—he is like a prisoner condemned for life to guard other prisoners.

Note well that in Russia the word "prison" signifies something more than it does elsewhere. One shudders to think of all the subterranean cruelties, robbed even of our pity by the discipline of silence in a country where every man at birth is apprenticed to discretion. One must come here to hate reserve; so much caution reveals a secret tyranny whose image appears before me everywhere. Each movement of the face, each reservation, each inflection of the voice warns me of the danger of trust and naturalness.

It is not just the sight of the houses that brings my thoughts back to the painful conditions of human existence in this country.

When I suffer from the dampness of my room,

I think of those poor wretches exposed to the dampness of the subterranean cells of Kronstadt, of the Fortress of Petersburg, and of many other political tombs whose names I do not know. At every step I see raised before me the phantom of Siberia, and I think of all that the name of this political desert signifies, this abyss of miseries, this graveyard of the living—a world of fabulous griefs, a land peopled by infamous criminals and sublime heroes, a colony without which this Empire would be as incomplete as a palace without cellars.

Such are the somber pictures which presented themselves to my imagination while the touching relations of the Czar with his subjects were vaunted before us. No, certainly I am not disposed to allow myself to be dazzled by the imperial popularity; on the contrary, I am disposed to lose the friendship of the Russians rather than the freedom of mind with which I judge their ruses and the means they employ to deceive us and to deceive themselves. But I fear their anger very little, for I do them the justice of believing that, at the bottom of their hearts, they judge their country more severely than I because they know it better. While loudly accusing me, they will quietly absolve me; that is enough for me. A traveler who would allow himself to be indoctrinated here by the people of the country might traverse the Empire from one end to the other and return home without having seen anything but a series of façades; that is what I should do to please my hosts. I am aware of this, but at that price their hospitality would be too dear for me. I would rather sacrifice their approbation than lose the real, the unique fruit of my trip—experience.

Provided a foreigner appears foolishly active, rises early after a late night, does not miss a ball after having stayed throughout the maneuvers— in short, provided he exerts himself to the point of being unable to think, he is welcomed everywhere; he is judged with good will; he is entertained; a crowd of people he doesn't know will shake his hand everytime the Czar speaks to him or smiles at him, and when he leaves he will be declared a distinguished visitor. But let him beware of giving evidence that his enthusiasm for this rôle is waning—at the first sign of fatigue or clear-sightedness, at the slightest indication of indifference, not weariness but the ability to become weary, he would see rise up against him, like an angry serpent, that most caustic of minds, the Russian.

Mockery, that feeble consolation of the oppressed, is the peasant's delight here, as sarcasm is the elegance of the grandee—irony and imitation are the only native talents I have found in the Russians. The foreigner, once the butt of the venom of their censure, would never recover from it; he would be passed over tongues like a deserter; disgraced, overthrown, he would finish by falling under the feet of a mob of ambitious people, the most merciless and the most callous in the world.

I take pleasure in digressions, as you have long known, and I never like to put aside the collateral ideas that a subject offers me—this kind of disorder intrigues my imagination which is enamored of everything that resembles freedom.

The site of Peterhof is the most beautiful natural picture I have seen in Russia up to the present. A slight cliff looks out over the sea, nearly a third of a league away at the end of the park. The palace is built on the edge of this little cliff, fashioned almost to a point by nature. On this point, they have cut magnificent ramps; you descend from terrace to terrace down to the park where you find groves—majestic in the thickness of their foliage and in their extent. This park is decorated with fountains and artificial cascades in the style of those at Versailles, and it is rather varied for a garden designed in that style. There are certain raised points, certain structures which command a view of the sea, the coasts of Finland, then the arsenal of the Russian marine, the island of Kronstadt with its ramparts of granite on a level with the water. Farther away, nine leagues to the right, lies Petersburg, the white city, which from this distance appears gay and brilliant, and which, with its heaps of palaces with painted roofs, its islands, its temples with plaster columns, its forests of minaret-like bell towers, toward evening resembles a forest of pines whose silvery pyramids have been lighted by fire.

When I think of all the obstacles that man has overcome here to live in a community, to build a city, to house more than a king in these dens intended for bears and wolves—as Catherine was

166

told—and to support a magnificence in keeping with the pride of great princes and of great peoples, I do not see a lettuce or a rose without being tempted to cry out the miracle. If Petersburg is a whitewashed Lapland, Peterhof is the palace of Armide under glass. I cannot believe myself out-of-doors when I see so many pompous, delicate, brilliant things; and when I think that at a few degrees to the north the year is divided into one day, one night, and two twilights of three months each —then especially, I cannot keep from being filled with admiration.

One does a league by carriage in the imperial park without passing through the same lanes twice. Pray then, picture this park all ablaze. In this glacial country deprived of bright light, illuminations are a conflagration; one would say that the night must make up for the day. The trees disappear under a decoration of diamonds; in each path there are as many lanterns as leaves; it is Asia, not real Asia or modern Asia, but the fabulous Bagdad of "A Thousand and One Nights," or the more fabulous Babylon of Semiramis.

It is said that on the day of the Czarina's festival, six thousand carriages, thirty thousand pedestrians, and a countless number of boats leave Petersburg to come and set up encampments around Peterhof. It is the only day and the only place where I might see a crowd in Russia. A bourgeois bivouac in a completely military country is a curiosity. I do not mean that the army is missing at the festival; a part of the guard and the corps of cadets are likewise lodged around the royal residence.

167

All these people, officers, soldiers, merchants, serfs, masters, nobles, wander together through a woods where night is driven away by 250,000 lamps.

It is also said that in thirty-five minutes all the lanterns of the park are lighted by 1,800 men; the section of the illuminations which faces the castle is lighted in five minutes. This part comprises, among other things, a canal which is opposite the principal balcony of the palace and plunges for a great distance in a straight line through the park toward the sea. This perspective has a magic effect—the sheet of water in the canal is so bordered with lamps and reflects such a glowing light that one takes it for fire. Ariosto would perhaps have an imagination vivid enough to paint so many marvels for you in the language of fairies. There is taste and fantasy in the use they have made here of this prodigious mass of light. Various groups of lanterns, advantageously dispersed, have been given original shapes—there are flowers as big as trees, suns, vases, bowers of vine branches imitating Italian pergolas, obelisks, columns, walls chiseled in the Moorish manner; in short, an entire world of fantasy passes before your eyes without anything holding your attention, as the wonders follow one after the other with incredible rapidity. You are entertained by a fortification of fire, by draperies, by laces of precious stones; everything shines, everything burns, everything is of flame and diamonds; one fears lest this magnificent spectacle finish in a heap of ashes like a fire.

168

But the most amazing thing, seen from the palace, is the great canal which looks like motionless lava in a blazing forest.

At the end of this canal, on an enormous pyramid of colored lights (I believe it is seventy feet high) rises the monogram of the Empress, which shines with a brilliant whiteness above all the red, green, and blue lights around it—like a cluster of diamonds surrounded by colored gems. All of this is on such a grand scale you doubt what you see. You say to yourself, such efforts for an annual fête are impossible; what you see is too big to be real; it is the dream of a lovesick giant told by a mad poet.

The incidents to which the fête gives place are just as amazing as the festival itself. For two or three nights all this crowd I have told you about camps around the village and spreads out a fairly good distance from the palace. Many women sleep in their carriages and some of the peasants sleep in their carts; all these vehicles enclosed by the hundreds in fenced off spaces form encampments which are very amusing to wander through and would be worthy of reproduction by some clever artist.

The cities of a day that the Russians improvise for their festivals are much more amusing and have much more national character than the real cities built in Russia by foreigners.

My discomfort is increased since I have been living among Russians by the fact that everything reveals to me the real worth of this oppressed people. The idea of what they could do if they were free provokes the anger I feel when I see what they are doing today.

The ambassadors, with their families and their suites, as well as the foreign guests are lodged and entertained at the Czar's expense. A large and charming building in the form of a square pavilion, called the English Palace, is reserved for this purpose. This year the number of foreigners being greater than usual they could not all find quarters in the English Palace; consequently, I have not slept there, but I dine there every day with the diplomatic corps and seven to eight hundred other people at a perfectly appointed table. Certainly that is magnificent hospitality!

In any other country such a great gathering of people would produce a commotion, a deafening tumult. In Russia everything takes place with gravity, everything assumes the character of a ritual; silence is indispensable. To see all these young people gathered together for their pleasure, or for the pleasure of others, not daring to laugh, or sing, or quibble, or play, or dance, or run is like seeing a troop of prisoners on the point of leaving for their destination. Another reminder of Siberia! The thing I miss in all I see is certainly not grandeur or magnificence, or even taste and elegance, it is gaiety.

On the day of the ball and the great illumination, at seven o'clock in the evening, all the guests gather at the imperial palace. Personages of the court, the diplomatic corps, foreign guests, and the so-called representatives of the people admitted to the fête are introduced pell-mell into the great apartments.

There, squeezed by the crowd, you wait, a rather long time, for the appearance of the Emperor and the imperial family. As soon as the master, the sun of the palace, emerges, space opens up before him; followed by his noble cortège, he passes freely through the rooms, where an instant before one would have believed it impossible to make way for another person, and without even being grazed by the mob.

We thought during a large part of the day that the illumination would not take place. Toward three o'clock in the afternoon, as we were at dinner at the English Palace, a squall burst on Peterhof. The trees in the park were in violent motion, their tops were twisted in the air, their branches grazed the ground; and, while we were indifferently watching the effects of this spectacle, it never crossed our minds that the sisters, the mothers, the friends of a number of persons seated calmly at the table with us were perishing on the water because of this same burst of wind. Our carefree curiosity was approaching gaiety while a large number of boats which had left Petersburg to come to Peterhof were capsizing in the middle of the Gulf. Today two hundred people are admitted to have been drowned; some say fifteen hundred, others two thousand. No one will ever know the truth, and the papers will not even mention the disaster—that would distress the Czarina and imply blame to the Czar.

The secret of the disasters of the day was guarded during the entire evening. Nothing leaked out until after the fête; and this morning the court seems neither more nor less sad. In the court, etiquette demands, above all, that no one speak of what fills the thoughts of all; even outside the palace, confidences are exchanged only in a few passing words and in whispered tones. The habitual sadness of the life of people in this country comes from the fact that they themselves count life for nothing; each one feels that his existence hangs by a thread and makes up his mind to that, so to speak, at birth.

A SERF DOES NOT COMPLAIN . . .

Petersburg, July 29, 1839

ACCORDING to the latest news I was able to get this morning on the disasters of the Peterhof festival, they exceeded my suppositions. However, we will never know the exact circumstances of this event. Any mishap is treated here as an affair of State.

Furthermore, the secrecy that the police believe they must enforce here concerning misfortunes on which the human will has no bearing misses its goal in that it leaves the field open to the imagination. Thus, some say that day before yesterday only thirteen persons perished, while others speak of twelve hundred, of two thousand, and still others of a hundred and fifty. You can appreciate our uncertainty in all matters, since the circumstances of an event which happened, so to speak, under our eyes will always remain uncertain even for us.

I never cease to be astonished in seeing that there exists a people indifferent to the point of calmly living and dying in the dim light granted to it by its masters' police. Up to now, I believed that man could no more do without truth for the spirit than air and sun for the body; my journey to Russia disabuses me. Here, to lie is to protect the social order, to speak the truth is to destroy the State.

173

Here is an episode the authenticity of which I guarantee: Nine persons of the same family and from the same house—they arrived in Petersburg recently from the province—masters, women, children, and servants had imprudently embarked on a boat without a bridge and too frail to resist the sea. The squall came up; not one has reappeared. For three days they have been making searches along the shores, and this morning they had not yet found a single trace of these ill-fated people who were claimed only by their neighbors as they have no relatives in Petersburg. In the end, the skiff which had carried them was found; it was capsized and grounded on a sandbank near the beach, three leagues from Peterhof and six from Petersburg; of the people no trace—no more of the sailors than of the passengers. There, then, are nine deaths well established, not counting the sailors; and the number of small boats submerged like this one is considerable. They came this morning to affix the seals to the door of the empty house. This house is near mine, a circumstance without which I would not have been able to recount this story to you, for I was ignorant of it, as I am of many others. The twilight of policy is less transparent than that of the polar sky. However, everything thoroughly weighed, frankness would be a better plan, for when a little is hidden from me, I suppose that much is hidden.

Can you imagine the thousands of stories, the discussions, the gossip of all kinds, the conjectures, the shouts to which such events would give rise in any country other than this one, and especially in France? What the papers would say and how many voices would reiterate that the police never do their duty, that the boats are poor, the boatmen grasping, and that the authorities, far from remedying this dangerous state of affairs, only aggravate it, by carelessness or by cupidity. Here nothing! A silence more terrifying than the disaster itself. Two lines in the paper with no details; and, at the court, in the city, and in the drawing rooms of high society, not a word—if it is not mentioned in those places, it would hardly be spoken of elsewhere. There are no cafés in Petersburg where one comments on the newspapers—indeed real newspapers do not exist. The minor employees are more timid than the grandees, and that which one dares not mention in the houses of the chiefs is mentioned even less in the houses of the subordinates. The merchants and the shopkeepers remain and they are cautious, like everyone who wishes to live and prosper in this country. If they speak about grave and, consequently, dangerous subjects, it is only in a whisper and that in private.

This time the silence of the police is not pure flattery, it is also the effect of fear. The slave fears the bad humor of his master and applies himself with all his might to keeping him in a protected cheerfulness. The chains, the cell, the knout, Siberia are indeed close to an irritated Czar, or at the very least the Caucasus—this temperate Siberia for the use of a despotism which is softening every day according to the progress of the century.

175

Russia is a nation of mutes; some magician has changed sixty million men into automatons who await the wand of another magician to be reborn and to live. Nothing is lacking in Russia . . . except liberty, that is to say life.

The evil of deception extends farther than one thinks: the Russian police, so quick to torment the people, are slow to enlighten them when addressed in an effort to clear up some suspicious act.

Here is an example of this calculated inertia. During the last carnival, a woman of my acquaintance had let her maid go out on Shrove Sunday. At nightfall the girl did not return. The next morning, the lady, very worried, sought information from the police.

The reply was that no accident had occurred in Petersburg the preceding night, so it was impossible that the lost maid would not soon return safe and sound.

The day passed in this false security without news. Finally, the following day, a relative of the young girl, a young man rather well-informed about the secret maneuvers of the police of the country, had the idea of going to the surgical amphitheater, where one of his friends let him in. Scarcely inside, he recognized the corpse of his cousin, on the point of being dissected by the students.

As a good Russian, he kept enough control of himself not to betray his emotion.

"Who is this corpse?"

"Nobody knows. It is the body of a girl who was found dead night before last in such and such a street; it is believed that she was strangled while trying to defend herself against some men who tried to do her violence."

"Who are these men?"

"We do not know; one can only form conjectures on this incident as proofs are lacking."

"How did you get this corpse?"

"The police sold it to us secretly, so do not mention it."

The usual refrain, which becomes like a parasitic phrase articulated by a Russian or by an acclimatized foreigner.

The cousin kept quiet, the mistress of the victim did not dare protest; and, today, six months later, I am perhaps the only person she has told about the death of her maid, because I am a foreigner.

You see how the subordinate agents of the Russian police perform their duty. These perfidious employees had a double advantage in trafficking in the body of the murdered woman; first, they extracted a few rubles out of it; second, they concealed a crime which would have brought a severe reprimand upon them if word of the event had been spread abroad.

Reprimands addressed to men of this class are, I believe, accompanied by rather rough demonstrations designed ineffaceably to engrave the words on the memory of the unfortunate fellow who hears them.

A Russian of the low class is beaten as much as he is greeted in his life. The blows of the stick (in Russia the stick is a big split reed) and the tipping

of the hat, distributed in equal doses, are effica-
ciously employed in the social education of this
people, docketed rather than policed. One can be
beaten only in a certain class and by a man of a
certain other class. Here, ill-treatment is as for-
mally regulated as a customs duty; this is reminiscent of Ivan. The dignity of the caste is admitted,
but, up to the present, no one has thought of including in the laws, or even in usage, the dignity
of man. You remember what I told you about the
politeness of the Russians of all classes. I leave it
to you to imagine what the value of this urbanity
is, and I limit myself to describing some of the
scenes which pass under my eyes every day.

In the street, I saw two droshky (the Russian
hack) coachmen ceremoniously lift their hats
upon meeting: this is the accepted usage—if they
are slightly intimate, they bow with a friendly air
on passing one another, the hand on the mouth
and kissing it while making a very soulful and ex-
pressive little sign with their eyes. So much for social propriety. Now for justice: a little farther
on I saw a messenger on horseback, an orderly or
some other of the lowest government employees,
get down from his mount, run to one of these two
well-trained coachmen and strike him brutally
with a whip, a stick, or his fist, raining blows pitilessly on his chest and head, and in the face;
meanwhile, the poor man, who would not have
drawn back quickly enough, allows himself to be
mercilessly belabored without the least complaint
or resistance out of respect for the uniform and
caste of his attacker. But the attacker's anger is not

always disarmed by the prompt submission of the delinquent.

Have I not seen one of these dispatch carriers, a courier of some minister or the glorified flunky of some aide-de-camp of the Emperor, pull a young coachman from his seat and beat him unceasingly until his face was covered with blood? The victim submitted to this assault in veritable agony but without the least resistance, as one obeys a supreme decree, as one accedes to some natural disturbance; meanwhile, the passers-by were not in the least moved by such cruelty; even one of the victim's comrades, watering his horses nearby, ran at a sign from the irate courier to hold the horses of this public personage during the entire time that it pleased him to prolong the attack. Go to any other country and ask the help of a man of the people in arbitrarily punishing one of his comrades! But the employment and dress of the man who administered the blows gave him the right to beat the hackman with a vengeance; so the punishment was legitimate. But I say—so much the worse for the country where such actions are legal.

This scene that I have just described to you took place in the best quarter of the city at the promenade hour. When the poor beaten man was released, he wiped away the blood that was streaming down his cheeks, calmly remounted his seat, and resumed his greetings to every new person he met.

The offense, such as it was, had not, however, caused any serious disturbance. Note that this abomination was committed with perfect order in the presence of a silent crowd which, far from dreaming of defending or pardoning the guilty man, dared not tarry long to watch the punishment. A nation governed by Christian principles would protest against this social discipline which destroys all individual liberty. But here the influence of the priest is limited to obtaining from the people and from the aristocracy signs of the cross and prostrations.

Despite the cult of the Holy Spirit, this nation always has its God on earth. Like Batu, like Timur, the Czar of Russia is idolized by his subjects; Russian law has never been christened.

Thanks to the terror which hovers over all heads, submission serves everyone: victims and executioners—all believe they have need of the obedience which perpetuates the injustice they inflict and the injustice they suffer.

It is known that the intervention of the police between persons who are quarreling exposes the combatants to much more dreaded punishment than the blows they bear in silence: one avoids noise because an outburst of anger would summon the hangman who really punishes.

Here, however, is a tumultuous scene which chance made me a witness to this morning:

I was passing along a canal covered by boats loaded with wood. Some men were taking this wood to shore to stack on their carts. One of these porters picked a quarrel with his comrades and all began to fight openly, like the street porters in France. The aggressor, feeling himself the weakest, sought refuge in flight; with the agility of a squirrel, he scrambled up the mainmast of the boat; up to this point I found the scene amusing. Perched on a crossarm, the fugitive defied his less nimble adversaries. These men, seeing themselves foiled in their hope of vengeance and forgetting that they were in Russia, exceeding all the limits of their politeness—that is to say their accustomed caution, manifested their fury by paroxysms of shouts and savage threats.

At regular intervals along all the streets of the city uniformed police agents are stationed. Two of these agents, sort of city patrolmen, drawn by the vociferations of the fighters, arrived on the scene of the quarrel and summoned the principal offender down from his high perch. He did not obey; the patrolman jumped aboard; the rebel still clung to the mast. The officer repeated his summons; the rebel persisted in his defiance. The furious policeman tried to climb the mast and succeeded in gripping one of the porter's feet. And what do you think he did then? He pulled his adversary with all his strength, without precaution and without concern for the manner in which the poor man might fall; the culprit, despairing of escaping the punishment which awaited him, finally abandoned himself to his fate. He flipped over and fell backward and headfirst twice the height of a man onto a pile of wood, where his body lay as motionless as a sack.

I leave it to you to imagine whether the fall was hard. His head rebounded on the logs and the echo of the blow reached me, although I had stopped at a distance of about fifty feet. I thought the man was killed—blood covered his face; however, recovering from the first shock, this poor trapped savage got up. What one could see of his face under the blood stains was of a terrible pallor. He began to bellow like a bull; his blood-curdling screams lessened my sympathy—it seemed to me that this was nothing more than a brute and that I was wrong to soften toward him as toward one of my fellow men. The more the man bellowed, the more my heart hardened: how true it is that the objects of our compassion must conserve some semblance of their own dignity in order for us to take a serious part in their suffering! Pity is an association, and where is the man, however compassionate he may be, who wishes to associate himself with something he despises?

They finally mastered the culprit, although he put up a desperate and fairly long resistance. A little boat, brought up at that very instant by some other police agents, quickly approached. The prisoner was bound and, with his hands tied behind his back, was thrown on his face in the bottom of the boat. This second fall, much harder than the first, was followed by a hail of blows. That is not all, and you are not at the end of the preliminary torture. The sergeant who had seized the victim no sooner saw him prostrated than he jumped on his body. I came nearer; thus I witnessed what I am about to tell you. This butcher, having descended to the bottom of the hold and walked on the body of the criminal, began to trample this poor man with repeated blows, crushing the wretch with his feet as one treads grapes in a press. During this horrible execution, the fierce howls of the tortured one increased at first; but when they began to grow weaker, I felt that my own strength was failing and I fled. Not being able to prevent any of this, I had already seen too much. . . . There you have a picture of what happened under my own eyes, in plain view, during a recreational stroll, for I had wished to rest at least for a few days from my profession of traveling correspondent. But how could I suppress my indignation? It has made me take up my pen again immediately.

I admit that such actions are accepted in Russian morals, for I have been unable to catch one expression of blame or horror on the face of a single spectator at these odious scenes; and there are men of all classes among these spectators.

In broad daylight, in the open street, to beat a man to death before trying him—this appears very natural to the public and to the police of Petersburg. It is as though there were a mutual understanding among all to allow such things to take place under their eyes without question. Elsewhere, everybody protects the citizen against the public agent who abuses him; here, the public agent is protected against the rightful complaint of a maltreated man. A serf does not complain.

I make a solemn declaration as to the correctness of the details which I have reported. I have neither added nor kept back a single gesture in the account you have just read, and I hurried to include it in my letter while the smallest details were fresh in my mind.

The morals of a people are produced slowly by the reciprocal action of laws on customs and customs on laws; they do not change at the wave of a wand. Those of the Russians, despite all the pretensions of these half-savages, are cruel and will remain so for a long time yet. It is scarcely more than a century since they were real Tartars; it was only Peter the Great who began to force men to introduce women into gatherings. Beneath their modern elegance, many of these newcomers to civilization are still bears; they have turned their skins inside out, but one has only to scratch a little to find the bristling fur.

Now that they have allowed the Age of Chivalry, from which the nations of the Occident profited so well in their youth, to pass them by, these people need an independent and conquering religion. Russia has faith; but political faith does not emancipate the spirit of man; it confines it in the narrow circle of its native predilections. With the Catholic faith, the Russians would soon acquire general ideas based on reasonable instruction and on liberty proportionate to their lights. I am personally convinced that from this height, if they were able to attain it, they could dominate the world. The sickness is profound, and the remedies employed up to now have acted only on the surface; they have covered the wound without healing it. Real civilization extends from the center to the circumference, whereas Russian civilization goes from the circumference toward the center: this is masked barbarism, nothing more.

Does it follow that because a savage has the vanity of a man of the world he also has his culture? I have said this before; I repeat it, and I shall probably repeat it again: the Russians are much less interested in being civilized than in making us believe they are civilized. As long as this disease of public vanity gnaws at their hearts and warps their minds, they will have a few grandees who can play at elegance at home and abroad and will in reality remain barbarians: but unfortunately this savage has firearms.

You are not at the end; I have not finished my sentimental journey. Yesterday, I was taking a walk with a Frenchman of great intelligence, who knows Petersburg well. Placed as instructor in a family of high nobles, he is in a position to know the truth which we birds of passage pursue in vain.

We were walking at random and having arrived midway on the Nevski Prospect, we slackened our pace so as to tarry longer on this brilliant promenade. I was admiring my surroundings when a black, or rather dark green, carriage came alongside us. It was long, squarish, fairly low, and enclosed on all sides. It looked like an enormous bier placed on a cart chassis. Four little openings, about six inches square, with iron bars, let air and light into this rolling tomb. A child of eight years, or ten at the most, drove the two horses hitched to this contraption, and, to my surprise, a goodly number of soldiers escorted it. I asked my companion what purpose such a peculiar outfit might serve; my question was not out before a pale face showed itself at one of the gratings to take care of the reply: This carriage is used for transporting prisoners to their destination.

"It is a Russian police van," my companion said to me. "Without doubt, something of this nature exists in other countries, but it is an odious object and hidden from view as much as possible. Doesn't it seem to you that here they make a point of displaying it? What a government!"

"Think," I replied, "of the difficulties this government encounters."

"Ah! you are still the dupe of their golden words; I can very well see that the Russian authorities will do anything they wish with you."

"I try to put myself in their place: nothing is more deserving of consideration than the point of view of men who govern, for they have not chosen their lot. Every government is obliged to start with accomplished facts; the government here did not create the order of things that it is called upon to defend energetically and cautiously to perfect. If the rod of iron, which directs this still brutish people, ceased for an instant to bear down upon them, the entire social order would be overturned."

"They tell you that; but you may be sure this pretended necessity suits them: those who complain most about the severities and say they are forced to use them, would relinquish them only with regret. In their hearts, they love governments without counterweight; that kind of government

186

functions more easily. Are you unaware of what happened on the Volga a short time ago?"

"I heard talk of serious troubles promptly repressed."

"Without doubt; but at what price? And if I told you that these fearful disorders were the result of a word from the Czar?"

"You could never make me believe that he had approved such horrors."

"That is not what I mean to say; all the same, a word, which I agree he may have pronounced innocently, caused the disaster. Here are the facts. Despite the injustices of the officers of the crown, the lot of the Czar's peasants is still preferable to that of other serfs; and, as soon as the sovereign becomes the proprietor of some new domain, the inhabitants of these lands acquired by the crown become the object of envy of all their neighbors. Recently, the Emperor bought a considerable property in the district which has since revolted. Immediately peasants were delegated from all parts of the region to the new administrators of the imperial lands to beg the Czar also to buy the neighboring domains with their inhabitants. Serfs chosen as ambassadors were sent as far as Petersburg. The Emperor received them, welcomed them with kindness; however, to their great regret, he did not buy them. 'I cannot,' he told them, 'acquire all of Russia; but a time will come, I hope, when every peasant in this Empire will be free; if that depended only on me, the Russians would enjoy, from today, the independence that I wish for them and that I am working with

187

all my might to procure for them in the future.' "

"Well, this response seems to me full of reason, sincerity, and good will."

"No doubt, but the Czar should know to whom he is addressing his words and not cause the throats of his nobility to be cut through tenderness for his serfs. This discourse interpreted by barbaric and envious men set an entire province on fire. Then it was necessary to punish the people for the crimes they had been made to commit. 'The *Father* wishes our deliverance,' the deputies returning from their mission cried out on the shores of the Volga. 'The Czar aspires only to act for our good; he told us this himself; so, it is the landowners and all their agents who are our enemies and who oppose the good plans of the *Father!*' Thereupon the peasants believed they were performing a pious duty in throwing themselves on their masters. In consequence, all the landowners and all the overseers of an entire district, along with their families, were massacred. They put one on the spit to roast him alive; they boiled another in a cauldron; they disemboweled overseers; they killed officers and administrators in various ways; they laid violent hands on everyone they met, put entire villages to fire and blood; in short, they devastated a province, not in the name of liberty—they do not know what that is, but in the name of deliverance and to the cry of *Long Live the Czar,* words clear and well-defined for them."

"It was probably some of these cannibals that we just saw pass in the police wagon. Try to con-

trol such savages with the gentle methods you
demand from Western governments!"

"The spirit of populations must be changed
gradually; instead of that, the Russians find it
more convenient to change their domicile; on
every occasion of this kind, they deport entire villages or districts in mass; no population is sure of
retaining its territory. The result of such a system
is that man, attached as he is to the yoke, in his
slavery does not even have the sole compensation
attributed to his condition—an established location, fixed habits, and attachment to his home. By
an infernal combination, he is mobile without being free. A word from the sovereign uproots him
like a tree, tears him from his native soil, and
sends him to perish or languish at the end of the
world. What becomes of the inhabitant of the
fields transplanted to a village where he was not
born, to a man whose life is tied to all the objects
which surround him? The peasant exposed to
these hurricanes of supreme power no longer
loves his hovel, which is the only thing he could
love in this world; he detests his life and does not
recognize his duties, for it is necessary to give
some happiness to man to make him understand
his obligations: misery teaches him only hypocrisy and revolt. If self-interest, well understood, is
not the basis of morality, at least it is its support.
If I were permitted to give you the authentic details I collected yesterday on the events at ——,
you would shudder to hear them."

"It is hard to change the mentality of a people;
it is not a matter of a day or even of a reign."

"Are they working on it in good faith?"

"I believe so; but with caution."

"What you call caution, I call insincerity. You do not know the Emperor."

"Accuse him of being inexorable but not of being insincere; and, frequently, inexorability is a virtue in a prince."

"That cannot be denied; but I do not wish to lose my theme. You believe the character of the Emperor sincere? Recall his conduct at the death of Pushkin."

"I am not familiar with the circumstances of that event."

While chatting in this manner, we arrived at the Champs de Mars—a vast plain which seems deserted although it occupies the center of the city. It is so vast people are lost there; one can be seen approaching from a long way off; consequently, it is possible to talk there with more safety than in one's own room. My guide continued:

"Pushkin was, as you know, the greatest of the Russian poets."

"We are not the judges of that . . ."

"Deserved or not, his reputation was great. He was still young and of a fiery temperament—you know he had Moorish blood from his mother. His wife, a very beautiful woman, inspired in him more passion than confidence; with his poetic soul and African character, he was carried away by jealousy. The poor fellow, exasperated by appearances and false reports, poisoned by a perfidy which recalls Shakespeare's Othello—this

190

Petersburg, July 29, 1839

Russian Othello lost all restraint and wanted to force the man by whom he felt himself wronged to a duel. This man was a Frenchman and his brother-in-law besides; his name was d'Antes. A duel in Russia is a serious matter; all the more serious since, instead of conforming with custom although against the law as in our country, it conflicts with traditional ideas; Russia is more oriental than chivalrous. A duel is illegal here, as it is everywhere, and there is less support from public opinion than elsewhere.

"D'Antes did what he could to avoid the clash. Vigorously pressed by the incensed husband, he refused satisfaction with a fair degree of dignity; but he continued his assiduous attentions. Pushkin became almost crazy: the continued presence of this man whom he wished dead appeared to him as an endless outrage, and he risked everything to drive him from his house. Things finally reached such a point that the duel became unavoidable. So, the two brothers-in-law fought each other, and d'Antes killed Pushkin; the man condemned by public opinion triumphed and the offended husband, the national poet, the innocent man succumbed.

"This death created a public scandal and universal mourning. Pushkin, the Russian poet par excellence, the author of the most beautiful poetry in the Russian language, the first native talent whose name had resounded with some eminence in Europe . . . in Europe! . . . in short, the glory of the present, the hope of the future, everything was lost; the idol was struck down in

his temple, and the hero, smitten in his prime, fell
under the hand of a Frenchman. What hatred,
what passions came into play! Petersburg, Moscow, the whole Empire was moved.

"A general mourning attested the merit of the
deceased and confirmed the glory of the country,
which could say to Europe: I have had my poet!
. . . and I have the honor to mourn him!

"The Czar, the man in Russia who best knows
the Russians and who best understands flattery,
took pains to participate in the public grief. He
ordered a service: I am not sure that he did not
even carry his pious coquetry to the point of going
to this ceremony in person in order to publicize
his regrets by making even God a witness to his
admiration for the national genius, snatched too
soon from his glory.

"However that may be, the sympathy of the
ruler flattered the Muscovite spirit to such an extent that it awakened an ardent patriotism in the
heart of a young man endowed with a great deal
of talent. This too credulous poet, inflamed by
this act of august protection accorded the first of
the arts, became so bold as to believe himself inspired. In the naïve expansiveness of his gratitude,
he even dared to write an ode . . . admire the
audacity! . . . a patriotic ode to thank the Czar
for making himself the protector of letters. He
ended this remarkable piece by singing the praises
of the vanished poet—nothing more. I have read
these verses, and I can attest to you the innocent
intentions of the author; at least if you do not
look upon it as a crime for him to hide in the bot-

tom of his heart what seems to me a perfectly permissible hope for a young imagination. I think I guessed what he was thinking without his saying it—that one day, perhaps, Pushkin would be reborn in him and the son of the Czar would reward the second poet of Russia as the present Emperor had honored the first. . . . A rash person! . . . to aspire to fame, to avow passion for glory under despotism! It is as if Prometheus had said to Jupiter: 'Be careful, defend yourself; I am going to steal your thunder!' So, here is the kind of reward the young aspirant to victory, that is to say to martyrdom, received. The poor fellow, for insolently connecting himself with the public love of his master for the arts and belles-lettres, brought about his own disgrace and received *in secret* the order to develop his poetic tendencies in the Caucasus—this temperate branch of old Siberia.

"After staying there two years, he returned with his health ruined, his soul crushed, his imagination radically cured of its absurd fancies, hoping that his body would likewise be cured of the fevers of Georgia. After this sketch, do you still have confidence in the official words of the Czar, in his public deeds?"

This is approximately what I replied to my compatriot's recital:

"The Emperor is a man; he shares human weaknesses. Something in the direction of the ideas of this young poet must have shocked him. You may be sure they were European rather than national. The Czar does the contrary of Catherine II; he defies Europe instead of flattering it. This is a fault, I agree. . . . But this fault is pardonable, especially if you reflect upon the evil done to Russia by princes who were possessed throughout their lives by a craze for imitation."

"You are incorrigible," my friend cried out. "You, too, believe in the possibility of a Russian civilization. The chances were good before Peter I, but he destroyed the fruit in its seed. Go to Moscow. It is the center of the old Empire, but you will see that minds there turn toward industrial speculations and that the national character is as effaced there as it is in St. Petersburg. Czar Nicholas commits today, in another sense, an error similar to that of Czar Peter I. He counts the history of an entire century for nothing—the century of Peter the Great. History has its fatalities; everywhere the past extends its influence over the present. Woe to the prince who does not wish to yield to it!"

The hour was late. We separated and I continued my walk, musing all alone on the lively feeling of opposition which must germinate in souls accustomed to reflect in the silence of despotism. The characters that such a government does not brutalize grow stronger.

I returned to write to you, as I do nearly every day. Nevertheless, much time will pass before you receive my letters in view of the fact that I conceal them as if they were plans for a conspiracy, meanwhile awaiting an occasion when I can safely send them to you—a thing so difficult that

I fear I shall be obliged to bring them to you myself.

Can one enjoy without uneasiness the luxury of a magnificent residence when one thinks that at a distance of some hundreds of leagues from the palace people are killing each other and that the entire social order would dissolve without the terrible means employed to protect it? (This has to do with the revolt of the peasants which then occupied all minds in Russia.)

With this obedient people, the influence of social institutions is so great in all classes, the involuntary formation of habits dominates character to such a point that even the recent outbursts of vengeance seem to be regulated by a certain discipline. Calculated murder is executed in cadence; men kill other men militarily, religiously, without anger, without emotion, without words, with a calm more terrible than the delirium of hatred. They clash together; they are overturned; they are crushed; they run over each others' bodies, as machines turn regularly on their pivots. This physical impassiveness in the midst of the most violent actions, this monstrous audacity in conception, this coldness in execution, this silence of fury, this mute fanaticism, is, if one may so express himself, conscientious crime. A certain order contrary to nature presides in this astonishing country of the most unprecedented excesses; tyranny and revolt march in time, each regulating its step to that of the other.

Here even the earth, the monotonous aspect of

195

the land, bespeaks symmetry: the complete absence of undulation in a terrain everywhere the same and usually barren, the lack of variety in vegetation always poor in northern soils, the complete absence of picturesque irregularities in the eternal plains where one would say one lone site obsesses the traveler and follows him like a dream from one end of the Empire to the other—in short, all that God has failed to do for this country contributes to the imperturbable uniformity of the political and social life of the people.

As everything is alike, the immense extent of territory does not prevent everything being done from one end of Russia to the other with magic punctuality and accord. If one ever succeeded in organizing a real revolution among the Russian people, the massacre would be regulated like the movements of a regiment. One would see villages changed into barracks and organized murder, completely armed, coming out of thatched cottages to advance in line and in good order; finally, the Russians would be prepared to plunder from Smolensk to Irkutsk just as they parade on the square of the Winter Palace in Petersburg. From so much uniformity a harmony is produced between the natural disposition of the people and their social habits, the effects of which could be prodigious either for good or for evil.

Everything is obscure in the future of the world; but one thing is certain—the world will see some strange scenes played before nations by this predestinated nation.

It is nearly always through blind respect for

power that the Russians disturb the public order. Thus, if one must believe the whispered rumors, without the word of the Emperor to the peasants' deputies, the peasants would not have taken up arms.

This prince knows the character of his people better than anyone else, and I cannot imagine myself that he would have provoked the revolt of the peasants even without intending to do so. However, I should add that several well-informed persons disagree with my opinion in this matter.

I add that the bloody scenes are still renewed daily at several points in the same district where order has just been disrupted and restored by such frightful means. You see that it ill becomes the Russians to reproach France for her political disorders and draw conclusions from them favorable to despotism. If freedom of the press were accorded to Russia for twenty-four hours, what you would see would make you recoil with horror. Silence is indispensable to oppression. Under an absolute government such indiscretion would be tantamount to high treason.

If better diplomats are found among the Russians than among highly civilized peoples, it is because our papers warn them of everything that happens and everything that is contemplated in our countries. Instead of disguising our weaknesses with prudence, we reveal them with vehemence every morning; whereas, the Russians' Byzantine policy, working in the shadow, carefully conceals from us all that is thought, done, and feared in their country. We proceed in broad daylight; they advance under cover: the game is one-sided. The ignorance in which they leave us blinds us; our sincerity enlightens them; we have the weakness of loquacity; they have the strength of secrecy. There, above all, is the cause of their cleverness.

THE SECRET LIFE OF RUSSIA

Petersburg, August 1, 1839

IT WOULD BE impossible to imagine the dreariness of St. Petersburg when the Czar is away. Frankly, this city is never what could be called gay; but without the court it is a desert, besides which, as you know, it is always threatened with destruction by the sea. So, this morning while walking on the lonely quays and the empty boulevards, I said to myself, "So Petersburg is going to be submerged; the people have fled, and water is coming back to take possession of the marshes; this time Nature has taken her revenge on the efforts of art." It was not that at all; Petersburg is dead because the Emperor is at Peterhof, nothing more.

Do not think that the Czar's absence makes speech any freer; he is always present in spirit—thus, in the absence of his eyes, his thought makes the sunlight. In a word, the Czar is the benevolent God, he is life, he is love for this unhappy people. Can you imagine life reduced to the hope of bowing before the master to thank him for a glance?

If I put myself in the place of the only man whose right to live freely is recognized, I tremble for him. What a terrible rôle to play—providence for sixty million souls! This divinity, born of a political superstition, has only two choices: to prove that he is a man by allowing himself to be crushed, or to force his disciples to conquer the world in order to prove that he is God. Thus, the whole of life in Russia is only the school of ambition.

But along what road did the Russians pass in order to arrive at this self-abnegation? What human means could have brought them to such a political result? The means? . . . here it is—the *tchin*. The tchin is galvanism, the life apparent of bodies and minds; it is the passion which outlives all passions!

The tchin is a regimented nation, a military order applied to an entire society, even to the castes who do not go to war. In a word, it is the division of the civilian population into classes which correspond to ranks in the army. Since this hierarchy has been instituted, a man who has never even seen a drill can obtain the rank of colonel.

Peter the Great (one must always go back to him to understand present-day Russia), took it into his head one day that the aristocracy thought too much and were too independent. Wishing to eliminate this inconvenience—the most serious of all in the view of a spirit active and sagacious in its sphere but too limited to understand the advantages of liberty, however profitable it may be to nations and even to the men who govern—this great master of arbitrariness could think of nothing better, in his deep but restricted insight, than to divide the people, that is to say the country, into different classes, irrespective of the name, of the birth of individuals, or of the illustriousness of families. Thus, the son of the greatest lord of the Empire could be a member of an inferior class while the son of one of his peasants could rise to the top classes, according to the good pleasure of the Emperor. In this division of the people, each man received his position through the benevolence of the prince; and that is how Russia became a regiment of sixty million men. This is what is called the *tchin,* and it is the greatest work of Peter the Great.

The tchin is composed of fourteen classes and each of these classes has privileges which pertain only to it.

The fourteenth class is the lowest. It is placed immediately above the serfs and gives its members the sole advantage of being called free. This freedom means only that no one can strike a member of this class without incurring criminal proceedings. In return, every individual who forms a part of this class must write the number of his class on his door, so that no superior can be led into temptation or error; forewarned in this manner, the beater of a free man would be guilty and would be liable to penalty.

This fourteenth class is made up of the most menial employees of the government: postal clerks, letter carriers, and other subordinates charged with carrying or executing the orders of superior administrators. It corresponds to the grade of noncommissioned officer in the imperial army. The men who compose it are servants of the Czar, not serfs of an individual, and they have the feeling of their social dignity; as for human

201

dignity, as you know, it is not yet known in Russia.

All the classes of the tchin correspond to equivalent military ranks. Thus the hierarchy of the army is found, so to speak, in parallel with the hierarchy that reigns in the entire State. The first class is at the peak of the pyramid and is composed, today, of a single man: Marshal Paskievitch, Viceroy of Warsaw.

I repeat, it is solely the will of the Czar which brings about advancement of the individual in the tchin. Thus, a man rising step by step to the highest rank of this artificial nation can attain the highest military honors without having served in any army.

The favor of advancement is never asked for, but is always maneuvered.

There is in this an immense power of fermentation which is put at the disposal of the chief of State. Doctors complain of not being able to produce fever in certain patients in order to cure them of chronic ailments: Czar Peter inoculated all his people with the fever of ambition in order to make them more pliable and to govern them as he liked.

Such a social organization produces a fever of envy so violent, a straining of minds toward ambition so constant, that by now the Russian people must be inept in everything except the conquest of the world. I always come back to this term because such a goal is the only thing that can explain the excessive sacrifices imposed here on the individual by society. If inordinate ambition dries up the heart of man, it can also exhaust the minds and delude the judgment of a nation to the point of making it sacrifice its liberty to victory. Without this ulterior design, admitted or not, which many men obey, perhaps in ignorance, the history of Russia seems to me an inexplicable enigma.

Here a capital question arises: is the idea of conquest, which is the secret life of Russia, itself a lure to seduce dense populations or must it some day be realized?

This doubt obsesses me endlessly, and, in spite of all my efforts, I have not been able to resolve it. All I can tell you is that since I have come to Russia I see the future of Europe in black. However, my conscience obliges me to say that this opinion is opposed by some very wise and experienced men.

These men say I exaggerate Russian power, that each society has its liabilities to disaster and the destiny of this one is to push her conquests toward the East, then to be divided herself. These minds that persist in refusing to believe in the brilliant future of the Slavs agree with me concerning the favorable and pleasing characteristics of this people; they admit that it is a people endowed with an instinct for the picturesque; they grant its feeling for music; they conclude these bents can help in developing the fine arts up to a certain point but are not sufficient for the realization of the hopes of domination that I attribute to this people or that I impute to its government. In addition they say: "The Russians lack scientific

203

genius. They have never shown creative ability; being lazy and superficial by nature, if they apply themselves it is more through fear than through inclination; fear makes them capable of any undertaking, any boast, but likewise it prevents their going far along any path. Genius like heroism must be fearless, it lives on freedom; whereas, fear and slavery have a reign and a sphere limited by the mediocrity of which they are the weapons. The Russians are good soldiers but bad sailors. In general they are more resigned than reflective, more religious than philosophical; they have more submissiveness than will, their minds lack energy as their souls lack freedom. The thing that seems hardest and least natural to them is applying their intelligence seriously and focusing their imagination in order to use it profitably: always children, they could for a moment be victorious in the realm of the sword but never in the realm of the mind. A people which has nothing to teach the peoples it wishes to subjugate is not the stronger for long.

"Physically even French and English peasants are more robust than the Russians: the Russians are more agile than muscular, more ferocious than energetic, more cunning than enterprising. The Russians have passive courage, but they lack daring and perseverance. The two Turkish campaigns have sufficiently demonstrated the weakness of the colossus: in brief, a society which did not enjoy liberty at birth, where every great political crisis has been provoked by the influence of a foreign civilization, a society deprived of strength in its bud cannot have a long future."

From all of that, it is concluded that Russia, strong at home, formidable as long as she contends only with Asiatic populations, would be crushed by Europe any day she should decide to throw off her mask and wage war to back up her arrogant diplomacy.

I have cited what seem to me the strongest arguments opposed to my fears by the political optimists. I have not weakened their case in the least; they still accuse me of exaggerating the danger. Actually my opinion is shared by equally serious men who unceasingly reproach the optimists for their blindness and exhort them to recognize the evil before it becomes incurable.

I see the colossus close at hand, and I have difficulty persuading myself that this creation of Providence has for an end only diminishing the barbarism of Asia. It seems to me that it is mainly destined to castigate the evil civilization of Europe by a new invasion; eternal oriental tyranny threatens us endlessly, and we will suffer it if our extravagances and our iniquities make us deserve such a punishment. It is said that the Russians have nothing to teach us. That may be true; but they have a great deal to make us forget. Furthermore, are they not more capable of obedience and patience than we? In policy, the resignation of the people is the strength of the government.

Do not expect a complete travelogue from me. I neglect to mention many celebrated and interesting things because they have made but little impression on me. I wish to remain free to describe only the things that impress me forcibly.

One can see nothing here without ceremony and advance preparation. To go anywhere, no matter where, at the moment you have the desire is impossible; if it is necessary to foresee four days in advance where one's fancy will take one, one may as well have no fancy. But, in the end, one is resigned to this while living here. Russian hospitality, bristling with formalities, makes life difficult for the most favored foreigners; it is a polite pretext for hampering the movements of the traveler and limiting his license to observe. They do you the so-called honors of the country. Thanks to this fastidious politeness, the observer cannot visit places or look at anything without a guide; never being alone he has trouble judging for himself, which is what they want. To enter Russia, you must deposit your free will along with your passport at the frontier. Would you like to see the curiosities of the palace? They will provide you with a chamberlain who will do the honors from top to bottom and, by his presence, will force you to observe each thing in detail, that is to say, to see nothing except from his point of view and to admire everything without choice. Would you like to visit a camp, which has no interest for you beyond the site of the barracks, the picturesqueness of the uniforms, the beauty of the horses, the attitude of the soldier in the tent? An officer, maybe even a general, will accompany you. A hospital? The doctor in charge will escort you. A fortress? The governor will show it to you, or rather, politely conceal it from you. A school, any kind of public establishment? The director, the inspector, will be forewarned of your visit; you will find him armed and his mind well prepared to brave your examination. A building? The architect will take you over all its parts and will, himself, explain everything you have not asked in order to avoid instructing you on the things you are interested in learning.

The result of this oriental ceremony is that to avoid making a career of seeking permissions, you give up seeing many things—first advantage! Or, if your curiosity is sufficiently robust to make you persist in bothering people, you will at least be watched over in your investigations from such close range they will result in nothing; you will communicate officially only with the heads of the so-called public establishments, and they will allow you no liberty beyond expressing, before legitimate authorities, the admiration which is required by politeness, by prudence, and by gratitude—of which the Russians are most jealous. They refuse you nothing, but they accompany you everywhere: courtesy becomes a means of surveillance here.

Thus they tyrannize over you under the pretext of honoring you. Such is the lot of privileged visitors. As for unsponsored visitors—they see nothing at all. This country is organized in such a fashion that, without the immediate intervention of government agents, no foreigner can travel agreeably or even safely.

The Russians are still convinced of the efficaciousness of the lie; this illusion astonishes me in people who have used it so much. It is not that their minds lack finesse or comprehension; but, in a country where the governors have not yet understood the advantages of liberty even for themselves, the governed must recoil before the immediate inconveniences of sincerity. One is forced to repeat every instant: here people—great and small—all remind us of the Greeks of the Byzantine Empire.

In Russia secrecy presides over everything: secrecy—administrative, political, social; discretion—useful and useless; silence—superfluous for assuring necessary security; such are the inevitable consequences of the primitive character of this people, corroborated by the influence of its government. Every traveler is indiscreet; so it is necessary, as politely as possible, to keep track of the always too inquisitive foreigner lest he see things as they are—which would be the greatest of inconveniences. In brief, the Russians are disguised Chinese; they do not wish to acknowledge their aversion to observers from distant places. If they dared, like the real Chinese, to brave the accusation of barbarism, they would refuse us entry to Petersburg as the Chinese have excluded us from Peking; and they would admit to their country only craftsmen, taking care not to permit the worker, once received, ever to return to his own country.

I observed from the beginning that any Russians of the lower classes, suspicious by nature, detest foreigners through ignorance and national prejudice; I have since found that any Russian of the upper classes, equally suspicious, fears foreigners because he believes them hostile; he says: "The French, the English, are convinced of their superiority over all peoples." This is sufficient motive for the Russian to hate the foreigner. A barbaric jealousy, an envy—childish but impossible to allay, governs most Russians in their relations with people of other countries; and as you sense this unsociable tendency everywhere you finish, while feeling sorry for yourself, by showing the distrust that you inspire. You conclude that a confidence which never becomes reciprocal is fraudulent; hence you remain cold and reserved.

All Russians are born imitators; consequently, they are observers above everything else. This talent, which is characteristic of infant peoples, often degenerates into a rather low espionage; it produces obtrusive and impolite questions which are shocking on the part of people who are, themselves, always impenetrable and who respond only by subterfuges. One would say here that even friendship has a certain intimacy with the police. How can one feel at ease with men who are so cautious, so discreet in everything that concerns them and so inquisitive with regard to others? If they saw you assume more natural manners with them than they have with you, they would believe you their dupe.

The excessive defiance of people with whom you have dealings here, no matter to what class they belong, warns you to be on your guard: the danger you run is revealed to you by the fear you inspire.

No one can leave Russia if he has not apprized all his creditors of his plan, that is to say if he has not had his departure announced in the newspapers three times with an interval of a week between each publication. This can be avoided only by paying the police to shorten the delay; and even so the insertion must appear at least once or twice. You will be allowed post horses only on presentation of an official certificate attesting that you owe no one. So many precautions denote the bad faith which reigns in this country.

A NIGHTMARE OF THINGS
TO COME

Petersburg, August 2,1839

THE DAY of the Peterhof fête, I asked the Minister of War what I should do in order to obtain permission to see the fortress at Schlüsselburg.

He replied to me: "I will let His Majesty know of your desire."

His tone of caution mixed with surprise made me find the reply significant. My request, simple as it had appeared to me, had importance in the eyes of a minister. Think of visiting a fortress, historic since the detention and death of Ivan VI, which happened under the reign of the Empress Elizabeth: what an enormous daring!

I realized that, without suspecting it, I had touched a sensitive string and I remained silent.

Some days afterwards, that is to say day before yesterday, just as I was preparing to leave for Moscow, I received a letter from the Minister of War which heralded the permission to see the *sluices* of Schlüsselburg.

The ancient Swedish fortress, renamed Key of the Baltic by Peter I, is situated precisely at the source of the Neva on an island in Lake Ladoga, of which this river is, properly speaking, the outlet—a sort of natural canal by which the lake sends its waters to the Gulf of Finland. But

211

this canal, the Neva, is enlarged by an abundant jet of water which is regarded as the real source of the river; one sees it gush forth below the waters directly under the walls of the fortress of Schlüsselburg, between the river and the lake. By means of water-gates, boats avoid danger and follow the lake without passing over the source of the Neva.

This is the fine construction I was being permitted to examine in detail: I had asked for a State prison; they responded with water-gates.

The Minister of War ended his note by announcing to me that the general aide-de-camp, director of the lines of communication of the Empire, had been ordered to provide me with means of making the trip with ease.

This mark of protection was too much like a proof of defiance to flatter me as much as it annoyed me. So, while champing at the bit and crushing the Minister's letter of recommendation in my hands, I was saying: "Prince X, whom I met on the boat of Travemünde, was decidedly right when he exclaimed that Russia is the land of useless formalities."

I went to the general aide-de-camp to claim the execution of the supreme word.

The director was not receiving, or he had gone out; I was put off until tomorrow. Not wishing to lose another day, I insisted. They told me to come back in the evening. I came back and finally got as far as this important personage. He received me with the politeness that men of position have accustomed me to here, and, after a visit of a quarter of an hour, I left his office armed, note this, with the necessary orders for the engineer at Schlüsselburg but not for the governor of the castle! While conducting me as far as the antechamber, he promised me that a subordinate officer would be at my door the following morning at four o'clock.

I did not sleep. I was seized by an idea which will appear insane to you: the idea that my protector could become my executioner. If this man, instead of conducting me to Schlüsselburg, eighteen leagues from Petersburg, should show, on leaving the city, an order to deport me to Siberia to allow my troublesome curiosity to expire there, what would I do, what would I say? It will be necessary to begin by obeying, I thought, and later, upon arriving at Tobolsk, if I arrive there, I will protest. Politeness does not reassure me; on the contrary, for I have not forgotten the caresses Alexander bestowed on one of his ministers seized by a messenger at the very exit of the Emperor's office. Alexander had, himself, given the order to take the minister to Siberia immediately upon his departure from the palace, without taking him even for a moment to his home. Plenty of other examples of arrests of this nature came to my mind to justify my presentiments and trouble my imagination.

Nor is being a foreigner sufficient security: I recalled the circumstances of the removal of Kotzebue [German poet, 1761-1819] who, at the beginning of this century, was also seized by a courier and transported from Petersburg to

Tobolsk for a stroke of the pen such as mine. (I believed myself already on the road.)

It is true that the exile of the German poet lasted only six weeks; and in my youth I laughed at him for his lamentations; but on this night I no longer laughed. Whether the possible analogy of our destinies had made me change my point of view, or whether age had made me more just, I pitied Kotzebue from the bottom of my heart. Such torture should not be judged by its duration: the journey of eighteen hundred leagues in a *telega* on wooden wheels, in this climate, is itself a trial that many bodies would not be able to stand; but, without stopping at this initial discomfort, what man would not have compassion for a poor foreigner taken from his friends, his family, who for six weeks believed he was doomed to end his days in deserts without names, without bounds, among criminals and their guards, indeed even among the administrators of more or less elevated rank? Such a prospect is worse than death and is enough to cause death or, at the very least, to derange the mind.

My ambassador will reclaim me; yes, but for six weeks I shall have suffered the beginning of an eternal exile! Add to this the fact that, despite all protests, if they are seriously interested in doing away with me, they will spread the rumor that while sailing in a small boat on Lake Ladoga I capsized. That is known to happen every day. Will the French Ambassador try to recover my body from this abyss? They will tell him that they searched in vain for my body. The dignity of our nation thus covered, the Ambassador will be satisfied and I will be lost.

What was the offense of Kotzebue? He had made himself feared by publishing opinions which the Russians thought were not wholly favorable to the established order in Russia. And, who guarantees that I have not incurred precisely the same censure—or the same suspicion, which would be enough? This is what I was saying to myself while, unable to sleep, I was striding up and down my room. Am I not also mad, to think and to write? If I arouse the least suspicion here, can I hope to be shown more consideration than they have had for so many others more powerful and more prominent? I have in vain repeated to one and all that I will publish nothing about this country. No doubt, the more I feign admiration for what they show me the less they believe me; it is useless to flatter myself: they cannot think that everything pleases me in equal proportions. The Russians are familiar with cautious lies. Furthermore, I am spied upon; every foreigner is. Consequently, they know I am writing letters and holding them; they also know I never leave the city, not even for a day, without taking these mysterious papers with me in a large portfolio; they will perhaps be curious to know my true thoughts. They will prepare a trap for me in some forest; they will attack me; they will ransack me in order to take my letters, and they will kill me in order to silence me.

Such were the fears that obsessed me throughout night before last, and, although yesterday I visited the fortress of Schlüsselburg without mishap, my fears were not so unreasonable that I can feel myself entirely safe for the rest of my journey. I have in vain tried to tell myself that the Russian Police, cautious, enlightened, well-informed, indulge only in the violent measures they believe to be necessary; that I am attaching a great deal of importance to my remarks and to my own person to think that they could upset the men who govern this Empire. These grounds for safety, and many others that I shall spare myself the trouble of mentioning, seem to me more specious than sound. Experience has shown me only too well how excessively powerful men are preoccupied with minutiae; everything is important to him who wishes to hide the fact that he rules through fear, and anyone who values opinion cannot disdain that of an independent man who is a writer. A government which lives by mystery and whose strength is dissimulation, if not feint, is terrified by everything; everything seems consequential to it; in short, my self-concern conspires with my reflections and my memories to convince me that I run some risk here.

If I stress these anxieties, it is because they paint this country for you. Suppose my fears to be only fancies, at least they are fancies which could harass my mind only in Petersburg or in Morocco; that is what I wish to point out.

Yesterday at five o'clock in the morning, I set out in a barouche drawn by four horses abreast.

My courier sat in front by the driver, and we

rapidly crossed Petersburg, leaving behind us the elegant quarter, then the manufacturing quarter, then the immense cotton mills, as well as many other factories, directed for the most part by the English. This part of the city resembles a colony: it is the city of manufacturers.

As a man is appreciated here only according to his relations with the government, the presence of the courier on my carriage produced a great effect.

I noticed, with alarm, the marvelous efficaciousness of this power charged with my protection, and I thought that he would obey with equal punctiliousness if he had received the order to do away with me. The difficulty one experiences in getting into this country is annoying but not frightening; the thing that impresses me more is the difficulty one might have in getting out. The common people say: "The doors leading into Russia are wide; those leading out are narrow." However big this Empire, I am cramped; the prison is vast in vain, for the prisoner always finds himself pinched for room. This is a figment of my imagination, I agree, but I had to come here to be subjected to it.

Under the guard of my soldier, I rapidly followed the shores of the Neva. One goes out from Petersburg by a kind of village street, a little less monotonous than the routes I have covered up to now in Russia. A few vistas on the river across rows of birch trees, a series of mills, factories in considerable number which appear to be very active, hamlets built of wood, vary the landscape slightly. Do not imagine a nature truly picturesque in the ordinary sense of the word; this part of the country is less desolate than that one sees from the other side—that is all.

The appearance of certain villages surprised me. They have a real richness and even a sort of rustic elegance which is pleasing. The houses, always of wood and strung out along the road, appear well kept. They are painted on the side facing the street and the rooftops are loaded with ornaments that might be called pretentious; for, in comparing this exterior sumptuousness with the scarcity of comfortable furnishings and the lack of cleanliness which strike one inside these toy houses, one regrets seeing the taste for the superfluous hold sway over a people who are still unacquainted with the necessary.

On close inspection, one also sees that these dwellings are really extremely poorly constructed. They are made of beams and joists scarcely squared, scooped out at both ends, and tied together to form the corners of the cabin; these timbers rudely piled up one on the other leave cracks which are carefully stopped up with tar-smeared moss. This spreads a fearful odor throughout the entire dwelling and even outside.

I had sent a relay to a village ten leagues from Petersburg: four fresh horses all rigged awaited me there. In this village, I found a sort of Russian market and went in. In traveling I like to lose nothing of my first impressions: to experience them I tour the world and to renew them I describe my travels. So, I got out of my carriage to

218

see this rural center. This was my first opportunity to observe Russian peasants on their own ground. Peterhof was not real Russia; the crowd gathered there for a fête altered the usual aspect of the land and brought the customs of the city to the country. So this was my introduction to the fields.

First I noticed a vast shed entirely of wood, with board walls on three sides, boards under the feet, boards over the head. I entered this enormous market which occupied a large part of the rustic settlement. In spite of the currents of air, I was overwhelmed by the odor of onions, sour cabbage, and old greasy leather that the Russian villagers and the villages themselves exude.

A low and rather small room adjoined this vast shed; I entered it and felt as if I were in the principal room of some flatboat sailing on the river, or in a tunnel. Everything was of wood: the walls, the ceiling, the floor, the seats, the table were no more than a crudely worked assemblage of thick planks and staves of various lengths. The odor of sour cabbage and pitch was always prevalent.

In this hole, practically cut off from air and light by the low doors and garret-like windows, I found an old woman busy serving tea to four or five bearded peasants covered with sheep skins —the wool turned inside (it has been rather cold for several days, the beginning of August). These men, mostly small in stature, were seated at a table, their leather cloaks draped over them in various manners.

The air of the Russian peasant, at once gentle

219

and savage, is not devoid of grace. His elegant stature, his strength which does not detract from his agility and suppleness, his broad shoulders, his sweet smile, the mixture of tenderness and fierceness which is found in his savage and sad expression, make his appearance as different from that of our laborers as the place he lives and the land he cultivates are different from the rest of Europe. Here everything is new to a foreigner. The people have a certain charm that one senses but that is not expressed; it is an oriental languor mixed with the romantic dreaminess of the people of the North, and all of this in the uncultivated but noble form which constitutes the merit of primitive talents. This people inspires interest but not confidence—another shade of feeling I have come to know here. The men of the people in Russia are amusing rogues. One could do a lot with them if one did not deceive them; but when the peasants see that their masters or the masters' agents lie even more than they themselves, they become calloused in ruse and baseness.

Filth is great in this country; the dirtiness of their houses and their clothes struck me more than that of the individuals. The Russians take a fair amount of care about their persons. While their steam baths appear disgusting to us—I prefer pure water to great clouds of steam—this boiling fog washes the body and fortifies it, although at the same time prematurely wrinkling the skin. Nevertheless, thanks to the use of these baths, one often sees peasants who have clean beards and clean hair, whereas one cannot say as much for their clothes. Warm clothing is costly; consequently, it must be worn for a long time and gets dirty long before it is worn out.

In certain districts the men, while working, wear a tall headdress of dark blue cloth shaped like a balloon and resembling that of a Buddhist priest. There are several other styles of headdress, and all these toques and bonnets of various forms are rather agreeable to the eye.

But what shall I tell you about the women? Up to now, those I have seen seemed repulsive. I hoped to encounter some pretty villagers on this excursion. But here, as in Petersburg, they have short, fat figures; and their dresses are belted just above the bust which falls loose under the skirt— it is hideous! To this voluntary deformity, add men's boots, made from disgustingly greasy leather, a kind of overcoat of sheepskin, similar to that of the cloaks of their husbands, and you will have an idea of a supremely unattractive person. Unfortunately, this idea will be correct. To achieve the acme of ugliness, the woman's sheepskin is cut less gracefully than the little redingote of the man, and (this comes no doubt from a praiseworthy economy) it is also usually more wormeaten; it literally falls in tatters. Such is their attire.

Actually, most of the women one meets in the government circles of Petersburg are of the Finnish race. I am assured, however, that in the interior of the country, which I am going to visit, there are a great many pretty peasants.

The route from Petersburg to Schlüsselburg is

Journey for Our Time

bad in some parts. There is sometimes deep sand, sometimes shifting mud on which they have thrown planks, inadequate for pedestrians and dangerous for carriages; these pieces of wood, badly fastened down, sway up and down and splash muddy water to the very depths of the calash. But that is the least of the discomforts of the road; there is something worse than the planks. I want to tell you about the unsplit green logs, placed crosswise on certain portions of the spongy terrain where the soil has no solidity and would swallow up any covering other than a roadway of logs. Unfortunately, this rustic and mobile parquet over the mire is constructed from odd scraps, badly joined and uneven. The tottering structure dances continually under the wheels in this bottomless, perpetually soaked terrain which becomes elastic at the least pressure. At the pace one travels in Russia, a carriage is soon destroyed on such roads: people break their bones and from verst to verst the bolts of the carriages fly out on all sides, the wheel rims are split, the springs burst out—this should reduce carriages to their simplest form, to something as primitive as the Russian cart.

Except for the famous *chaussée* from Petersburg to Moscow, the Schlüsselburg road is still one relatively free of these dreadful logs. I counted many bridges of rotten planks, one of which seemed really dangerous to me. But human life is of little importance in Russia. With sixty million children can one have the feeling of a father?

222

On my arrival at Schlüsselburg, where I was expected, I was received by the engineer in charge of the operation of the water-gates.

The weather was gray, cold, windy. Scarcely out of my carriage in front of the engineer's house —a good dwelling entirely of wood, I was shown into a comfortable salon where the engineer offered me a light repast. I ate and warmed myself in silence. "I'm sorry to hurry you," my host said to me, "but we do not have too much time for visiting the works which I have been ordered to show you in detail."

I had foreseen the blow without being able to ward it off; I took it with resignation and let myself be conducted from water-gate to water-gate, always thinking with a useless regret of the fortress, the tomb of the young Ivan, which they did not want me to go near. This unavowed purpose of my trip was always present in my mind, and you will soon see how I achieved it.

The number of squares of granite that I saw during this afternoon, of sluice-gates fitted into grooves in blocks of this same stone, flagstones of the same material used to pave the bottom of a gigantic canal, is scarcely important to you, and I am extremely glad as I would not be able to tell you. By means of a system of canals, colossal like everything that is done in this Empire, they have succeeded, since Peter the Great, in joining, without danger for boats, the Caspian Sea to the Baltic Sea by the Volga, Lake Ladoga, and the Neva.

Europe and Asia are thus crossed by waters which join the North to the South. This idea, bold

223

in conception and prodigious in realization, has resulted in the production of one of the marvels of the civilized world. It is beautiful and good to know about, but I found it boring to see, especially under the guidance of one of the executors of the masterpiece; the professional man accords to his work the esteem that it deserves without doubt, but for a simple curiosity seeker, like myself, admiration is stifled under the minute details which I am sparing you.

When I believed I had scrupulously granted what was expected of my time and my praises to the wonders I was obliged to review in order to respond to the favor they believed they were doing me, I returned to the prime motive of my trip, and disguising my aim—the better to achieve it—I asked to see the source of the Neva. This desire whose insidious innocence could not conceal its indiscretion was at first evaded by my engineer who replied: "It springs up under the water at the exit of Lake Ladoga, at the bottom of the canal separating the lake from the island where the fortress is erected." This I already knew.

"It is one of the natural curiosities of Russia," I replied. "Would there be no means of visiting this source?"

"The wind is too strong; we will not be able to make out the bubblings of the spring; calmer weather would be necessary for the eye to distinguish a jet of water which bursts forth at the bottom of the waves. However, I shall do what I can to satisfy your curiosity."

224

At these words, the engineer summoned an extremely pretty little boat, rowed by six elegantly dressed oarsmen, and we set off to see the source of the Neva, so to speak, but really to approach the walls of the fortress, or rather of the enchanted prison to which they had, with the most artful politeness, refused me access. But the difficulties served only to increase my eagerness; if I had received word that I could free some wretched prisoner from this place, my impatience could hardly have been more intense. We turned around the fortress in order, we said, to come as near as possible to the source of the Neva. Our boat soon brought us directly over this whirlpool. The oarsmen were so skillful with the oars that, in spite of the bad weather and the smallness of our boat, we barely felt the beating of the waves, although they were as agitated in this spot as in the middle of the sea. Not being able to distinguish the source whose whirlpool had been hidden by the movement of the waves which carried us away, we first took a turn on the big lake; later, on our return, the wind, a little calmed, permitted us to perceive some billows of foam at a rather great depth. We were rowing above the very source of the Neva.

When I had thoroughly admired the site of Schlüsselburg, praised this natural phenomenon, contemplated, with the aid of a telescope, the position of the battery placed by Peter the Great to bombard the fortress of the Swedes, finally having expressed due appreciation for everything that scarcely interested me: "Let's go to see the inside

225

of the fortress," I said with a most offhand and worldly air. "It is on a site which seems to me most picturesque," I added a little less adroitly, for above all in the art of finesse one must do nothing in excess. I felt the full force of the searching look the Russian cast upon me; the mathematician become diplomat replied:

"This fortress has nothing of interest for a foreigner, sir."

"No matter, everything is worthy of curiosity in a country as interesting as yours."

"But if the commander is not expecting us, they will not let us enter."

"You can ask permission to bring a traveler into the fortress; furthermore, I believe the commander is expecting us."

In fact, we were admitted on the first message of the engineer, which made me suppose that my visit had been, if not announced as certain, at least indicated as probable.

Received with military ceremony, we were led under an arch and through a rather poorly protected doorway. After crossing a grass-covered court, we were taken into . . . the prison? Not at all, into the quarters of the commander. He did not know a word of French, but he received me with decorum, pretending to take my visit for a courtesy of which he alone was the object; he had the engineer translate to me the thanks he could not express himself. These wily compliments seemed to me more strange than satisfying. I had to be ceremonious and appear to talk with the wife of the commander, who likewise spoke scarcely any French. We had to take chocolate and busy ourselves with everything except visiting the prison of Ivan, this fabulous reward for all the troubles, all the schemes, all the politeness, and all the tiring details of the day. Never was access to a fairy palace more ardently desired than I desired entry to this dungeon.

Finally when the time of a reasonable visit seemed to me to have passed, I asked my guide if it was possible to see the interior of the fortress. A few words, a few glances were rapidly exchanged between the commander and the engineer, and we left the room.

I believed I had reached the goal of my efforts. The fortress of Schlüsselburg has nothing of the picturesque; it is an enclosure of not very high Swedish walls whose interior resembles a kind of garden where various low buildings have been dispersed: to wit, a church, a house for the governor, a barracks, and finally some invisible cells masked by towers whose height did not exceed that of the rampart. Nothing indicates that violence and mystery are at the bottom of things here; it is not revealed in their appearance. The almost serene appearance of this State prison seems to me more fearful to the mind than to the eye. The grilles, the drawbridges, the crenelles, in sum, the rather theatrical apparatus which decorated the terrible castles of the Middle Ages are not found here at all. On leaving the governor's sitting room, they started by showing me the "superb ornaments of the church"! The governor took the trouble to tell me himself that the four copes which were solemnly spread before me cost thirty thousand rubles. Tired of so much affectation, I spoke quite simply about the tomb of Ivan VI; to that they responded by showing me a crack made in the walls by Czar Peter's cannon when he, in person, seized the Swedish fortress, Key of the Baltic.

"Ivan's tomb," I took up again, without being disconcerted, "where is it?"

This time they took me behind the church near a Bengal rosebush: "It is here," they told me.

I concluded that victims do not have tombs in Russia.

"And Ivan's room?" I continued with some insistence, which must have seemed as peculiar to my hosts as their scruples, their reticence, and their evasions were to me.

The engineer told me in a low voice that they could not show me Ivan's room because it was in a part of the prison at present occupied by State prisoners. The excuse appeared legitimate to me, and I was expecting it. But the thing that surprised me was the governor's anger; maybe he understands French better than he speaks it, maybe he had wished to deceive me in pretending to be ignorant of my language, or maybe he had grasped the sense of the explanation that had just been given me, for he severely reprimanded my guide whose indiscretion, he added, might someday become fatal. My guide, piqued by the reprimand, choosing a favorable moment found the means of telling me this, adding that the governor had warned him in a very significant manner to abstain, henceforth, from speaking of *public matters* and from bringing foreigners into a State prison. This engineer has all the necessary characteristics to become a good Russian, but he is young and does not know the elementals of his profession. But it is not of the engineer that I wish to speak.

I sensed that I would have to yield. I was the weaker; I recognized myself vanquished and I gave up the visit to the cell where the ill-fated heir to the throne of Russia had died an imbecile because they had found it more convenient to make him an idiot than to make him Emperor. It was unbelievably impressive to see how the Russian government is served by its agents. I recalled the expression of the Minister of War the first time I dared mention my desire to visit a castle made historic by a crime committed at the time of the Empress Elizabeth; and I weighed, with admiration mixed with fright, the confusion of ideas in our country against the absence of all thought or personal opinion, the blind submission which governs the conduct of the officials of the Russian administration, as well as the subordinate employees. The unity of action in this government was overpowering to me. Shuddering, I wondered at the tacit agreement of superiors and subordinates to wage war on ideas and even on facts. I now felt as anxious to leave as an instant before I had been impatient to enter; and as there was nothing to interest me further in a fortress where they had not wished to show me anything more than the sacristy, I asked to be returned to Schlüsselburg.

I was afraid of being forced to become one of the inhabitants of this place of secret tears and unknown sorrows. In my ever increasing anguish, I no longer aspired to anything more than the physical pleasure of walking and breathing. I was forgetting that even the country I was going back to was a prison: a prison so much the more dreadful in that it is bigger and one enters and leaves its borders with more difficulty.

A Russian fortress! The impression this produces on the imagination differs vastly from that experienced in visiting the fortresses of really civilized, sincerely humane peoples. More than the open acts of barbarism, the puerile precautions they take in Russia to dissimulate what they qualify as secrets of State confirms me in the idea that this government is nothing but hypocritical tyranny.

If, instead of seeking to disguise the truth under a false propriety, they had simply taken me to the places they are permitted to show; if they had replied with frankness to my questions on an act accomplished a century ago, I would have been less concerned about what I was not able to see; but what they kept from me, too artificially, proved to me the contrary of what they wished to make me believe. All these vain detours are revelations to the eyes of the experienced observer. The thing that made me indignant was that the men who used these subterfuges with me could believe I was the dupe of their childish ruses. I am assured, and I have this on good authority, that the subterranean cells of Kronstadt

230

confine, among other prisoners of State, some unfortunates who have been relegated there since the reign of Alexander. Those poor wretches are brutalized by a torture the atrocity of which nothing can excuse or justify; if they happened to come out of the earth, they would rise up like so many vengeful specters who would make the despot himself recoil with fright and the structure of despotism fall in ruins. Anything can be defended by pretty words and even by good reasons; but say what they will, a régime so violent that it must be sustained by such means is a profoundly vicious régime.

The victims of this odious policy are no longer men: these ill-fated beings, deprived of the rights of common law, rot away, strangers to the world, forgotten by all, abandoned to themselves in the night of their captivity, where imbecility becomes the fruit and the last consolation of an interminable weariness; they have lost their memory and even their reason—this human light that no man has the right to extinguish in the soul of his fellow man. They have forgotten their own names; the guards even amuse themselves by asking the prisoners their names with a brutal and always unpunished derision, for, in the depths of these abysses of iniquity, there reign such disorder and darkness that all traces of justice have been erased.

The authorities are ignorant even as to the charge against certain prisoners; but they hold them forever because they do not know to whom to return them and because they deem it less troublesome to perpetuate the crime than to publish it. They fear the ill effect of belated justice, and they aggravate the evil to avoid being forced to justify their abuses: atrocious pusillanimity which calls itself respect for *propriety,* caution, obedience, discernment, sacrifice to the public good, to reasons of State . . . how can I know what more? Despotism, when it speaks, is discreet: are there not two names for everything in human society? Thus they tell us there is no death penalty in Russia. To bury alive is not to kill! When one thinks on one hand of so much unhappiness, on the other of so much injustice and hypocrisy, one no longer recognizes the guilty in prison: the judge alone appears criminal, and, to cap it all, one realizes this iniquitous judge is not brutal just for his own pleasure. That is what bad government can do to men interested in its continuance! But Russia moves on to meet her destiny; this is the answer to everything. Certainly, if one measures the grandeur of the end by the extent of the sacrifices, one should foresee for this nation the empire of the world.

On my return from this sad excursion, a new corvée awaited me at the engineer's house; a ceremonial dinner with people of the middle class. In my honor the engineer had gathered together some of his wife's relatives and a few of the local landowners. Russian thought, disguised with care by the tact of people in the upper circles, was revealed here in its true colors. This society was more honest and less polite than that of the court, and I saw clearly what I had only sensed elsewhere: the spirit of examination, sarcasm, and criticism which dominates the relations of Russians with foreigners. They hate us as any imitator hates his model; their scrutinizing looks are searching for faults which they want to find in us. When I discovered this trend of mind, I was by no means inclined toward indulgence. I was thinking that perhaps the people who are to decide the future of Russia will come from this level of society. The middle class is new-born in this Empire and God alone knows the influence it will have on the destiny of Russia . . . and of the world.

THE CZAR'S TWO FACES

Petersburg, August 2, 1839—Midnight

I HAVE just taken a last look at this extraordinary city. I have said goodbye to Petersburg . . . Adieu! What a magic word! It lends an indefinable attraction to both places and persons.

Petersburg seemed to me less beautiful, but more astonishing than Venice. These are two colossi erected by fear: Venice was the work of just simple fear—the last of the Romans preferred flight to death, and the fruit of the fear of these ancient giants became one of the wonders of the modern world; Petersburg is likewise the product of fear, but a pious fear, for the Russian policy knew how to make obedience a dogma. The Russian people are considered very religious and they may be; but what is a religion that is forbidden to instruct? They never preach in the Russian churches. The Gospels would reveal liberty to the Slavs.

Sometimes I feel myself ready to share the superstition of this people. Enthusiasm becomes contagious when it is general, or even if it only appears to be general; but this evil no sooner overtakes me than I think of Siberia, that indispensable auxiliary of Muscovite civilization, and I promptly regain my calm and my independence.

Political faith is firmer here than religious faith; the unity of the Orthodox church is only appar-

234

ent: the sects, reduced to mutism by the skillfully calculated silence of the dominant Church, dig their way under ground; but nations are mute only for a time—sooner or later the day of discussion arises; religion, policy, all speak and all explain themselves in the end. Thus, as soon as speech is restored to this silenced people, one will hear so much dispute that an astonished world will think it has returned to the confusion of Babel. It is through religious dissensions that a social revolution will someday occur in Russia.

When I am near the Emperor, when I see his dignity, his beauty, I wonder at this marvel.

However, I examine the objects of my respect with scrupulous care; consequently, when I gaze upon this personage, unique in the world, from close at hand, I believe his head has two faces, like that of Janus, and that the words violence, exile, oppression, or their total equivalent—Siberia—are engraved on the face I do not see.

This idea pursues me endlessly, even when I am talking to him. In vain I force myself to think only of what I am saying; against my will, my mind wanders from Warsaw to Tobolsk, and the name of Warsaw alone brings back all my defiance.

Do you know that at this very hour the roads of Asia are once again covered with exiles, recently snatched from their homes, who, on foot, seek their tomb like herds driven from the pasture to the slaughterhouse? This renewal of wrath is due to a so-called Polish conspiracy of *young fools,* who would have been heroes if they had

235

succeeded, although their efforts, it seems to me, were all the more courageous for being desperate. My heart bleeds for the banished, for their families, for their country. What will happen when the oppressors of this corner of the world, where chivalry formerly flourished, will have populated Tartary with the most noble and the most courageous among the children of old Europe? Then, achieving the peak of their glacial policy, they will enjoy their success: Siberia will have become the kingdom and Poland the desert.

Should not one blush with shame in pronouncing the word *liberalism* when one thinks that there exists in Europe a people who were independent and who no longer know any liberty other than that of apostasy? When the Russians turn against the West the weapons they employ with success against Asia, they forget that the methods which aid their progress with the Kalmucks become a crime against humanity in the land of a long civilized people. I abstain, you observe with what care, from using the word *tyranny;* although it would be in place, it would only lend weapons against me to men hardened to the protests that they never cease to provoke.

But why should I be alarmed? Beyond a few pages they will not read what I write; they will file the book away and forbid its being spoken of; the book will not exist; it will never have existed for them nor in their country. Like their church, their government protects itself by imposing silence; this policy has succeeded heretofore and should succeed for a long time to come in a country where distances, isolation, swamps, woods, and winters take the place of conscience in the men who rule, and of patience in those who obey.

The Volga incidents continue. These horrors are attributed to the provocations of Polish emissaries: an imputation which reminds one of the justice of La Fontaine's wolf. The cruelties; the excesses of both sides serve as an introduction to the convulsions of the eventual denouement and suffice to forewarn us of the nature it will take. But in a nation governed like this one passions boil a long time before breaking out; while the danger approaches from hour to hour, the evil is prolonged, and the crisis delayed. Even our grandchildren may not see the explosion; but we can say today that explosion is inevitable, while we cannot predict the time.

A TRUE TALE OF HEROISM
AND HORROR

Petersburg, August 3, 1839

I SHALL NEVER get away. Providence always intervenes . . . still another delay! But this one was legitimate; you will not blame me for it. I was on the verge of getting into my carriage when one of my friends insisted upon seeing me and came in. He wished me to read a letter at that very instant, and what a letter, My Lord! It was from Princess Troubetskoy, who addressed it to a member of her family charged with showing it to the Emperor. I wanted to copy it in order to publish it without changing a word, but my friend did not wish to permit this.

"It would spread over the entire earth," he said, frightened by the effect the letter had produced on me.

"All the more reason to make it known," I replied.

"Impossible. It involves the existence of several persons; it was lent to me only to show you and on my word of honor to return within half an hour."

Unhappy country where every foreigner appears as a savior to the eyes of a band of oppressed because he represents truth, public attention, liberty to a people deprived of all these benefits.

Petersburg, August 3, 1839

Before telling you what this letter contained, I must first tell you in a few words a lamentable story.

Prince Troubetskoy was condemned *to the mines* fourteen years ago. At that time he was young and had just taken a very active part in the revolt of the fourteenth of December.

The conspiracy was foiled by the Czar and it was necessary to proceed to the punishment of the criminals. Prince Troubetskoy, one of the most compromised, could not clear himself. He was sent as a convict to the mines of the Urals for fourteen or fifteen years and for the rest of his life to Siberia, in one of the distant colonies that the malefactors are destined to populate.

The prince had a wife whose family is one of the most eminent in the country. It was impossible to persuade the princess not to follow her husband into the tomb. This noble wife obtained the "favor" of being buried alive with her husband. The thing that astonishes me, now that I have seen Russia and caught a glimpse of the ruling spirit in this government, is that by some residue of shame they should have thought it necessary to respect this act of devotion for fourteen years. That they countenance patriotic heroism is perfectly understandable, they profit by it. But to tolerate a sublime virtue which is not in agreement with the political views of the sovereign is a negligence for which they should reproach themselves.

Maybe they acceded to the fear of incensing powerful families or to I do not know what kind of prudence or mercy; be that as it may, the princess left with her husband, the convict; and even more amazing, she arrived. A prodigious journey, which was in itself a terrible trial—you know that these journeys are made in a telega, a little open cart without springs; one rolls along for hundreds, thousands of leagues on wooden wheels which not only break the cart but the body. The unfortunate woman bore this fatigue and many others after that; I had a glimpse of her privations, her sufferings, but I cannot describe them to you as I lack the details and I do not wish to draw on my imagination for anything—the truth in this story is sacred to me.

They had no children in Petersburg; they had five in Siberia.

For fourteen years the couple have lived, so to speak, beside the Ural mines, for the arms of a worker like the prince further the production of the pickax very little; he is there for the sake of being there . . . that is all; but he is a convict and that suffices. . . . You will see shortly to what this condition condemns a man . . . *and his children!*

Good Russians are not lacking in Petersburg, and I have met among them those who regard the life of persons condemned to the mines as very bearable and who complain that the hardships of the conspirators in the Urals are exaggerated. The true patriots unconditionally approve the political prison of Russian invention. These courtiers of the hangman always find the penalty too mild for the crime.

Whatever the delights of Siberia may consist of, the health of Princess Troubetskoy has been affected by her sojourn at the mines: it is difficult to understand how a woman accustomed to the luxury of the élite in a voluptuous country has been able to bear for such a long time the privations of all kinds to which she has subjected herself by choice. She wished to live, she has lived. She has conceived and given birth; she has raised her children in a zone where the duration and severity of the winter seem to us contrary to life. The thermometer there falls each year to from 33 to 40 degrees below zero. This temperature alone would be enough to destroy the human race. But this saintly woman had many other worries.

At the end of seven years of exile, when she saw her children growing up, she thought she should write to a member of her family humbly to beseech the Czar to allow them to be sent to Petersburg or some other large city in order to receive a suitable education.

The supplication was carried to the feet of the Czar, and the worthy successor of Ivan and of Peter I replied that the children of a convict, convicts themselves, are always sufficiently erudite.

Upon receiving this reply, the family . . . the mother . . . the condemned, remained silent for seven more years. Humbled humanity, honor, Christian charity, religion alone protested for them, but silently; not a voice was raised to protest against such *justice*.

However, today a new misery has just torn a last cry from the depths of this abyss.

241

The prince has done his time as a convict and now the so-called liberated exiles are condemned —they and their young family—to form a colony in one of the most remote corners of the desert. The site of their new residence, chosen purposely by the Czar himself, is so wild that the name of this cavern is not yet even marked on the maps of the Russian General Staff, the most faithful and the most minute of geographic maps.

You understand that the condition of the princess (I name only her) is more miserable since she *is permitted* to live in this solitude (note that in this language of the oppressed, interpreted by the oppressor, permissions are obligatory). At the mines she warmed herself under the earth; there, at least, she had silent consolers in her sorrow, witnesses to her heroism. She met human looks which contemplated and respectfully deplored her inglorious martyrdom, thus making it more sublime. Without having need to speak, she felt herself in communication, for governments do their worst in vain, pity will come to light wherever there are human beings.

But how to arouse pity in bears, pierce impenetrable woods, melt the eternal ice, clear the spongy peat mold of a morass without bounds, protect oneself from mortal cold in a hovel? How, finally, to subsist alone with her husband and her five children, at a hundred leagues, perhaps farther, from all human habitation, unless it is that of the overseer of the colonies—for that is what one calls colonizing in Siberia.

Today, this father and this mother, deprived of

all assistance, without physical strength against such adversities, punished in their children whose innocence serves only as an aggravation to the torture of the parents—these martyrs no longer know how they can support themselves and their family. These little convicts by birth have in vain borne numbers instead of names if they no longer have a country, a place in the State; nature has given them bodies which must be nourished and clothed. In the mines one could still take care of them; in their new exile everything is lacking. In this extreme destitution, she sees no farther than their misery; the father, his heart withered by so much adversity, lets her act according to her inspiration. Pardoning with a heroic generosity the cruelty of the first refusal, the princess writes a second letter from the depths of her hovel. This letter is addressed to her family but intended for the Emperor. This was to put herself at the feet of the enemy, to forget what she owed to herself; but who would not exonerate this ill-fated woman?

The princess's letter reached its destination. The Czar read it, and it was to see this letter that my departure was prevented. I do not regret the delay; I have never read anything simpler or more touching. Actions such as hers need no words. She makes use of the privilege of a heroine; she is laconic even in asking for the life of her children. In a few lines she sets forth her situation, without declamation, without complaint. She places herself above all eloquence; the facts alone speak for her. She finishes by imploring as a sole

243

favor, the permission to live within range of an apothecary in order, she says, to be able to get medicine for her children when they are sick. The neighborhood of Tobolsk, Irkutsk, Orenburg would seem to her a paradise. In the final words of her letter she no longer addresses the Czar; she forgets everything except her husband; she responds to the thoughts in their hearts with a delicateness and a dignity that would justify the forgiveness of the most execrable crime: and she is innocent! And the ruler to whom she addresses herself is all-powerful and has only God to judge his acts. "I am very miserable," she says; "however, if it were to be done over, I would still do it."

In this woman's family there is a person courageous enough—and anyone who knows Russia should pay homage to this act of piety—a person courageous enough to dare to carry this letter to the Czar and even to support with humble supplication the request of a disgraced relative. One does not speak of it to the ruler except with terror as one would speak of a criminal, although one is honored, in the eyes of everyone other than the Emperor of Russia, to be related to this noble victim of conjugal duty.

So, after fourteen years, this woman, ennobled by so many heroic sufferings, obtains from the Emperor Nicholas, as a final response, the words that you are about to read and that I have heard from the very mouth of a person to whom the courageous relative of the victim has just repeated them: "I am astonished that you still dare to speak to me . . . (twice in fifteen years! . . .) of a family whose head has conspired against me." The person who repeated this to me is worthy of confidence; furthermore, the facts speak for themselves—the letter has changed nothing in the lot of the exiles.

Away with hesitation, away with uncertainty! For me Czar Nicholas is finally judged. . . . He is a man of character and will—he needs to be to constitute himself the jailer of a third of the globe; but he lacks magnanimity. The use that he makes of his power proves this to me only too well.

I will complete my journey, but without going to Borodino, without attending the entry of the court into the Kremlin; without speaking further to you of the Emperor. What would I tell you of this prince that you do not know now as well as I? Think, in order to give yourself an idea of the people and life of this country, that there are many other stories which take place here of the kind you have just read; but they are, and will continue to be, unknown. It has required a combination of circumstances that I regard as providential to reveal to me the facts and the details that my conscience obliges me to record here.

I am going to gather together all the letters I have written to you since my arrival in Russia and which you have not received, since I have held them through caution; I shall add this one to the lot and make a well-sealed package which I shall place in reliable hands—not an easy thing to find in Petersburg; then, I shall finish my day by writing you another letter, an official letter which will

245

leave tomorrow by the post. All the people, all the things that I see here will be praised to the utmost in this letter. You will see by this letter that I admire this country without restraint, everything that is found here and everything that is done. The thing that amuses me is that I am convinced the Russian police and you yourself will be equally duped by my enthusiasm for authority and my praises without discernment and without restriction. (I was thinking, not without grounds, that these detailed flatteries seized at the frontier would insure my tranquillity during the rest of my journey.)

If you do not hear me mentioned again, think that I have been taken to Siberia—that alone could upset my trip to Moscow which I shall not delay further as my courier has come back to tell me that the post horses will be at my door tomorrow morning irrevocably.

NOTE: Since the publication of the first edition of this book, a person attached to the French Embassy at the time of the Emperor Alexander has related to me the following event of which he was one of the witnesses:

After the riot on his accession to the throne, the Emperor Nicholas condemned the five principal leaders of the plot to death. It was decided that they would be hanged at two o'clock in the morning on the glacis of the citadel at the edge of a twenty-five-foot moat. The condemned men were stationed on a bench a few feet high under the gallows. All the preparations for the punishment finished, Count Tchernichev, charged by his master with presiding at the execution, began his function as chief of the executioners by giving the agreed signal. The drums beat and the bench was withdrawn from under the feet of the criminals. Instantly three of the ropes break; two of the released victims fall to the bottom of the moat, the third is stopped on the bluff. The people who had been permitted to watch this lugubrious scene are excited, their hearts beat with joy and gratitude in thinking that the Emperor had taken this means of reconciling the rights of humanity with the obligations of policy. But Count Tchernichev has the roll of the drums continue. The executioners descend to the moat, pick up two of the victims, one of whom has his legs broken and the other his jawbone shattered. They assist the prisoners in resuming their places under the gallows and re-attach the ropes around their necks. But while the third criminal, having remained intact, submits to the same operation, this doomed man collects all his forces and, with heroic fury, cries out in such a manner as to make himself heard in spite of the drums: "Unhappy land where one does not even know how to hang!" He had been the soul of the conspiracy; his name was Pestel.

This energy of the conquered and this barbarity of the triumphant power—therein is Russia in its entirety! But to complete the picture, I must tell you the result of this scene: Mr. Tchernichev was created a Count and named Minister of War.

THEY MEAN TO SEIZE BY ARMED FORCE THE COUNTRIES ACCESSIBLE TO THEM; AND THENCE TO OPPRESS THE REST OF THE WORLD BY TERROR

Pomerania, Post House, 18 leagues from
Petersburg, August 3, 1839

To TRAVEL the road from Petersburg to Moscow is to give oneself during entire days the sensation experienced in riding the roller coaster in Paris.

My courier has ideas, a bearing, a face which do not allow me to forget the spirit which reigns in this country. On arriving at the second relay, one of our four horses, harnessed abreast, missed his footing and fell under the wheel. Happily the coachman, in control of those who remained to him, stopped them on the spot. In spite of the advanced season, it is still blistering hot in the middle of the day and the dust makes the air stifling. I thought the fallen horse had suffered a sunstroke and that if one did not bleed him at once he would die. I summoned my courier, and, pulling from my pocket a case containing a veterinary blade, I offered it to him, telling him to use it immediately if he wished to save the poor beast. He replied to me with malicious coolness, without taking the instrument I offered him, and without even looking

248

at the horse: "It is completely useless; we are at the relay."

Thereupon, instead of helping the poor postilion loose the animal, he went into the neighboring stable to have another team prepared for us. The Russians are still far from having, as do the English, a law for the prevention of cruelty to animals; in fact, people should have someone to plead their cause in Russia as the cause of dogs and horses is pleaded in London. My courier would not believe such a law exists.

This man inspires me with little confidence; officially he is called my protector, my guide; but I see in him a disguised spy, and I think that at any instant he could receive the order to declare himself constable or jailer. Such ideas disturbed the pleasure of traveling; but I have already told you that they come to me only when I write. En route, the movement which carries me away and the rapid succession of sights distract me from everything else.

The Russian people impress me as men of agreeable talents who believe themselves born exclusively for physical strength. Together with the indifference of the Orientals, they possess a feeling for the arts, which is equivalent to saying that nature has endowed them with the need of freedom; but instead of giving them freedom, their masters turn them into instruments of oppression. A man raised ever so little above the level of the mob, immediately acquires the right—even more, he contracts the obligation—to maltreat other

men to whom he is charged to transmit the blows
that he himself receives from above; he is free to
seek some recompense in the ills he inflicts for
those to which he submits. Thus the spirit of iniquity descends from rank to rank into the very
foundations of this unfortunate society which subsists only through violence—the kind of violence
that forces the slave to lie to himself in order to
give thanks to the tyrant. From such arbitrary
acts, which make up each individual existence, is
born what they call here the public order, that is
to say a dismal tranquillity, a frightening peace,
for it is like the peace of the tomb; the Russians
are proud of this calm. As long as man has not decided to crawl, he must be proud of something,
even if only to retain his right to be called a human being. And if anyone succeeded in proving to
me the necessity for injustice and violence in order to obtain important political ends, I would
conclude that patriotism, far from being the civic
virtue that it has been called up to the present, is
high treason against humanity.

The Russians excuse themselves in their own
eyes by the thought that the government to which
they submit tends to promote their ambitious
hopes.

They wish to rule the world by conquest; they
mean to seize by armed force the countries accessible to them, and thence to oppress the rest of
the world by terror. The extension of power they
dream of is in no way either intelligent or moral;
and if God grants it to them, it will be for the woe
of the world.

Pomerania, August 3, 1839

The spectacle of this society, all the springs of which are taut like the trigger of a weapon that one is about to fire, frightens me to the point of dizziness.

THE SUBJUGATION OF THE
RUSSIAN CHURCH

Klin, a village a few leagues from Moscow
August 6, 1839

STILL ANOTHER DELAY and always for the same
reason. My carriage breaks down regularly every
twenty leagues!

Any mind seriously preoccupied with the ideas
developing in the political world can only profit
by examining this society close at hand. Here is a
society governed, in principle, in the manner of
the most ancient States named in the annals of the
world, but already entirely penetrated by the ideas
fermenting in the most revolutionary modern nations. The patriarchal tyranny of the governments
of Asia, in contact with the theories of modern
philanthropy; the characters of the peoples of the
Orient and of the Occident, incompatible by nature and nevertheless violently chained one to the
other in a semibarbaric society controlled by fear:
this is a spectacle one can enjoy only in Russia;
and certainly no thinking man would regret the
trouble he must take to come to study it at close
range.

The social, intellectual, and political state of
present-day Russia is the result, and—so to speak
—the summary of the reigns of Ivan IV, nicknamed the Terrible by Russia itself; of Peter I—

252

called the Great by men who glorify themselves in aping Europe; and of Catherine II—deified by a people who dream of the conquest of the world and who flatter us while waiting to devour us. Such is the fearful heritage of which Czar Nicholas disposes. God knows to what end!

In general, the education that a people receives determines in a large measure the morality of each individual. From this it follows that a frightening and mysterious mutual responsibility for rights and wrongs has been established by Providence between governments and subjects, and that there comes a moment in the history of societies when the State is judged, condemned, exterminated like an individual man.

It is necessary to repeat often that the virtues, the vices, the crimes of slaves do not have the same significance as those of free men; thus, when I examine the Russian people, I can verify as a fact, which does not imply here the same blame that it would imply in France, that in general self-respect, refinement, and nobility are lacking, and these qualities are supplanted by patience and cunning: such is the right of interpretation, the unquestionable right of any honest observer; but I admit that, right or wrong, I am going still further—I either condemn or I praise what I see; it is not enough to describe, I wish to judge.

"The Russian people are gentle," they say. To that I reply, "I give them no credit for that, it is the habit of submission." Others say to me, "The Russian people are gentle only because they dare not show what is in their hearts—the basis

253

of their feelings and of their ideas is superstition and ferocity." To this I reply, "Poor people! They are so badly reared."

That is why the Russian peasants arouse great pity in me although they are the happiest people —that is to say, they have less to complain of than any others—in Russia. The Russians will exclaim and protest in good faith against my exaggerations, for there are no evils not attenuated by habit and ignorance of contrary virtues; but I, I also am of good faith, and the point from which I consider matters permits me to perceive, although on the run, things which escape the accustomed eyes of the natives.

From all that I see in this world and especially in this country, it seems that happiness is not the true goal of the mission of man here below. The goal is entirely religious: it is moral improvement —the struggle and the victory.

But since the usurpations of the temporal authority, the Christian religion in Russia has lost its spiritual value. It is stationary; it is one of the wheels of despotism—nothing more. In this country where nothing is neatly defined, purposely so, one has trouble in understanding the true relations of the church with the Chief of State who has made himself also the arbiter of the faith, without however positively proclaiming this prerogative; he has arrogated it to himself, he exercises it in fact, but he does not dare claim it as a right. He has kept a synod—this is a final homage rendered by tyranny to the King of Kings and to His ruined Church. Here is how this religious revolution is recounted in Lévesque, which I was reading a while ago.

I had gotten down from my carriage at the post and, while they looked for a blacksmith to repair one of the rear axles of my carriage, I was leafing through "History of Russia" from which I extracted this passage. I am copying it for you without changing a word.

"1721. After the death of Adrien, the last patriarch of Moscow, Peter I managed continuously to defer arranging for the election of a new patriarch. During twenty years of delay, the religious veneration of the people for the chief of the Church had cooled imperceptibly.

"The Emperor believed himself able at last to declare that this office was abolished forever. He divided the ecclesiastical power, previously united entirely in the person of a great pontiff, and caused all matters which concern religion to proceed from a new tribunal called the Holy Synod.

"He did not declare himself the head of the Church; *but he was that in effect* through the oath that the members of the new ecclesiastical college took to him. Here is the oath: 'I swear to be a faithful and obedient servant and subject of my natural and true sovereign . . . *I recognize that he is the supreme judge of this spiritual college.*'

"The synod is composed of a president, two vice-presidents, four counselors and four assessors. These members, removable for ecclesiastical causes, are very far from having together the power that the patriarch alone possessed, and which the metropolitan formerly enjoyed. They

255

are not even called into consultation; their names do not even appear in the acts of the sovereignty; even in matters submitted to them they have only an authority subordinate to that of the sovereign. As no exterior symbol distinguishes them from other prelates and as their authority ceases from the time when they no longer sit on their tribunal, finally, as this tribunal itself is not very imposing, they cannot inspire in the people any very special veneration."

In our time, the Russian people are the firmest in religious belief of all the Christian peoples; you have just seen the principal cause of the negligible efficacy of their faith. When the Church abdicates freedom, it loses moral potentiality; the slave gives birth only to slavery. One cannot repeat this enough, the only veritably independent church is the Catholic Church which, alone, has thus conserved the trust of true charity; all the other churches form a constitutive part of the States which use them as political means to support their power. These churches are excellent auxiliaries of the government; complaisant toward the holders of the temporal power, princes or magistrates, hard toward the subjects, they call the Divinity to the aid of the police; the immediate result is certain, it is good order in society. But the Catholic Church, just as powerful politically, comes from higher and goes further. National churches make citizens; the Universal Church makes men.

In Russia, respect for authority is still today the sole spring of the public machine; this respect is necessary without doubt, but in order to civilize profoundly the hearts of men they must be taught something more than blind obedience.

I spent the night meditating on the great problem of relative virtues and vices, and I concluded that in our era a very important point of political morality has not been sufficiently clarified: namely, the share of merit or responsibility which falls on each individual in his own actions and that which belongs to the society into which he is born. If society glories in the great things produced by some of its children, it should also share responsibility for the crimes of some of the others. In this respect, antiquity was more advanced than we are now; the scapegoat shows us to what extent the Jewish nation stood in awe of joint responsibility for crime. From this point of view, the death penalty was not only the punishment, more or less just, for the criminal; it was a public atonement, a protest of society against all participation in crime and in the thought that inspires it. This helps us to understand how social man has been able to arrogate to himself the right legally to dispose of the life of his fellow man; an eye for an eye, a tooth for a tooth, a life for a life: the law of retaliation, in a word, was politic; a society that wished to endure should cast the criminal from its bosom. When Jesus Christ came to put His charity in the place of the rigorous justice of Moses, He well knew that He was shortening the duration of the kingdoms of the earth, but He was opening to men the Kingdom of Heaven. . . . Without eternity and immortality, Christianity would cost the world more than it brings to it.

This is what I was dreaming about tonight while wide-awake.

A cortège of indecisive ideas, phantoms of the mind, half-active, half-benumbed, filed slowly through my head. The gallop of the horses which were drawing me seemed to me faster than the work of my sluggish mind—the body had wings, the mind was of lead and I was leaving it, so to speak, behind me, while rolling through the dust more quickly than the imagination crosses space. The steppes, the marshes with their whitened pines and their deformed birch trees, the villages, the cities were fleeing before my eyes like fantastic figures without my being able to account for what had brought me before this moving spectacle where the soul was not keeping up with the body, so quick was the sensation. This reversal of nature, these mental illusions whose cause was material, this optical game applied to the mechanism of ideas, this displacement of life, these voluntary fancies were prolonged by the monotonous songs of the men driving my horses—sad notes similar to the psalm-singing in our churches, or rather to the nasal accents of the old Jews in the German synagogues.

This chanting without rhythm, a sort of declaimed reverie in which the man confides his sorrows to the beast, the only kind of friend he does not distrust, filled my soul with a melancholy more profound than sweet.

Even Moscow will not repay me for the trouble I have taken to visit it. Let's give up Moscow, order the postilion to turn around and leave in all haste for Paris. I was there in my dreams when day came. . . . My servant tells me that my carriage is repaired; I am leaving, and if I am not destined to make my entry to Moscow in a handcart or on foot, my next letter will be dated from that holy city of the Russians where I have been led to hope I shall arrive in a few hours.

Do you see me busy hiding my papers because any of my letters, even one which would appear most innocent to you, would suffice to send me to Siberia? I take care to shut myself up when I write; and when my courier or someone of the post knocks at my door, I lock up my papers before opening the door and pretend to be reading. I am going to slip this letter between the crown and the lining of my hat. I certainly hope these precautions are superfluous, but I believe it necessary to take them—that is in itself enough to give you an idea of the Russian government.

ASIA STOMPED THE EARTH AND OUT OF IT CAME THE KREMLIN!

Moscow, August 7, 1839

HAS IT NEVER HAPPENED to you on nearing some port on the Channel or the Bay of Biscay to perceive the masts of a fleet behind low dunes which were hiding from you the city, the jetties, the beach, the sea itself with the hulls of the ships it was carrying? You could make out above the natural rampart only a stripped forest bearing brilliant sails of white, slender beams, many-colored flags, floating pennants, banners of lively and varied colors; and you stood astonished before this apparition of a fleet on dry land. Well, that is exactly the effect the first sight of Moscow produced on me—a multitude of bell-towers shone alone above the dust of the road and the mass of the city disappeared under this swirling cloud, while beyond the farthest distances of the landscape the horizon was obliterated behind the haze of the summer sky, always a little veiled in these parts.

The irregular plain, scarcely inhabited, half cultivated, barren to the eye, resembles dunes where some meager clusters of fir trees might grow and where fishermen might build their scattered huts, not very solid but sufficient to conceal their poverty. In the midst of this solitude, suddenly I saw spring up thousands of painted towers and sparkling domes, whose bases I did not

260

see. This was the city. The low houses still remained hidden in the undulations of the earth,
while the airy spires of the churches, the bizarre
shapes of the towers of the palaces and of the old
convents already attracted my eyes like a fleet at
anchor of which one can make out only the masts
soaring into the sky.

This first view of the capital of the Empire of
the Slavs, which rises brilliantly in the cold solitudes of the Christian East, produces an impression one cannot forget.

You have before you a sad landscape, but vast
like the ocean, and to animate the emptiness, a
poetic city whose architecture has no name, just
as it has no model.

To help you appreciate the strangeness of the
picture, I must remind you of the orthodox design
of every Greek church. The top of these structures is always composed of several towers which
vary in form and height, but the number is at least
five; this sacramental number is sometimes greatly
exceeded. The bell-tower in the middle is the
highest one; the four others surround the principal
tower respectfully from lower levels. Their form
varies, but the top of these symbolic towers rather
often resembles a pointed hat placed on a head;
one can also compare the great bell-tower of certain churches, painted and gilded on the outside,
to a priest's miter, to a tiara decorated with gems,
to a Chinese pavilion, to a minaret, to the headdress of a Buddhist priest; often also it is quite
simply a little cupola in the form of a ball terminated by a point. All these shapes, more or less

261

bizarre, are topped by great gilded crosses of openwork brass which, in their complicated design, remind one a little of filigree. The number and the disposition of these campaniles always has a religious meaning; they signify the degrees of the ecclesiastical hierarchy. It is the patriarch surrounded by his priests, his deacons and his subdeacons, raising his radiant head between the earth and the sky. A variety full of fantasy characterizes the design of these ornate roofs, but the original intention, the theological idea is always scrupulously respected. Brilliant chains of gilded or silvered metal unite the crosses of the lower spires to the cross of the principal tower; this metallic net stretched over an entire city produces an effect impossible to reproduce in a picture, and even more impossible to describe; words are almost as distant from colors as from sounds. Imagine then, if you can, the effect of this holy cohort of bell-towers, which, without representing the human form with precision, grotesquely outlines a group of personages assembled on the top of each church, as well as on the roofs of the smallest chapels. It is a phalanx of phantoms hovering over the city.

But I have not yet told you what is most singular in the appearance of the Russian churches—their mysterious domes are, so to speak, armored, so elaborate is the work on their covering. One would say that it is like a damascened armor, and one rests speechless with astonishment in seeing this multitude of roofs shining in the sun—tooled, scaly, enameled, bespangled, zebra-striped, streaked by bands and paints of diverse colors, but always very lively and very brilliant.

Picture for yourself rich tapestries spread from top to bottom the length of the most outstanding edifices of a city whose masses of architecture stand out against the water-green background of the solitary countryside. The desert is illuminated by this magic network of jewels set in a base of metallic sand. The play of light reflecting on this aerial city produces a kind of phantasmagoria in full day which reminds one of the splendor of the lamps shining in a gem-cutter's shop: these glimmering, iridescent lights give to Moscow an appearance different from that of any of the other great cities of Europe. You can imagine the effect of the sky seen from the center of such a city—a glory comparable to that of old pictures, one sees only gold.

I hope I have said enough about it to make you understand and share my surprise at the first vision of Moscow—that is my sole purpose. Your astonishment will increase if you recall to your memory what you have read everywhere: that this city is a country in itself and that the fields, the lakes, the woods contained within it put considerable distances between the various edifices which adorn it. An additional illusion results from such dispersion; the entire plain is covered with a silvery haze; three or four hundred churches thus spaced form to the eye an immense semicircle. Thus when one approaches the city for the first time toward the sunset hour when the sky is stormy, as I did, one thinks he sees a rainbow of

fire hovering over the churches of Moscow—this
is the aureole of the holy city.

But at three quarters of a league from the entrance to the city the prestige vanishes. One
stops before the very real Petrovski Palace, a
heavy castle of crude brick built by Catherine II
in a bizarre taste—a modern design overloaded
with ornamentation which stands out in white on
the red of the walls. This decoration of plaster, as
nearly as I could tell, and not of stone, has something of the gothic; but it is merely extravagant
and not good gothic. The building, is square as
a die, a regularity of plan which does not make the
general aspect more imposing and more especially
does not make it lighter. This is where the sovereign stops when he must make a ceremonial
entry to Moscow.

Past Petrovski, the disenchantment constantly
increases, to such an extent that on entering Moscow one ends by no longer believing what he has
perceived from a distance: one was dreaming and
upon awakening finds himself again in what is the
most prosaic and most boring thing in the world
—a big city without monuments, that is to say
without a single object of art worthy of considered
admiration. Before this heavy and clumsy copy of
Europe, you ask yourself what has become of the
Asia that appeared before you for an instant.
Moscow, seen from outside and as a whole, is a
creation of the sylphs; it is a dream world; seen
nearby and in detail, it is a vast commercial city,
hilly, dusty, badly paved, poorly constructed,
meagerly populated, which denotes without doubt

the work of a powerful hand, but at the same time the thought of a mind which lacked the idea of beauty necessary to produce a masterpiece. The Russian people have the strength of hands, that is to say the strength of numbers; but they lack the power of imagination.

Nevertheless, in the chaos of plaster, bricks, and planks called Moscow, two points steadily attract the eye—the Church of St. Basil (I will describe its appearance to you shortly) and the Kremlin, the Kremlin of which Napoleon himself was able to blow up only a few stones!

This prodigious monument with its white walls, uneven and jagged, and its tiered crenelles, is by itself as big as a city. I am told that it is a league in circumference. Toward the end of the day, the hour when I was entering Moscow, the bizarre masses of palaces and churches enclosed in this citadel stood out clearly against a misty landscape, simple in line, poor in plan, vast in expanse but cold in tone—which does not, however, prevent our being scorched by the heat, stifled with dust, and devoured by mosquitoes.

I shall never forget the shudder of terror that I have just experienced in seeing the cradle of the modern Russian Empire for the first time: the Kremlin is worth the trip to Moscow.

At the gate of this fortress but outside its walls, according to my courier—I have not yet been able to go there—stands the Church of St. Basil, *Vassili Blagennoi;* it is known also under the name of the Cathedral of the Protection of the Holy Virgin. In the Greek rite they lavish the

265

title of cathedral on churches; each quarter, each monastery has its own, each city has several; this one of Vassili is unquestionably the most unusual, if it is not the most beautiful in Russia. I have seen it only from a distance, but the effect it produces is prodigious. Imagine an agglomeration of little unequal towers, together composing a bush, a bouquet of flowers; imagine rather a kind of irregular fruit, all bristling with protuberances, or better still a crystallization of a thousand colors whose metallic polish gives off reflections which glisten in the rays of the far-away sun like Bohemian or Venetian glass, like the most variegated Delft faïence, like the most highly polished enamel of China. It is like gilded scales of fish, the skins of serpents stretched on piles of misshapen stones, heads of dragons, shells of chameleons, altar ornaments, priests' robes, and the whole is topped by spires so painted that they resemble rich materials of reddish brown silk. In the narrow spaces between these campaniles, decorated as one would adorn persons, you see glittering roofs painted dove-gray, rose, azure, and always well polished; the scintillation of these tapestries dazzles the eye and fascinates the imagination. "Certainly, the land where such a monument is called a place of prayer is not Europe; it is India, Persia, China, and the men who go to worship God in this box of glazed fruits are not Christians!" Such is the exclamation which escaped me in seeing this strange Church of Vassili for the first time. Since I have entered Moscow, I have no other desire than to examine this masterpiece of caprice close by. This monument must indeed be of a most extraordinary style to have distracted me from the Kremlin at the moment when this formidable castle appeared before me for the first time.

The Kremlin is not just a palace like any other, it is a complete city, and this city is the very heart of Moscow; it serves as the frontier of two parts of the world, the East and the West: the old world and the modern world are present there. Under the successors of Genghis Khan, Asia for the last time rushed upon Europe; in withdrawing she stomped the earth and out of it came the Kremlin!

The princes who today possess this sacred asylum of oriental despotism say that they are Europeans because they drove from Muscovy the Kalmucks—their brothers, their tyrants, and their teachers; with all due deference to them, nothing so resembles the Khans of Sarai as their adversaries and successors, the Czars of Moscow, who have borrowed from them even their title. The Russians called the khans of the Tartars czars. Karamsin says on this subject:

"This word is not an abridgement of the Latin Caesar, as many scholars believe without foundation. It is an old oriental name which we have learned through the Slavonic translation of the Bible. Given first by us to the emperors of the Orient, and later to the khans of the Tartars, it signifies in Persian *throne, supreme authority,* and it is observed in the termination of the names of the kings of Assyria and Babylon, such as Nabopolassar, Nebuchadrezzar, etc." And as a note he

267

adds: "See Boyar, Russian Origin. In our translation of the Holy Scriptures, one writes Kessar instead of Caesar, Tsar or Czar is altogether another word."

Once in the center of Moscow, I crossed a boulevard which resembles all boulevards, then I followed a fairly gentle slope at the bottom of which I arrived in an elegant quarter, built in stone and with streets laid out by the rule and line. Finally, I was brought into Dmitriskoi: the street where a good and attractive room in an excellent English inn was awaiting me.

As soon as I was installed, I began to write to you in order to relax. The night is approaching, it is moonlight, I am interrupting my letter to take a walk through the city. I shall come back and tell you about it.

Having gone out toward ten o'clock alone, without a guide, walking at random, as is my custom, I started down the long broad streets, badly paved, like all the streets in Russian cities, and hilly in addition; but these bad streets are laid out regularly. The straight line is not wanting in the architecture of this country; however, the chalk line and the square have disfigured Moscow less than they have marred Petersburg. In Petersburg these feeble-minded tyrants of modern cities found a bare table; but here they had to fight against old national monuments. Thanks to these invincible obstacles of history and of nature, the aspect of Moscow has remained that of an ancient city. It is the most picturesque of all the cities of the Empire, and the Empire continues to recognize it as the capital in spite of the almost supernatural efforts of the Czar Peter and his successors —such is the strength of the law of nature against the will of men, even the most powerful men.

The first thing that struck me in the streets of Moscow was that the population is more lively and more openly gay than in Petersburg. Here one breathes an air of liberty unknown in the rest of the Empire. This explains to me the secret aversion the sovereigns have for this city.

I slowly followed some strollers and after having descended and climbed many slopes at the heels of a crowd of idlers whom I mechanically took for my guide, I came toward the center of the city onto a vacant square where a garden walk begins. This seemed to me a splendid promenade; one heard music in the distance; one saw numerous scintillating lights, and several open cafés which recalled Europe. But I could not interest myself in these attractions, for I was under the walls of the Kremlin, this colossal mountain erected for tyranny by the arms of slaves. A public promenade, a sort of English-style garden has been made around the walls of this ancient fortress of Moscow for the modern city.

Do you know what the walls of the Kremlin mean? This word *walls* gives the idea of something too ordinary, too paltry; it misleads you. The walls of the Kremlin are a chain of mountains. . . . This citadel built at the frontier of Europe and Asia is to ordinary ramparts what the Alps are to our hills in France. The Kremlin is the Mount Blanc of fortresses. If the giant one calls the Russian Empire had a heart, I would say that the Kremlin is the heart of this monster: it is its head.

I should like to be able to give you an idea of this mass of stone which stands out in relief like steps in the sky. Singular contradiction! . . . this asylum of despotism rises in the name of liberty, for the Kremlin was a fortress erected as an obstacle to the Kalmucks by the Russians. Its walls had two purposes—they facilitated the independence of the State and served the tyranny of the sovereign. They boldly follow the deep curves of the terrain; when the slopes of the hillside become too steep, the rampart lowers itself in steps; these stairs which mount between the earth and the sky are enormous; this is a ladder for giants about to make war on the gods.

The line of this first belt of constructions is cut by fantastic towers, so high, so strong and so bizarre in shape that they have the appearance of cliffs of various forms and glaciers of a thousand colors; the darkness, no doubt, contributed to enlarging objects and giving them unnatural shapes and colors: I say colors because night, like engraving, has its coloring.

I walked through the public gardens on the slopes of the old citadel of the Czars; I saw towers, then other towers, tiers then other tiers of walls, and my eyes looked down on an enchanted city. To speak of a fairyland is to say too little . . . the eloquence of youth astonished and surprised by everything would be needed to find

270

words equal to these prodigious sights. Over a long vault that I had just crossed, I saw a suspended road by which pedestrians and carriages enter the holy city. This spectacle was incomprehensible to me; nothing but steep slopes, arches which serve to support roads by which one comes out of the Moscow of today—the Moscow of the people—to enter the Kremlin, the Moscow of history, the marvelous Moscow. These waterless aqueducts support still other tiers of edifices, even more fantastic. I glimpsed, supported by one of these suspended passages, a low round tower completely bristling with crenelles made of lance blades; the brilliant whiteness of this singular decoration stood out on a blood-red wall—a screaming contrast which the always translucent obscurity of the Northern nights did not prevent my discerning. This tower was a giant rising by a full head over the fort whose guardian he appeared to be. When I was satiated with the pleasure of daydreaming, I endeavored to find my way back to my hotel, where I started writing to you, an occupation little suited to calming my agitation.

What doesn't one see while walking around the Kremlin in the moonlight? Everything is supernatural and one believes in specters in spite of oneself. Who would be able to approach without religious awe this sacred boulevard of which one stone, detached by Bonaparte, rebounded to St. Helena to crush the rash conqueror there in the middle of the ocean.

After seeing what I saw this evening, one would do well to return straight away to one's own country. The emotion of the journey is spent.

THE CITADEL OF SPECTERS

Moscow, August 8, 1839

AN EYE INFLAMMATION that I developed between Petersburg and Moscow is painful and bothers me. But in spite of this, today I wanted to retrace my steps of yesterday evening in order to compare the Kremlin of broad day with the fantastic Kremlin of the night. Shadow enlarges and displaces all things, but the sun restores their proper forms and proportions.

On this second test, the fortress of the Czar surprised me again. The moonlight enlarged and gave relief to certain masses of stone, but it hid others from me; and while rectifying several errors and realizing that I had figured too many vaults, too many arcades, too many suspended roadways, porticos and caverns, I found enough of all these things to justify my enthusiasm.

There is everything at the Kremlin—it is a landscape of stones.

The solidarity of its ramparts surpasses the strength of the stony masses that support them; the number and the form of its monuments are a marvel. This labyrinth of palaces, of museums, of dungeons, of churches, of cells is frightening. . . . Mysterious noises come out of the depths of the caverns; such dwellings cannot be suitable for beings like us. There one dreams of the most

272

astonishing scenes, then shivers in remembering
that these scenes are by no means pure invention. The sounds one hears seem to come out of
the tomb; one believes in everything except what
is natural.

Be completely convinced that the Kremlin of
Moscow is not at all what they say it is. This is
not a palace; it is not a national sanctuary where
the historical treasures of the Empire are conserved; it is not the boulevard of Russia, the revered sanctuary where sleep the saints, the protectors of the fatherland; it is less and it is more
than all that—it is quite simply the citadel of specters.

From a distance the Kremlin, on its hill, appeared to me a princely city built in the middle of
the city of the people. This tyrannical castle, this
proud pile of stones, towers above the abode of
the community of men by the height of its cliffs,
its walls, its campaniles; and, contrary to what
happens to monuments of ordinary dimensions,
the closer one comes to this indestructible mass
the more one is amazed. Like the skeletal remains
of certain gigantic animals, the Kremlin proves to
us the history of a world which we cannot keep
ourselves from still doubting, even while finding
its ruins. In this prodigious creation strength takes
the place of beauty, caprice of elegance; this is
the dream of a tyrant, but it is forceful like the
mind of one man who commands the mind of a
people; there is something disproportionate about
it.

Heritage of the fabulous times when falsehood

was king without control: jail, palace, sanctuary, bulwark against the foreigner, fortress against the nation, support of tyrants, prison of peoples—that is the Kremlin!

A sort of Acropolis of the North, a barbarian Pantheon, this national sanctuary could be called the Alcazar of the Slavs.

Such then was the preferred abode of the old Muscovite princes; but even these formidable walls were not enough to calm the terror of Ivan IV.

The fear of an all-powerful man is the most terrible fear in the world; so one does not approach the Kremlin without shuddering.

Towers of all forms, round, square, with sharp spires, belfries, dungeons, turrets, watchtowers, sentry boxes on minarets, steeples of all heights, different in color, in style, in purpose; palaces, domes, lookouts, walls crenelated and pierced; loopholes, machicolations, ramparts, fortifications of all kinds, bizarre fantasies, incomprehensible inventions, kiosks beside cathedrals, everything spells disorder and violence; everything betrays the eternal vigilance necessary to the security of the singular beings who are condemned to live in this supernatural world. But these innumerable monuments of vanity, of caprice, of voluptuousness, of glory, of piety, in spite of their apparent variety express only one sole and same thought which dominates everything here: war sustained by fear. The Kremlin is, without contradiction, the work of a superhuman being, but of a malevolent being. Glory in slavery, such is the allegory featured in this satanic monument, as extraordinary in architecture as the visions of St. John are extraordinary in poetry—it is a habitation suitable for the personages of the Apocalypse.

In vain each little tower has its individual character and its particular use; all have the same significance—armed terror!

To live in the Kremlin is not to live; it is to protect oneself; oppression creates revolt; revolt necessitates precautions; precautions increase the danger; and of this long series of actions and reactions is born a monster, despotism which has built itself a house in Moscow—the Kremlin! The giants of the antediluvian world, if they came back on earth to visit their feeble successors, after having vainly searched for some traces of their primitive asylums, would still be able to dwell in the Kremlin.

Intentionally or not, everything has a symbolic sense in the architecture of the Kremlin; but the thing that remains real, after you have overcome your first dread and are able to delve into the midst of these wild splendors, is a mass of cells pompously named palaces and cathedrals. The Russians try in vain—they do not get out of prison.

The climate itself is an accomplice of tyranny. The cold of this land does not permit the construction of vast churches, where the faithful would be frozen during prayer; here the spirit is not lifted to the sky by the pomp of religious architecture; in this zone, man can build to God only dark dungeons. The somber cathedrals of the Kremlin, with their narrow vaults and their thick walls, resemble caves; they are prisons just as the palaces are gilded jails.

Of the wonders of this frightening architecture it must be said, as travelers say of the inner Alps: these are beautiful horrors.

THE KREMLIN—MASTERPIECE
OF DESPOTISM

Moscow, August 8, 1839—Evening

MY EYE has become more and more inflamed. I have just had a doctor who ordered me to stay in for three days. I plan to use these three days of forced leisure to finish a work started for you at Petersburg and interrupted by the agitations of the life I led there. This is the résumé of the reign of Ivan IV, the tyrant *par excellence* and the soul of the Kremlin. It is not that he built this fortress, but that he was born there, that he died there, and that he comes back there—his spirit lives in the Kremlin.

The plan of the Kremlin was conceived and executed by his grandfather, Ivan III, and by men of this stamp. I wish to make use of these colossal figures, as of mirrors, to show you the Kremlin, for I feel I must give up simply trying to describe it; my words are not up to the task. Besides, this roundabout way of completing a description seems novel to me, and I think it is valid. So far I have done what I could to give you an idea of the place itself, but I must now show it to you in a different way—namely, in giving you the history of the men who inhabited it.

If from the arrangement of a house we can deduce the character of the person who lives in it, can we not by an analagous operation of the mind figure out the aspect of edifices by examining the men for whom they were constructed? Our passions, our habits, our genius are certainly powerful enough to engrave themselves ineffaceably on the very stones of our dwellings. Certainly, if a monument exists to which this process of the imagination can be applied, it is the Kremlin. One sees Europe and Asia face to face there and the genius of the Greeks of the Byzantine Empire unite them.

All things considered, whether one looks at this fortress in a purely historical light or whether one contemplates it from the poetic or picturesque point of view, it is the most national monument of Russia, and, consequently, the most interesting for Russians as well as for foreigners.

I have told you that Ivan IV did not build the Kremlin. This sanctuary of despotism was reconstructed in stone under Ivan III in 1485 by two Italian architects, Marco and Pietro Antonio, called to Moscow by the *Great Prince* who wished to re-erect the ramparts, formerly of wood, of the fortress founded in more ancient times under Dmitri Donskoi.

But if this palace is not the work of Ivan IV, he is its idea. It was through a spirit of prophecy that the great king Ivan III erected the palace of the tyrant, his grandson. There have been Italian architects everywhere; but nowhere have they produced anything which resembles the work they accomplished in Moscow. I add that elsewhere there have been unjust, arbitrary, bizarre, abso-

lute monarchs, but that the reign of none of these
monsters resembles the reign of Ivan IV. The
same seeds germinating in different climes and in
different soils produce plants of the same species
but of different dimensions and appearances. The
world will never see two such masterpieces of despotism as the Kremlin, nor two nations as super-
stitiously patient as the Muscovite nation was
under the fabulous reign of its tyrant.

The results are felt to this day. If you had accompanied me on this journey, you would have
discovered, with me, in the depths of the souls of
the Russian people the inevitable ravages of arbitrary power pushed to its utmost consequences.
The first result is a savage indifference toward
sanctity of the word, sincerity of sentiment, justice
of deed; the second result is deceit triumphant in
all the actions and transactions of life—the absence of probity, bad faith, fraud in all its forms;
in a word, a deadened moral sense. It seems to me
I see a stream of vices flowing out through all the
gates of the Kremlin to inundate Russia.

Other nations have tolerated oppression; the
Russian nation has loved it; she still loves it. Is
not this fanaticism of obedience characteristic?
Here, however, it cannot be denied that this popular mania has become, by exception, the principle of sublime actions. In this inhumane country,
if society has denatured man it has not shrunk
him. At times, he carries baseness to the point of
heroism; he is not good but he is not paltry; that
is also what one can say of the Kremlin. To look
at the Kremlin does not give pleasure but creates

fear. It is not beautiful; it is terrible, terrible like the reign of Ivan IV.

Such a reign blinds forever the human soul in a nation which has patiently submitted to it to the end. The last descendants of these men, branded by the hangman, will suffer from their fathers' betrayal of trust—treason against humanity degrades peoples unto their remotest posterity. This crime does not consist just in administering injustice but in tolerating it. A people which, under the pretext that obedience is the greatest of virtues, bequeaths tyranny to its descendants slights its own interests; it does worse than that—it fails in its obligations.

The blind patience of subjects, their silence, their fidelity to insane masters are poor virtues. Submission is praiseworthy and sovereignty venerable only in so far as they become the means of assuring the rights of humanity.

These are limitations that the Russians have never admitted nor understood; however, they are necessary to the development of real civilization. Without them, a moment would come when the social state would become more harmful than useful to humanity and the sophists would have a good case to send man back to the depths of the forests.

However, such a doctrine, no matter how moderate one may be in expounding it and wishing to put it into practice, is considered seditious in Petersburg, even though it is only the application of the Holy Scriptures. Thus the Russians of our

280

time are the worthy children of the subjects of
Ivan IV. That is one of the reasons which made
me decide to give you an abridged history of his
reign.

In France, I had forgotten these facts, but in
Russia one is forced to recall the frightful details.
This will be the subject of my next letter. Have
no fear of being bored; no story was ever more interesting, or, at least, stranger.

That madman exceeded the bounds, so to
speak, of the sphere in which beings received permission from God, under the guise of free will, to
do evil. Never has the arm of man extended so
far. The brutal ferocity of Ivan IV makes pale
that of Tiberius, Nero, Caracalla, Louis XI, Peter
the Cruel, and Henry VIII; in sum that of all the
tyrants ancient and modern as described by their
most incorruptible judges—Tacitus at their head.

Also, before recalling to you the details of these
incredible excesses, I feel I must emphasize my
accuracy. I shall cite nothing from memory. When
I undertook this journey, I filled my carriage with
the books I need and the principal source from
which I have drawn is Karamsin, an author who
cannot be rejected by the Russians as he is criticized for having understated rather than exaggerated facts unfavorable to the reputation of his
nation. An excessive caution, going even to the
point of bias, is the defect of this author. In Russia, patriotism is always tainted with complaisance.

One can, one should, then credit Karamsin
when he relates the monstrosities of the life of

281

Ivan IV. I affirm that all the facts you will read in
my summary are found reported in more detail
by this historian in his work entitled: *History of
the Russian Empire*.

THE SOUL OF THE KREMLIN

Moscow, August 11, 1839

IF YOU HAVE NOT MADE a special study of the annals of Russia, the work that you are about to read will strike you as the result of a monstrous scheme; however, it is only a summary of authentic facts.

But it is not this assemblage of abominations attested to by history, though it reads like fiction, that makes one ponder most in retracing the long reign of Ivan IV. No, it is the effect produced by this tyranny, unequaled, on the nation it decimated. Not only does it not disgust the generations, it fascinates them. This is a completely insolvable problem for philosophers, an eternal subject of wonder and dreadful meditations. This astounding fact seems to me to throw a new light on the mysteries of the human heart.

Ivan IV, still a child, came to the throne in 1533; crowned at the age of 17 on January 16, 1546, he died in his bed in the Kremlin after a reign of 51 years, January 18, 1584, at 54 years of age, and was mourned by the entire nation—the children of his victims not excepted.

This monstrous reign has fascinated Russia to the point of making her find an object for admiration even in the shameless power of the princes who govern her. Political obedience has become a cult, a religion for the Russians. It is only with

283

this people—at least I believe this is so—that one has seen martyrs in adoration before their executioners! Did Rome fall at the feet of Tiberius and Nero to beseech them not to relinquish their absolute power and to continue to burn and pillage, to bathe themselves calmly in its blood and bring shame upon its children? That is what you will see the Muscovites doing in the middle of the reign and at the height of the tyranny of Ivan IV.

He will wish to abdicate; on their knees they will beg him to continue to govern them according to his whims. Thus justified, thus assured, the tyrant will again take up his succession of executions. For him, to reign was to kill; he killed out of fear and out of duty; and this too simple charter was sanctioned by the assent of Russia and the grief and tears of the entire nation at the death of the tyrant. When Ivan, like Nero, decided to shake off the yoke of glory and virtue and reign solely by terror, he did not limit himself to quests for cruelties unknown before or after him, he also crushed the unfortunate victims of his furies with invective; he was ingenious, he was comical in atrocity; the horrible and the burlesque together enlivened his satiric and pitiless spirit. He pierced hearts with sarcastic words while, with his own hands, he was tearing bodies to pieces; and the subtlety of his words surpassed the barbarity of his acts in this fiendish work against his fellow men whom his terrified egotism took for so many enemies.

This does not mean that he did not, in the use of torture, improve upon all the means invented before him to make the body suffer and prolong the pain. His government was the reign of torture.

The imagination refuses to credit the duration of such a moral and political phenomenon. Ivan IV began, like the son of Agrippina, with virtue and that which perhaps even to a greater extent commands the love of an ambitious and vain nation—with conquests. At this period of his life, silencing the vulgar appetites and brutal terrors he had manifested from infancy, he submitted to the direction of wise and severe friends.

Pious counselors, prudent directors made the beginning of this reign one of the most brilliant and the happiest in the annals of the Muscovites. But the beginning was short compared to the rest, and the metamorphosis was quick, terrible, and complete.

Kazan, that formidable fortress of Islam in Asia, fell in 1552, under the attack of the young Czar, after a memorable siege; the energy that this prince deployed was astonishing even in the eyes of half-barbarian men. He supported his plan of campaign with an inflexibility of courage and sagacity of spirit that threw the most experienced captains into consternation and ended in commanding their respect.

At the outset of his military career, the audacity of his enterprises would have made any cautious courage seem childish; but soon he revealed himself as cowardly, as cringing, as he had been daring; he became fearful at the same time he became cruel. It was with him as with nearly all monsters; cruelty had its principal root in fear. All

285

his life he remembered what he had suffered in his childhood: the despotism of the boyars, their dissensions that threatened his life at a period when he lacked strength to defend himself. One would say that manhood brought him no other desire than to avenge the ignorance of his youth.

But if there is a profoundly moral fact in the history of this man's terrible life, it is that he lost daring in losing virtue.

Thanks to the perseverance of the young hero, criticized at that time by all his council, Astrakhan suffered the fate of Kazan. Russia, delivered from the proximity of its old rulers, the Tartars, shouted with joy; but this population of menials, able to escape one yoke only to pass under another, idolized its young sovereign with the conceit and timidity of the emancipated slave. At this age, the beauty of Ivan was in keeping with the vigor of his soul: he was the god of the Russians.

But suddenly the tired Czar ceased his activity and stood still in the midst of his glory. He was weary of his beneficent virtues; he succumbed under the weight of laurels and palms and renounced forever the pursuit of his saintly career. He preferred to distrust everyone and punish his friends for the fear they inspired in him rather than listen longer to their wise counsel. However, this madness was in his heart, not in his head; for in the midst of his most irrational actions, his conversations were full of sense, his letters full of logic—their incisive style painted the malignance of his soul but did honor to the penetration and lucidity of his mind.

286

His old counselors were the first butt of his blows; they appeared to him as traitors, or, that which was synonymous in his eyes, as masters. He condemned to exile, to death, these traitors to autocracy, these insolent ministers who had long taken it into their heads to think themselves wiser than their master; and the arrests seemed just in the eyes of the nation. They were just in the opinion of those incorruptible men to whom he owed his glory: he could not bear the weight of the recognition he owed them, and, lest he appear ungrateful to them, he killed them. . . . Then a wild fury took fire in him; the terrors of the child awakened the cruelty of the man; the ever-present memory of the dissensions and violences of the great who disputed the custody of his cradle showed him traitors and conspirators everywhere.

Self-adulation, with all its consequences, applied to the government of the State was the Czar's code of justice, ratified by the assent of the whole of Russia. In spite of his crimes, Ivan IV was to Moscow the elect of the nation; elsewhere he would have been regarded as a monster vomited up from Hades.

Tired of lying, he pushed the cynicism of tyranny to the point of dispensing with hypocrisy— the final precaution of common tyrants. He came out in the open with his cruelty; and, in order to rid himself of the necessity of blushing before the virtues of others, he abandoned the last of his austere friends to the vengeance of more indulgent favorites.

Then a rivalry in crime which makes one shud-

der was established between the Czar and his satellites; and (here God unveils himself again in
this almost supernatural history) just as his moral
life is divided into two periods, his physical appearance changed before his time: handsome in
his early youth, he became hideous when he became a criminal.

He lost an accomplished wife; he took another,
as bloodthirsty as he; this one died too. He remarried, to the great scandal of the Orthodox
Church, which does not permit three marriages.
He remarried five, six, seven times. The exact
number of these marriages is not known. He repudiated, he killed, he forgot his wives. None
could long withstand his caresses and his furies;
and, in spite of his notorious indifference toward
his old loves, he applied himself to avenging their
death with a scrupulous fury which spread new
terror in the Empire. However, usually the death
which served as a pretext for so many executions
had been caused or ordered by the Czar himself.
His bereavements were for him only an occasion
to spill blood and make others weep.

He had it announced everywhere that the pious Czarina, the beautiful Czarina, the ill-fated
Czarina had been poisoned by the ministers, by
the counselors of the Czar, or by boyars he wished
to dispose of.

The calumnies of Ivan IV were always proven
in advance; whoever was reached by the venom of
his words succumbed; cadavers were piled up
around him; but death was the least of the evils he
heaped upon the condemned. His unfathomable

288

cruelty discovered the art of making them long for the fatal blow. Expert in his tortures, he enjoyed the cunningly contrived suffering of his victims; he prolonged it with an infernal adroitness and, in his cruel anxiety, he liked their torture and feared their end as much as they wished it. Death is the only good that he accorded his subjects.

I must, however, describe to you, once and for all, some of these novel methods of torture devised by Ivan to use on the so-called criminals he wished to punish. He had them boiled in part while icy water was sprinkled on the rest of the body. He had them skinned alive *in his presence;* then he had their bared and palpitating flesh lacerated by thongs, while his eyes feasted on their blood and convulsions and his ears reveled in their screams. Sometimes he gave the finishing touch with stabs of his own dagger; but more often, reproaching himself for this act of clemency as a weakness, he spared the heart and the head as long as possible in order to make the torture last and ordered the limbs carved off, skillfully, without attacking the trunk; then he had these living fragments thrown one by one to famished beasts avid for this miserable flesh whose frightful shreds they tore away in the very presence of the half-minced victims.

These quivering torsos were sustained with care, with science, with atrocious intelligence, the longer to make them witness this human quarry for which they paid and for which the Czar competed with the tiger in ferocity.

He exhausted the butchers; there were not enough priests for the burials. Novgorod-the-Great was chosen to serve as an example of the wrath of the monster. The city in mass, accused of treason in favor of the Poles, but especially guilty for its long independence and glory, was deliberately infected with a pestilence derived from the host of arbitrary executions within its blood-stained walls; the waters of the Volkhov were polluted by the unburied corpses around the ramparts of the cursed city, and, as if death by torture were not devastation enough, a forced epidemic rivaled the scaffold in decimating entire populations and assuaging the wrath of the *Father*—term of endearment, or rather the title flattering Russians with cordiality automatically bestow on their all-powerful and well-loved sovereigns whatever they may be.

When Ivan avenged himself, he pursued the course of his *justice* to the last degree of relationship, exterminating entire families. He obliged sons to take the office of executioner against their fathers, and he found some who obeyed! He taught us that man can carry love of life to the point of killing, for fear of losing it, the very being from whom he holds that life.

Using human bodies for clocks, Ivan invented poisons regulated on the hour and succeeded in marking with satisfactory regularity the minutest divisions of his time by the death of his subjects, arranged with art from minute to minute along the road to the tomb he continuously held open under their feet. The most scrupulous precision reigned at this infernal amusement.

The monster was himself present at all these tortures he ordered: the smell of blood intoxicated him without satiating him; he was never gayer than when he had caused many victims to suffer and had seen them die.

The monster, after giving so many proofs of ferocity, should have been known by his people, and he was! Suddenly, whether to amuse himself in measuring the long-suffering stoicism of the Russians, whether in Christian repentance . . . (he affected respect for holy things) . . . or fear, or caprice, or fatigue, or ruse, one day he put down his scepter—that is to say his ax—and threw his crown to the ground. Then, but then only in all the course of this long reign, the Empire was aroused. The nation, threatened with deliverance, awakened with a start; the Russians, up to then silent witnesses, passive instruments of so many horrors, recovered their voice; and this voice of the people—which pretends to be the voice of God—suddenly was raised to deplore the loss of such a tyrant. Perhaps they doubted his good faith, with just cause feared his vengeance if they accepted his feigned abdication—who knows if all this love for the prince did not have its source in the terror which the tyrant inspired; the Russians refined fear in lending it the mask of love.

Moscow was menaced by invasion (the penitent had chosen his time well); anarchy was feared; in other words, the Russians foresaw the moment when, being unable to avoid liberty, they would be exposed to thinking, to deciding by and for themselves, to showing themselves men and, which is worse, citizens: that which would make the happiness of another people incensed this one. In brief, Russia at bay, enervated by its long negligence, fell distracted at the feet of Ivan, whom she feared less than she feared herself. She implored this indispensable master, she gathered up his bloodstained crown and scepter, gave them back to him and asked, as a unique favor, his permission to take back the yoke of iron that she would never tire of wearing.

Blinded by their monarchical idolatry, on their knees before the political idol they have made themselves, the Russians, those of our century as well as those of the century of Ivan, forget that respect for justice and the cult of truth are of more importance to all men, the Slavs included, than the fate of Russia.

Here once again in this old-style drama, the intervention of a supernatural power appears to me. Shuddering, one asks oneself what is the future reserved by Providence for a society which pays such a price for the prolongation of its life.

Too often I have occasion to make you note that a new Roman Empire smolders in Russia under the ashes of the Greek Empire. Fear alone does not inspire such patience. No, believe in my instinct, it is a passion that the Russians understand as no other people since the Romans have understood it—ambition. Ambition makes them sacrifice everything, absolutely everything, like Bonaparte, to self-preservation.

It is this sovereign law that subjects a nation to an Ivan IV: a tiger in the place of God rather than the annihilation of the Empire. Such was the Russian policy under this reign which made Russia; and the forbearance of the victims is even more appalling to me than the frenzy of the tyrant —policy of instinct or of calculation, it matters little to me. The thing I consider important and behold with terror is that this policy perpetuates itself, all the while adjusting to circumstances, and even today it would produce the same effects under a similar reign if it were given to the earth to give birth to another Ivan IV.

So . . . admire this picture, unique in the history of the world: the Russians, with the courage and baseness of men who wish to possess the world, pleading at the feet of Ivan that he continue to govern them, you have seen in what manner, and that he preserve for them a social order which would create hatred for society in any people not intoxicated with a fanatic presentiment of its glory.

All solemnly promise, great and small, boyars and merchants, castes and individuals, in a word the entire nation solemnly promises, with tears, with love, to submit to anything provided he does not abandon it to itself—this height of misfortune was the only reverse the Russians, in their ignoble patriotism, were unable to envisage cold-bloodedly, on the grounds that the inevitable disorder which would result from it would destroy their empire of slaves. Ignominy pushed to this degree approaches the sublime. It is a real Roman virtue; it perpetuates the State . . . but what a State! The means dishonors the end!

Meanwhile the ferocious beast, touched, took pity on the animals on which he had long been feeding and promised the herd to resume decimating it. He took back the power without concessions; on the contrary, under absurd conditions and all advantageous to his conceit and fury. Yet he made this people, as wildly enthusiastic for submission as others are frantic for freedom, this people thirsting for its own blood and eager to be killed for the amusement of the master, accept these conditions as favors because it became uneasy and trembled from the moment it breathed in peace.

Dating from this moment a methodical tyranny was initiated, so violent that the annals of mankind offer nothing comparable, considering that there was as much madness in submitting to it as in administering it. Prince and nation, at this period, the entire Empire became mad: and the results of the excesses continued.

The formidable Kremlin, with all its prestige, with its iron gates, its fabulous dungeons, its inaccessible ramparts raised to the sky, its machicolations, its crenelles, its caverns, seemed too weak a refuge to the mad monarch who wished to exterminate half the population in order to rule the other half in peace. In this heart, perverted by the force of terror and cruelty, where evil and the fright it engenders wreaked new havoc every day, an inexplicable defiance—for it is without apparent motive, or at least without positive motive—allied itself to an atrocity without aim; thus the most shameful cowardice pleaded in behalf of the blindest ferocity. A new Nebuchadnezzar the king changed into a tiger.

He retired first to a palace near the Kremlin which he had fortified like a castle; then to *a retreat,* in Alexandrova Sloboda, which became his habitual residence. There from among the most debauched, the most craven of his slaves, he selected for his guard a troop of *elite,* composed of a thousand men, which he called the elect: *opritchnina.* To this infernal legion, for seven consecutive years, he delivered over the fortune, the very life of the Russian people—I would say its honor if this word could have any meaning applied to men who had to be gagged to be ruled according to their liking.

Here is how Karamsin described Ivan IV for us in the year 1565, nineteen years after his coronation:

This prince (he says), big, well-built, broad-shouldered, with strong arms, full chest, beautiful hair, long mustaches, aquiline nose, small but shining gray eyes full of fire, had once been a pleasing figure. At this period, he was so changed one could scarcely recognize him. A somber ferocity was engraved on his deformed features; his eyes were dull; he was now almost bald, and he had left no more than a few hairs for a beard: inexplicable effect of the fury which was devouring his soul! After a new enumeration of the crimes committed by the boyars, he repeated his consent to keep the throne, enlarging at length upon the obligation imposed on the princes to maintain calm in their States and, to this effect, to take all the measures they deemed fitting, and stressing *the inconsequence of human life,* the necessity of looking beyond the tomb; finally, he proposed the establishment of the opritchnina, a name until then unknown. The consequences of this institution made Russia tremble anew. . . .

The Czar announced that he would choose a thousand satellites among the princes, gentlemen, and boyars, and would give them, in his own districts, fiefs from which the present proprietors would be transferred to other places.

He took possession of several streets even in Moscow, whence it was necessary to drive out the gentlemen and employees who were not inscribed among the thousand of the Czar. . . .

As if he had developed an aversion to the august sovereigns of the Kremlin and the tombs of his ancestors, he no longer wished to live in the magnificent palace of Ivan III; outside the Kremlin walls, he had a new palace constructed, surrounded by high walls like a fortress. This part of Russia and of Moscow, this *thousand* of the Czar, this new court, together formed the private estate of Ivan IV and was placed under his immediate control, receiving the name of opritchnina.

Moscow, August 11, 1839

Farther on, one sees the tortures of the boyars start again, that is to say one sees the reign of Ivan IV start again.

On the 4th of February, Moscow saw the conditions set forth by the Czar for the clergy and the boyars fulfilled in the borough of Alexandrov. The executions of the pretended traitors accused of having conspired with Kourbsky against the life of the monarch, the Czarina Anastasia and her children were begun. The first victim was the famous Voivode, Prince Alexander Gorbati-Shuiski, descendant of Saint Vladimir, of Vsevolod the Great and of the ancient princes of Souzdal. This man of great genius, a skillful soldier, inspired with equal ardor for religion and the fatherland, who had contributed strongly to the reduction of the Kingdom of Kazan, was condemned to death, as was his son Peter, a young man of seventeen. Holding hands, they presented themselves at the place of execution with calmness and dignity and without fear. To avoid witnessing the death of his father, the young Peter placed his head under the sword first; but his father made him draw back, saying with emotion: *No, my son, that I may not see you die.* The young man gave way to him and as soon as the prince's head was severed from its body, the son took it in his hands, covered it with kisses, and raising his eyes to the sky, serenely delivered himself into the hands of the executioner. The brother-in-law of Gorbati, Prince

297

Khovrin, of Greek origin, the great officer Golovin, Prince Soukhoi Kachin, grand cup-bearer, and Prince Gorensky were decapitated the same day. Prince Shevirev was impaled. It is reported that the poor man endured his horrible sufferings throughout an entire day, but that, sustained by religion, he disregarded them and chanted the canticle of Jesus. The two boyars, Princes Kourakin and Nemoi, were constrained to embrace the monastic state. A large number of gentlemen and boyars had their property confiscated and others were exiled. . . .

Karamsin also describes for us the way the Czar formed his new guard, which was not long restricted to a thousand, the number indicated at first, nor chosen from the high classes of society.

Young men were brought (he says), from whom no distinction of merit was asked but only a certain audacity. They were noted for their debauches and corruption, which made them fit to undertake anything. Ivan questioned them on their origin, their friends, and their patrons. Above all, it was required that they should have no connection with the great boyars; obscurity, even baseness of etraction, was ground for adoption. The Czar brought their number to six thousand men, who took oath to serve him for and against all, to denounce traitors, to have no relation with citizens of *the community*—that is to say with anyone not inscribed in the legion of the elect, to recognize neither relationship nor family when the sovereign was concerned. As compensation, their Czar turned over to them, not only the lands, but also the houses, the goods and chattels of twelve thousand landowners who, empty-handed, had been driven out of the places appropriated for the legion in such a way that a great number of them—men distinguished by their services and covered with honorable wounds—found themselves in the cruel necessity of setting out on foot, during the winter, with their wives and children, for distant and deserted domains. . . .

It is again in Karamsin that one must read the results of this infernal institution; but the developments with which the historian supports his recital cannot be fitted into a frame as narrow as this one.

This horde once loosed against the country, there was nothing but plunder and assassination everywhere; the cities were pillaged, always with impunity, by this new privileged class of tyranny. The merchants, the boyars with their peasants, the bourgeoisie—in short, everything that was not of the *elect* belonged to the *elect*. This terrible guard was like a single man whose soul was the Emperor.

Nocturnal rounds were made in Moscow and its environs to the profit of the robbers; merit, birth, fortune, beauty, advantages of all kinds were dangerous for those who possessed them.

The women, the girls who were beautiful and who had the misfortune to be considered virtuous, were taken away to serve as toys for the brutality of the Czar's favorites. This prince held these unfortunate women in his retreat; then, when he was tired of seeing them, those who had not perished in the shadow of the tortures invented expressly for them were sent back to their husbands and their families. These women, escaped from the claws of the tiger, returned to die of shame in their dishonored homes.

The instigator of such abominations, the Czar, wished his own sons to take part in these orgies of crimes; by this refinement of tyranny, he deprived his stupid subjects even of the future.

To hope for a better reign would be to conspire against the present sovereign. Perhaps, also, the Czar was afraid of finding a censor in a son less foul, less degraded than himself. Otherwise, must he sound the very depths of this abyss of corruption? Ivan derived a sensual pleasure in perverting; it was another kind of death. In destroying the soul he rested from the fatigue of killing the body, but continued to destroy. Such was the nature of his diversion.

In the conduct of affairs, the life of this monster was an inexplicable mixture of energy and cowardice. He threatened his enemies so long as he believed himself the stronger; vanquished, he sobbed, he prayed, he crawled, he shamed himself, his country, his people, and always without meeting resistance, without a single voice protesting against his villainy. Shame, that ultimate pun-

300

ishment of nations who fail themselves, did not open the eyes of the Russians.

The Khan of the Crimea burned Moscow; the Czar fled. He returned when his capital was a pile of ashes. His presence caused more terror among the remainder of the inhabitants than the presence of the enemy had created. No matter—not a murmur reminded the monarch that he was a man and had failed in abandoning his trust as King.

The Poles, the Swedes, one after the other, were exposed to the excess of his arrogance and his cowardice. In negotiations with the Khan of the Crimea, he stooped to the point of offering the Tartars Kazan and Astrakhan, which he had formerly torn from them with such glory. He toyed with glory as with everything else.

Later on he was to deliver Livonia—the prize of blood, the goal of his nation's struggles during the wars of several centuries—up to Stephen Batory [King of Poland, 1533-86]; but in spite of the repeated betrayals by its chief, Russia, always indefatigable in servility, was not for an instant disgusted with an obedience as onerous as it was debasing; heroism would have cost this nation, relentless against itself, less. And even in our lifetime, Karamsin believed himself obliged to mitigate the indignation that the dishonorable conduct of their chief should inspire in all Russians in these terms:

We have already made mention of the military institutions of this reign: Ivan, whose cowardice on the field of battle *covered* the flags

301

of his country with *shame*, nevertheless, left to
his country a better disciplined and much
larger army than it had ever had up to that
time.

This is a fact; but why does he not add a word
of protest in the name of humanity and national
honor?

It was under this reign that Siberia was, so to
speak, discovered and conquered by heroic Muscovite adventurers. It was in the destiny of Ivan
IV to leave this means of tyranny to his successors.

Let us finish the outline of Ivan's tyranny.

One day he had the idea of dressing himself
and his companions as monks; disguised in this
fashion, he continued to astound heaven and
earth by his inhumanity and his monstrous licen-
tiousness. He deadened indignation in the hearts
of the people; he tempted despair, but always in
vain. To the insatiable cruelty, to the madness of
the master, the slave opposed inexhaustible resignation. The Russians wished to live under this
prince; they loved him with his furies and his
scandalous behavior; taking pity on his fears, they
willingly gave their lives to reassure him. They
were happy enough, independent enough, men
enough, provided he was Czar and ruled over
them. Nothing quenched their inextinguishable
thirst for servitude—these people were martyrs of
self-humiliation; no brute was ever more acquies-
cent, more blind in his submission. Obedience car-

ried to this extreme is no longer patience, it is passion: and that is the answer to the enigma!

To complete the portrait of Ivan IV one must return to Karamsin; so, to finish my story, I am selecting a few of the most characteristic passages in his history.

Quarrels of pre-eminence took place in the service of the court. (You see etiquette rules in the cave of the savage beast.) The handsome Boris Godounov (later the assassin of the heir to the throne and usurper of the crown), new cupbearer and favorite of Ivan, had on this subject, in 1578, a suit with Prince Basil Sitzky whose son refused to serve at the table of the Czar on an equal footing with Boris; and, although Prince Basil had been vested with the dignity of boyar, Godounov was declared, by a letters-patent of the sovereign, higher *by several ranks* because Godounov's grandfather had been inscribed in the old registers before the Sitzkys. However, if he closed his eyes to the disputes of the voivodes on matters of pre-eminence, the Czar never pardoned shortcomings in military conduct. For example, Prince Michael Nosdrovoty, high-ranking officer, *was whipped in the stables* for having prepared the siege of Milten badly.

This incident, which took place in 1577, reminds me of another in the history of Russia, entirely modern as it happened in our lifetime. I am interested in comparing epochs in order to show you that there is less difference than you think between the past and present of this country. This incident occurred at Warsaw in the time of the Grand Duke Constantine and under the reign of the Emperor Alexander—the most philanthropic of the Czars.

One day Constantine was reviewing the guard and, wishing to demonstrate to a distinguished foreigner the degree of discipline observed in the Russian army, he got off his horse, approached *one of his generals* . . . and without warning him in any way, without voicing a reprimand, he calmly pierced the general's foot with his sword. The general stood motionless, without uttering a complaint. When the Grand Duke withdrew his sword, they took the wounded man away. This stoicism of a slave justifies the definition of the Abbé Galiani: *Courage,* said he, *is only a very great fear!*

The witnesses of this scene remained silent. The incident took place in the nineteenth century in Warsaw on a public square.

You see, the Russians of our era are the worthy descendants of the subjects of Ivan; and do not hold up to me as an objection the madness of Constantine. This insanity, granting it to be real, should have been known, since the conduct of this man from his early youth had been only a series of public acts of dementia. Thus, after so many proofs of mental derangement, to let him command armies, rule a kingdom, was to make a public show of a revolting disdain for humanity;

this is a mockery as degrading to those in authority as it is insulting to those who obey. Personally, I do not believe in the madness of the Grand Duke Constantine; and I see in his life only unrestrained cruelty.

I have often been told that insanity is hereditary in the imperial family of Russia: this is flattery. I believe this illness belongs to the very nature of the government and not to the defective constitution of individuals. Absolute power, when it is an actuality, would, in the long run, derange the soundest mind; despotism blinds men; people and ruler, all become drunk on the cup of tyranny. This truth seems to me to be clearly proven by the history of Russia.

Let us continue our extracts; a Livonian historian cited by Karamsin is speaking. This time we shall see, one after the other, an ambassador and a man subjected to punishment, both equally idolatrous of their master and executioner.

Neither torture nor disgrace could weaken the devotion of these men to their sovereign. We are going to cite a memorable testimonial: Prince Sougorsky, envoy to the Emperor Maximilian in 1576, fell ill as he was crossing Courland. Out of respect for the Czar, the Duke sought news of this envoy several times through his own minister who heard the sick man repeat endlessly: "My health is nothing provided the health of our sovereign flourishes."

The astonished minister said to him, "How can you serve a tyrant with so much zeal?"

"We Russians," replied Prince Sougorsky, "are always devoted to our Czars, kind or cruel."

In proof of what he propounded, the prince recounted the following incident. Some time before, Ivan had one of his *distinguished men* impaled *for a minor mistake;* this unfortunate man had endured twenty-four hours of terrible torture, all the while talking with his wife and children and repeating over and over: "Great God! protect the Czar!" That is to say (Karamsin himself adds) Russians gloried in the very thing foreigners criticized them for—blind and boundless devotion to the will of the monarch, even when in his most insane flights he trampled under foot all the laws of justice and humanity.

I shall give only one more excerpt—the correspondence of the Czar with one of his subjects.

The Khan of the Crimea had in his power Vassili Griaznoi, one of Ivan's favorites, who had been taken prisoner by the Tartars during a reconnaissance near Moloschnievody. The Khan offered to exchange him for Mouzza Divy, a proposition the Czar did not choose to accept, although he lamented the fate of Griaznoi and wrote him *friendly letters* in which he characteristically ridiculed the services of his unfortunate favorite. "You believed," he wrote him, "that it was as easy to wage war on the Tartars as to jest at my table; they are not like

Moscow, August 11, 1839

you; they do not fall asleep in a hostile land and continuously repeat: *It is time to go home!* . . . What a peculiar idea has come to you to vaunt yourself as a man of distinction! It is true, being obliged to drive out the perfidious boyars who surrounded me, I had to encircle myself with slaves like you of low extraction; but you should not forget your father and your grandfather. Do you dare compare yourself with Divy? Liberty would only give you back a voluptuous bed; whereas it would put a sword against Christians in Divy's hand. It should be enough that in protecting those of my slaves who serve me zealously I am prepared to pay a ransom for you."

The reply of the servant is worthy of the letter of the master. In it there is more than the picture of the heart of a vile man; one can draw from it an idea of the espionage practised by Russians in foreign countries ever since that time. Doubtlessly there are few who would be capable of committing Griaznoi's crimes, but I cannot help believing there are many who would write letters comparable at least in basic sentiments to that of this miserable creature. Here is the letter as Karamsin reports it.

My Lord, I have not slept in enemy territory: *I was carrying out your orders, gathering information for the security of the Empire;* trusting no one and vigilant night and day, I was captured with wounds and breathing my

307

last, abandoned by my cowardly companions in arms. In combat I exterminated enemies of Christianity, and during my captivity I have caused the Russian traitors who wished to destroy you to perish; *they were secretly slain by my own hand;* not a single one of them remains here among the living. I jested at my sovereign's table to amuse him; today, I am dying for God and for him. It is by a special grace of the Almighty that I still breathe; the ardor of my zeal for your service sustains me that I may return to Russia and *again amuse my prince.* My body is in the Crimea, my soul is with God and Your Majesty. I am not afraid of death; I fear only your disfavor.

Such is the *friendly* correspondence of the Czar with his subject.

Karamsin adds: "It was knaves of this sort that Ivan needed for his government, and, according to his belief, for his security."

But all the events of this stupendous reign, stupendous especially for its calmness and its long duration, are effaced before the most appalling of crimes.

We have already said that the degraded Ivan, trembling at the very name of Poland, ceded Livonia to Batory, almost without a struggle— Livonia, a province fiercely disputed for centuries with the Swedes, the Poles, its own inhabitants, and especially with its victorious sovereigns the Teutonic Knights. For Russia, Livonia was the door to Europe, the connection with the civilized world. It was from time immemorial the object of the Czars' covetousness and the goal of the efforts of the Muscovite nation. In an incomprehensible excess of terror, the most arrogant and, at the same time, the most cowardly of the princes gave up this prey and abandoned it to the enemy —not at the end of a disastrous battle, but spontaneously, with a stroke of the pen, although he was still rich, with countless forces and an inexhaustible treasury. So lend your attention to the scene which was the first result of this treason.

The Czarevitch—the cherished son of Ivan IV, object of all his favors whom he was rearing after his own image in the exercise of crime and in habits of the most disgraceful debauchery—felt some shame in the dishonorable conduct of his father and his sovereign; he did not risk remonstrance— he knew Ivan; but, carefully avoiding any word which could resemble criticism, he restricted himself to asking permission to fight the Poles.

"Ah! you find fault with my policy—that is in itself to betray me," replied the Czar. "Who knows if the idea of raising the standard of revolt against your father is not in your heart?"

Thereupon, inflamed with sudden wrath, he seized his ironbound staff and violently struck his son on the head; one of the favorites tried to restrain the tyrant's arm; Ivan repeated the attack; the Czarevitch fell mortally wounded.

Here began the only tender scene in the life of Ivan IV. Its pathos surpasses the natural: only the language of poetry could make one believe in virtues so sublime they were incomprehensible.

The prince was at death's door for more than a day. When the Czar saw that, with his own hand, he had killed the thing dearest in the world to him, he fell into a despair as wild and as violent as his wrath had been terrible. Howling savagely, he rolled in the dust; he mingled his tears with the blood of his doomed son, kissing the wounds, invoking heaven and earth to save the life that he had just taken away, summoning doctors, sorcerers, and promising wealth, honor, power to anyone who could give him back the heir to his throne, the sole object of his tenderness . . . of the tenderness of Ivan IV!

Everything was useless! The inevitable death approached; the father had struck the blow. God had judged the father and the son and the son was dying. But his suffering was drawn out; Ivan learned for once to suffer at the pain of another. The spirited victim struggled against death for four whole days.

But to what end to you think these four days were used? How do you think this child, perverted by his father—note this point—unjustly suspected, wounded, killed by his father; how do you think he avenged himself for the loss of all his hopes in this world and for the four days of torture to which heaven condemned him for the edification of the world and, if possible, for the conversion of his executioner?

He spent this time of suffering praying to God for his father, consoling his father who did not wish to leave his side, justifying his father, vindicating him by repeating—with a delicateness worthy of the son of a better man—that his punishment, severe as it appeared, was completely just, for a son who finds fault with the conduct of a crowned father, even in the depths of his heart, deserved to die. Death was present; it was no longer fear that spoke, it was political superstition.

When the final crisis drew near, the victim could think of nothing but concealing the horrors of his death from the eyes of his assassin, whom he venerated as the best of fathers and the greatest of kings; he begged the Czar to go away.

And, when instead of acceding to the insistence of the dying boy, Ivan, in his delirium of remorse, threw himself on his son's bed, then fell on his knees to ask a belated pardon from his victim, this hero of filial piety found supernatural strength in the sentiment of duty. Already in the jaws of death, he tarried at the crossing, hung on for an instant to the life he sustained as by miracle to repeat more vehemently, more solemnly, that he was guilty, his death justified and too easy. By force of soul, of filial love and respect for the sovereignty, he succeeded in disguising his agony; thus, up to the last moment, he hid from his father the torments of a body in which rebellious youth struggled violently against destruction. The gladiator fell with grace—not through mean conceit but through an effort of charity, solely to assuage the remorse in the heart of his guilty father. To his last breath he protested his loyalty, his submission to the legitimate sovereign of Russia, and finally he died kissing the hand that had killed him, praising God, his country, and his father.

The Czarevitch died in the retreat of tyranny called Alexandrova Sloboda outside Moscow.

What tragedy! Never has Rome, pagan or Christian, produced anything more noble than the long farewells of the son of Ivan IV to his father.

If the Russians cannot be human, they can sometimes raise themselves above humanity.

This experience did not chasten the character of the monster, who continued until the end of his days to cover himself with innocent blood and wallow in the most obscene debauchery.

At the approach of his own death, several times he had himself carried into his treasury. There, with dull eyes, he avidly contemplated his precious jewels—powerless riches escaped him along with life!

After living as a savage beast, he died as a satyr, outraging, by an act of revolting lechery, his own daughter-in-law, the young and chaste wife of his second son, Fedor, become, since the death of the Czarevitch Ivan, heir to the Empire. This young woman approached the dying man's bed to console him in his last moments . . . but suddenly she recoiled and fled with a scream of terror.

That is how Ivan IV died in the Kremlin, and . . . it is hard to believe this, he was mourned, mourned for a long time by the entire nation, nobles, peasants, bourgeoisie, and clergy, as if he had been the best of princes. . . .

So let us admit and not grow tired of repeating that unrestrained despotism has the effect of an intoxicating beverage on the human spirit. An Emperor of Russia would have to be an angel, or at least a genius, to keep his sanity after twenty years of ruling; but my astonishment and dismay increase in seeing the tyrant's dementia spread so easily to the men who submit to tyranny; the victims become the zealous accomplices of their executioners. That is the lesson one learns in Russia.

A detailed and completely accurate history of Russia would perhaps be the most instructive work one could offer for man's contemplation; but such a book is impossible to achieve. Karamsin, who attempted it, flattered his models, but even so his history covers only the early period terminating prior to the accession of the Romanovs. He died just at the time when it was becoming impossible for him to continue his work. Nevertheless, the restrained and abridged outline I have just traced for you is sufficient to depict the men and events to which the mind, in spite of itself, returns at the sight of the terrifying walls of the Kremlin.

SO MUCH GOLD, SO MANY DIAMONDS . . . AND SO MUCH DUST!

Moscow, August 11, 1839

TODAY I recommenced my sight-seeing by a methodic and detailed visit to the Kremlin . . . always the Kremlin! It is for me all Moscow, all Russia! It is a world!

I have never seen Constantinople, but I believe that after that city Moscow, in general appearance, is the most striking of all the capitals of Europe, the Byzantium of the mainland.

I never tire of the effect of the Kremlin seen from the outside. The outer walls, designed unevenly, rising and falling to follow the deep sharp curves of the hills and vales; so many levels of structures of strange style, carried one on the other, make up one of the most original and most poetic décors in the world. It is not for me, it is for artists to show you these wonders; words fail me in describing the effect; there are some things that the eyes alone can judge. However, it would be necessary for the artist to choose his points of view with discernment as, contemplated from the outside, the Kremlin is prodigious, from within it is flat and ordinary.

How can I convey to you my surprise when, upon entering the interior of this magic city, I ap-

314

proached the modern building which is called the Treasury and saw before me a little palace of sharp angles, rigid lines, Greek pediments decorated with Corinthian columns? This cold and shabby imitation of the antique, for which I should have been prepared, appeared so ridiculous to me I drew back several steps.

Finally, braving these dragons of bad taste with my eyes closed, I climbed up to the glorious arsenal where, arranged as if in a cabinet of curios, the most interesting historical trophies of Russia are found.

What a collection of armor, urns, and national jewels! What a profusion of crowns and thrones united in a single enclosure! The manner in which these objects are arranged adds to the impression they produce. One cannot help admiring the taste in decoration and, more than that, the political intelligence which directed the distribution—ever so little vain—of so many insignia and trophies; but patriotic pride is the most legitimate of all prides—one pardons a passion that helps to fulfill so many obligations. Here, the objects are only a symbol of a profound idea.

The crowns are placed on cushions supported by pedestals, and the thrones, arranged near the walls, are raised on individual platforms. To this evocation of the past only the men for whom all these things were made are lacking. Their absence merits a sermon on the vanity of human affairs. The Kremlin without its Czars is a theater without light and without actors.

The most venerable, if not the most imposing

315

of the crowns, is that of Monomachus; it was brought from Byzantium to Kiev in 1116.

Then come crowns on crowns, but all are subordinated to the imperial crown. Included in this royal constellation are the crowns of the kingdom of Kazan, Astrakhan, Georgia. The sight of these royal satellites, maintained at a respectful distance from the star which towers above them all, is particularly imposing—everything in Russia is symbolic; it is a poetic land . . . poetic like grief! The crown of Siberia is found among many others; this crown was created by the Russians as a symbol to be placed there in commemoration of a great historic feat accomplished by commercial adventurers and warriors under the reign of Ivan IV, the epoch from which dated not the discovery but the conquest of Siberia. All these crowns are covered with the most precious and most enormous jewels in the world. The entrails of this land are opened up to feed the vanity of the despotism whose retreat it is.

The throne and the crown of Poland form part of the superb imperial and royal firmament. So many crown jewels displayed in a small space shone in my eyes like the spread tail of a peacock. What bloodstained emptiness! I muttered to myself at each new marvel before which my guides forced me to stop.

The crowns of Peter I, of Catherine I, and of Elizabeth struck me particularly—so much gold, so many diamonds . . . and so much dust! The imperial globes, the thrones, the scepters, all gathered together to attest the greatness of things and the nothingness of men, and when one thinks that this nothingness extends to empires one no longer knows what straw to cling to under the torrent of time.

Urns chiseled in the style of Benvenuto Cellini, cups decorated with precious stones, weapons, armor, costly fabrics, rare embroideries, glassware of all countries and all centuries abound in this marvelous collection whose inventory a true connoisseur would not complete in a week. In addition to the thrones or chairs of all the Russian princes of all centuries, I saw the armor of their horses, their clothes, their furniture, and all these things, more or less rich, more or less rare, were dazzling. I make you think of the palace of *A Thousand and One Nights;* so much the better— I have no other means of describing this fabulous, if not enchanted, place to you.

But here the historical interest adds still more to the effect of so many wonders. How many curious feats are picturesquely registered there and attested to by venerable relics! From the helmet —the work of St. Alexander Nevski—to the stretcher which carried Charles XII to Poltava, each object brings back an interesting memory, a particular event. This treasury is a veritable album of the Kremlin.

In finishing the perusal of these vain relics of time, I am reminded, as if by inspiration, of a passage from Montaigne which I am copying for you, to complete by curious contrast this description of the magnificent things in the Muscovite treasury.

Of old, the Duke of Muscovy owed this courtesy to the Tartars—when they sent ambassadors to him he had to go on foot to meet them and present them with a goblet of mare's milk (a beverage they thought delicious), and if, while drinking this milk a few drops of it fell on the manes of their horses the Duke had to lick them up with his tongue.

The Emperor of All the Russias, with all his thrones, with all his pride, is, nevertheless, only the successor of these same Grand Dukes we see so humiliated in the sixteenth century.

During the era when the Grand Dukes of Moscow, on their knees, bore the shameful yoke imposed upon them by the Mongolians, the spirit of chivalry flourished in Europe, especially in Spain where blood ran in torrents for the honor and independence of Christianity. I do not believe, in spite of the barbarity of the Middle Ages, one would have found in Western Europe a single King capable of dishonoring the sovereignty by consenting to reign under the conditions imposed on the Grand Dukes of Muscovy in the thirteenth, fourteenth, and fifteenth centuries by their masters the Tartars. But in Russia, like everything else, glory is of recent date.

Other wonders awaited me elsewhere. I visited the Senate, the Imperial Palace, the ancient Palace of the Patriarch, all of which have no interest other than their names, and, finally, the little angular palace which is a gem and a toy. This structure reminds one a little of the masterpieces of Moorish architecture; it shines by its elegance in the midst of the heavy structures which surround it —one would say like a ruby mounted with cut stones.

To describe the contrast produced by so many diverse edifices piled up at a single point which forms the center of an immense city, and, in the midst of this confusion, paint for you the effect of this little palace, newly reconstructed but with decorations of an ancient style, approaching the Gothic and mixed with the Moorish, is impossible. Here Greek temples, there Gothic forts, farther on Indian towers, Chinese pavilions, the whole bizarrely enshrined in an interior enclosed by cyclopean walls—that is what I would have to show you in a word as one perceives it in a glance.

WHEN THE MUZHIKS
GET TIPSY . . .

Moscow, August 12, 1839

BEFORE COMING to Russia, I believe I had read most of the descriptions of Moscow published by travelers; however, I had not pictured the singular character of this hilly city, coming out of the earth as if by magic and appearing in the unvarying vast spaces, with its hills accentuated by the buildings they support and make stand out in the center of a rolling plain. It is a stage set. Moscow is almost the only hilly area in the central part of Russia. Do not, on the strength of this word, imagine Switzerland or Italy—this is an uneven terrain; nothing more. But the contrast of this unevenness in the midst of spaces where the eye and the mind lose themselves as in the prairies of America or the steppes of Asia, produces surprising effects. This city recalls the idea one has formed, without really knowing why, of Persepolis, of Bagdad, of Babylon, of Palmyra—romantic capitals of fabulous lands whose history is a poem and whose architecture is a dream. In short, in Moscow one forgets Europe—something I did not know in France.

Moscow is very proud of the progress of its factories; Russian silks compete here with those of the Orient and of the West. The city of merchants,

320

the Kitaigorod, as well as the street nicknamed Port des Maréchaux where the most fashionable shops are found, are counted among the interesting sights of this capital. I mention this only because I think the efforts of the Russian people to free themselves from the tribute they pay to the industry of others can have serious political and commercial consequences in Europe.

The freedom that reigns in Moscow is only an illusion; however, it cannot be denied that in the streets of this city there are men who seem to move spontaneously, men who think and act on their own impulse. In this respect Moscow is very different from Petersburg.

Moscow remains as though buried in the very center of the country of which it is the capital—hence the seal of originality stamped on its edifices, the air of freedom which distinguishes its inhabitants, and finally the little liking of the Czars for this domicile with its independent physiognomy. They prefer Petersburg, in spite of all its disadvantages, because they have need of being in continuous communication with the West of Europe. Russia, such as Peter the Great has made it, does not trust itself either to live or to instruct itself.

If the freezing and thawing snows did not make railways ineffectual in this country during six to eight months out of the year, you would see the Russian government anticipating others in the construction of these routes which shrink the earth; for, more than any other thing, Russia suffers from the disadvantage of distances. But they

will in vain multiply the railway lines, augment
the speed of transport, for a vast extent of territory is and always will be the greatest obstacle to
the circulation of thought—the soil does not allow
itself to be crossed in all directions as does the
sea. . . .

Certainly, if Moscow were a seaport, or even
the center of a vast network of these steel tracks—
electric conductors of human thought—which
seem destined to satisfy some of the impatience
of the century in which we live, one would not
see there what I saw yesterday at the English
Club: military men of all ages, elegant gentlemen,
serious men, and giddy youths, all making the
Sign of the Cross and meditating some instants before seating themselves at table, not a family table
but a public table, and among men. The persons
who abstain from this religious duty (there were
a goodly number of them) watched the others observe it without astonishment—you can well see
that there is still a distance of a good eight hundred leagues from Paris to Moscow.

I was not shocked; indeed, and in very good
faith, I admire the piety of the Russians. I made
this comment to the man who had presented me
to this circle.

We were talking in private after dinner at the
end of the club garden.

"Give me," I asked him, "an idea of the state
of religion in your country; tell me what is the
spiritual culture of the men who teach and explain the Gospels in Russia."

Although addressed to a very superior person,

this question would have been indiscreet in Petersburg; in Moscow, I felt I could risk it because there reigns here that mysterious liberty which one uses without being aware of it, which one neither alleges nor defines but which is real, although the false confidence it inspires can sometimes be dearly paid for. Here, in summary, is what my Russian philosopher replied to me—I use the word "philosopher" in its most favorable sense. After some years' sojourn in various countries of Europe, he has returned to Russia, very liberal, but very consistent. Here, then, is what he said to me:

"There has always been very little preaching in the schismatic Greek churches; and in our country, the political and religious authority is more opposed than elsewhere to theological discussions. As soon as one wished to explain the questions debated between Rome and Byzantium, silence was imposed on both sides. The subjects of dispute have so little gravity that the quarrel can perpetuate itself only by the force of ignorance. In several girls' or boys' schools, at the instigation of the Jesuits, some religious instruction has been given; but the use of these lectures is only tolerated and from time to time abrogated. A fact that will appear incomprehensible to you, although it is a positive reality, is that religion is not taught publicly in Russia. Consequently there are a multitude of sects whose existence the government does not permit you to suspect.

"Our priests are forbidden to write, even chronicles. Frequently some peasant interprets a

323

passage of the Bible which, taken in isolation and falsely applied, immediately gives place to a new heresy—most often Calvinist. When the village priest learns of this, the heresy has already won over some of the inhabitants of the community, and, thanks to the persistence of ignorance, it has even taken root as far as neighboring communities. If the priest complains, the infected peasants are immediately sent to Siberia. That ruins the landowner; so, if the landowner is foresighted, he silences the priest by more means than one. When, in spite of such precautions, the heresy reaches the point of breaking out before the eyes of the supreme authority, the number of dissidents is so considerable that it is no longer possible to act: violence would publish the evil without smothering it; persuasion would open the door to discussion, the worst of evils in the eyes of an absolute government; thus, one has recourse only to silence which hides the evil without curing it and which, on the contrary, furthers it.

"It is through religious dissensions that the Russian Empire will perish; thus, to envy us, as you do, the power of faith is to judge us without knowing us!"

Such is the opinion of the most discerning and most sincere men I have met in Russia.

I attended a popular festival around the monastery of Devitscheipol. The festival took place in commemoration of some saint, I don't know which one, whose relics and images are scrupulously visited between libations of kvas. On this particular evening there was a fabulous consumption of this national drink.

The miraculous Virgin of Smolensk—others say the copy—is conserved in this convent which has eight churches. Toward the end of the day, I went into the principal one.

This church houses the tombs of several czarinas and princesses, notably that of the ambitious Sophia, sister of Peter the Great, and the tomb of the Czarina Eudosia, the first wife of Peter the Great. This unfortunate wife, repudiated, I believe, in 1696, was forced to take the veil at Sousdal.

This evening the tents where the strollers of Devitscheipol huddled together were infested with diverse odors, the mixture of which produced a fetid air—perfumed Russian leather, alcoholic drinks, sour beer, fermented cabbage, the oil of the Cossacks' boots, the musk and amber of the nobles, who were there through idle curiosity and affected boredom if only through aristocratic vanity.

The greatest of the pleasures of these people is drunkenness, in other words, oblivion. Poor people! They have to dream to be happy. But the thing that proves the debonair disposition of the Russians is that when the muzhiks get tipsy, as calloused as they are, they grow tender instead of fighting and killing each other according to the custom of drunks in our countries. They weep and embrace—interesting and strange nation. It would be sweet to make them happy. But the task would be hard if not impossible. Find me the means of satisfying the vague desires of a giant, young, lazy, ignorant, ambitious and tied down to the point of being unable to budge either his feet or his hands! Never do I pity the lot of the people of this country without feeling equally sorry for the all-powerful man who governs it.

For want of definite documents, I amused instead of instructing myself at the festival; the physiognomy of the people, their costumes—half oriental, half Finnish—contributed endlessly to the diversion of the traveler. I congratulated myself on having gone to this festival, so lacking in gaiety but so different from all I have seen elsewhere.

Cossacks mingled in great numbers among the strollers and imbibers who filled the place. They formed silent groups around a few singers whose piercing voices chanted the melancholy words of a melody, very sweet in spite of the strongly marked rhythm. This air is the national song of the Cossacks of the Don. It is sweet and penetrating like the song of a nightingale when heard from a distance at night and in the depths of the woods. At times the accompanists repeated the last words of the stanza in chorus.

With every refrain, the effect augments: formerly in Paris one danced a Russian step that this music recalls; but on the spot national melodies produce a completely different impression. At the end of a few couplets one feels himself filled with an irresistible tenderness. The Cossacks of the

326

Urals also have special songs; I regret not having heard them.

This race of men is worthy of a study apart; the Cossacks, the majority of whom are married, form a military family, a subdued horde rather than a troop subjected to the discipline of a regiment. Attached to their chiefs like a dog to its master, they obey the command with more affection and less servitude than other Russian soldiers. In a land where nothing is defined, they believe themselves the allies, not the slaves of the imperial government. Their agility, their nomadic habits, the swiftness and nerve of their horses, the patience and adroitness of the man and of the beast, identified one with the other, hardened together to fatigue, to privations, constitute a force. One cannot help but admire whatever geographic instinct it is that aids these savage scouts of the army in guiding themselves without roads in the countries they invade: in the most deserted, the most barren, as well as in the most civilized and the most populated. In war, does not the name alone of Cossack spread terror in advance in the land of the enemy? Generals who know how to use such a light cavalry have an effective means of action that the captains of more civilized armies do not have.

The Cossacks are, it is said, naturally gentle; they have greater sensibility than one would have the right to expect from such a rough people; but their excessive ignorance makes me sorry for them and for their masters.

When I recall the advantage that officers here

327

take of the credulity of the soldier, all that I have of dignity in my soul rebels against a government which stoops to such subterfuges or does not punish those of its servants who dare resort to them.

I have it on good authority that several Cossack chiefs, leading their men out of the country during the war of 1814 to 1815, said to them: "Kill many enemies, strike your adversaries with fear. If you die in combat, you will, after three days, return to your wives and your children; you will be resuscitated in flesh and bone, in body and soul. What, then, have you to fear?"

Men accustomed to recognize the voice of God the Father in that of their officers took the promises made to them literally.

But one can imagine, without dismay and without disgust, the moral state of a nation whose armies were directed in that fashion less than twenty-five years ago? What goes on today? I do not know and I am afraid to find out.

THE MOST FAMOUS PILGRIMAGE IN RUSSIA

At the Monastery of Troitza
20 leagues from Moscow
August 17, 1839

IF IT WERE necessary to apologize for repetition and monotony, I should also have to beg pardon for traveling in Russia. Repetition of impressions is inevitable in all conscientious tours, but more so in this one than in any other. As I wish to give you the most accurate idea possible of this country, I must tell you exactly, hour by hour, what I experience; this is the only means of justifying what I shall think later. Furthermore, each new thing that recalls to me the same idea helps to prove that these ideas are correct.

After Kiev, Troitza is the most famous and frequented pilgrimage in Russia. During the summer the roads all around are lined with processions of travelers.

On leaving the inn one crosses a square and enters the religious center where one finds first a path lined with trees, then a few small churches called cathedrals, high campaniles separated from the churches to which they belong, and several chapels.

All the noted personages in Russian history have taken pleasure in enriching this monastery;

329

its treasury is overflowing with gold, diamonds, and pearls.

In spite of my long and vehement insistence, they refused to show me the library; my interpreter always gave me the same response: "It is forbidden!"

Tomorrow I hope to get to Yaroslavl; I will stay there a day or two in the hope of finding in the interior of Russia some real Russians. I took care in Moscow to arm myself with several letters of introduction for the capital of this province, one of the most interesting of the Empire because of its location as well as the industry of its inhabitants.

DISDAIN FOR WHAT THEY DO
NOT KNOW . . .

Yaroslavl, August 18, 1839

THE PREDICTION made in Moscow has come to pass; having completed barely a quarter of my journey, I arrived at Yaroslavl without a single part of my carriage intact. It will be repaired, but I doubt that it will take me to the end of the trip.

This city is an important commercial center for the interior of Russia; also, through it Petersburg communicates with Persia, the Caspian Sea, and all of Asia.

Like all Russian provincial cities, Yaroslavl is vast and appears empty. The same style of architecture prevails from one end of the Empire to the other. The following dialogue will show you the value the Russians attach to their so-called classical buildings.

A man of parts in Moscow told me he had seen nothing in Italy which was new to him.

"Are you speaking seriously?" I exclaimed.

"Quite seriously," he replied. "How could you expect that inhabitants of Petersburg and Moscow would be amazed by Italian architecture like other people? Do you not see models of this architecture at every step you take here, even in our smallest villages?"

After this explosion of vanity I kept quiet; I

331

was in Moscow; I wanted to laugh but it would have been dangerous to yield to this urge.

I congratulate myself on coming to Russia for only a short time; a long stay in this country would take away not only the courage but the desire to tell the truth about what I see and hear. Despotism inspires indifference and discouragement even in the minds most determined to fight against its crying abuses.

Disdain for what they do not know seems to me one of the most striking characteristics of the Russians. Instead of trying to understand they ridicule. . . .

The painted and gilded bell-towers, almost as numerous as the houses, in Yaroslavl, shine from a distance like those of Moscow, but the city is less picturesque than the old capital of the Empire.

The nearer one gets to this city the more one is struck by the beauty of the people, and the villages are rich and well built; I even saw a few stone houses, but they are still too few in number to change the unbroken monotony of the countryside.

AT NIZHNI THE COUNTRY ITSELF
IS BEAUTIFUL

Nizhni-Novgorod, August 22, 1839

THE SITE of Nizhni is the most beautiful I have
seen in Russia. Up to now I had enjoyed really
picturesque views only in the streets of Moscow
and along the quays of Petersburg and these were
man-made sites; but here the country itself is
beautiful.

I have been in this city only a few hours and
have already seen the governor—he seemed hos-
pitable and communicative for a Russian.

The Nizhni fair under his guidance and seen
from his point of view will have a double interest
for me: the interest of the sights themselves, which
are nearly all new for a Frenchman, and the interest I have in penetrating the minds of the men employed by this government.

TO CONCEAL IS USEFUL;
TO FEIGN IS ESSENTIAL

Nizhni, August 25, 1839

THIS YEAR, on the point of opening the fair, the
Governor summoned to his house the leading
businessmen in Russia, assembled at that time
in Nizhni, and set forth in detail for them the long
recognized and deplored disadvantages of the
monetary system in the Empire.

Having explained these disadvantages to his
audience and enumerated all the troublesome results deriving from them, the Governor added
that, in his constant solicitude for the welfare of
his peoples and the good order of his Empire, the
Emperor had finally just put an end to a disorder
the progress of which threatened to impede internal trade most seriously. The only remedy
known to be efficacious was the establishment of
a definite and irrevocable value for the minted
ruble. An edict accomplished this revolution in a
single day.

The good and wise men consulted on this grave
question replied that the measure, good in itself,
would destroy the most stable commercial fortunes if it were applied to deals previously nego-
tiated but to be completed only at the present
fair. All the while praising and admiring the profound wisdom of the Czar, they humbly demonstrated to the Governor that those of the mer-

334

chants who had effected sales at a price fixed on the old monetary standards and had made their contracts in good faith according to the relation existing at the previous fair between the paper ruble and the silver ruble would be exposed to reimbursements which were fraudulent in fact although authorized by law; and that these permitted frauds, depriving them of their profit or at the very least markedly reducing the gain they had a right to count on, could ruin them if the present edict were made retroactive.

The Governor replied, with the calmness and gentleness which preside in Russia at all administrative, financial, and political discussions, that he understood the views of the principal merchants interested in the business of the fair perfectly; but that, after all, the troublesome result feared by these gentlemen threatened only a few individuals . . . whereas a delay would always seem a little like resistance and such an example set by the most important commercial center of the Empire would bring in its wake disadvantages much more dreadful for the country than a few bankruptcies. Moreover, disobedience approved and supported, it must indeed be said, by men who up to this time had enjoyed the confidence of the Government would be a direct blow to respect for the sovereign, to the administrative and financial unity of Russia, that is to say to the vital principles of the Empire. He added that in view of these peremptory considerations he did not doubt that these gentlemen would be anxious to avoid, by their compliance, the monstrous accu-

335

sation of sacrificing the interest of the State to
their private interest, dreading the shadow of a
crime of treason to patriotism more than any pe-
cuniary sacrifices to which they might gloriously
expose themselves by their willing submission and
their patriotic fervor.

The result of this peaceful conference was that
the following day the fair was opened under the
retroactive rule of the new ukase which was for-
mally published with the advice and consent of
the principal merchants of the Empire.

The Governor himself told me this with the intention of demonstrating to me the ease with
which the machinery of a despotic government,
so libeled in countries ruled by liberal institutions,
functions. . . .

This administrator-courtier had the modesty
not to take into account his own finesse; he likewise avoided leaving me time to repeat to him
what the gossips whisper endlessly to me; namely,
that all financial measures of this kind give the superior authority a certain means of profiting, that
no one dares complain out loud about under an
autocratic régime. I do not know what secret maneuvers they had recourse to this time, but to give
myself an idea I imagine the situation of a deposi-
tary vis-à-vis a man who entrusts to him a considerable sum. If the man who has received this sum
has the power to triple at will the value of each of
the pieces of money which make up the sum, it is
obvious that he can reimburse the depositor while
keeping in his own hands two-thirds of the
amount given, to him. I do not say that such was

336

the result of the measure decreed by the Emperor, but I make this supposition among many others to help me understand the slander or, if you prefer, the calumnies of the discontented, or only their reticences. They add that the profit from this brusquely executed operation, which, by decree, reduced the former value of the paper money and proportionally increased the value of the silver ruble, is destined to indemnify the private treasury of the sovereign for the amount that he had to withdraw to rebuild *at his own expense* his Winter Palace, and to enable him to refuse, with the magnanimity that Europe and Russia have admired, the offers of the cities, of several private citizens, and of the principal merchants, all anxious to contribute to the reconstruction of a national monument since it serves as the residence of the chief of the Empire.

In order to live in Russia, dissimulation is not enough; feigning is indispensable. To conceal is useful; to feign is essential. I leave you to surmise and appreciate the efforts imposed upon gallant souls and independent minds obliged to resign themselves to enduring a régime where peace and good order are paid for by discrediting the human word—the most sacred of all the gifts of heaven for a man who holds anything sacred.

THE LAWS OF POLITENESS

Vladimir, between Nizhni and Moscow
September 2, 1839

THE TOWN of Vladimir is mentioned many times in history; its appearance is that of the eternal Russian town—a type all too well known to you. The country I have crossed since I left Nizhni also resembles what you know about Russia—a forest without trees, broken at great distances by towns without movement.

My frankness makes me guilty of a crime in the minds of the people of this country. Behold my ingratitude! The Minister gives me an official courier; the presence of this uniform is enough to spare me the annoyances of the journey, and in the eyes of the Russians this obliges me to be pleased with everything in their country. This foreigner, they think, would fail in all the laws of politeness if he permitted himself to criticize a country where so much consideration has been shown him. I still consider myself free to describe to you what I see and to judge it. Although my money and my letters of recommendation have procured a courier to tour the country with me, I want you to know that if I had started out to Nizhni with a simple manservant, who knew Russian as well as I know French, we would have been delayed by the ruses and knavish tricks of

338

the postmasters at every relay which was the least bit out of the way. First we would have been refused horses. Then, on our insistence, we would have been taken from stall to stall in all the stables of the post and would have been shown that all were empty. This would have annoyed us more than surprised us as we would have known in advance, but without being able to lodge a complaint, that the postmaster had taken care as soon as we arrived at the relay to have all the horses withdrawn to hiding places inaccessible to foreigners. At the end of an hour's discussion, we would have been brought a team, so-called free, which the peasant to whom it supposedly belonged would have condescended to let us have at a price two or three times higher than the tariff of the imperial posts. We would have refused the team and sent it back; then, to have peace and quiet, we would have finished by begging for the return of these precious beasts and by paying the men anything they wished. The same scene would have been repeated at each post. That is how inexperienced and unprotected foreigners travel in this country. It is, however, established and admitted that traveling by post in Russia is quick and costs very little.

Does it not seem to you, as it does to me, that after having appreciated as I should the favor of the Director-General of the Posts, I have the right to tell you what the annoyances are that his kindness has spared me?

The Russians are always on the defensive against truth, which they fear; but I, belonging to a society where life takes place in the broad light of day and where everything is published and discussed, am not bothered in the least by the scruples of these men in whose country nothing is said. . . . Any clear and accurate word is an event in a country where not only the expression of opinion, but even the recital of well-established facts is forbidden. A Frenchman must note this ridiculous situation but he is incapable of imitating it.

Moscow, September 6, 1839

Without awaiting the ceremonial entry of the Emperor to Moscow, I am leaving in two days for Petersburg.

*   *   *

My correspondence as a traveler ends here. The account which follows completes my memoirs and was written in various places, beginning in Petersburg in 1839, then in Germany, and later in Paris.

THE DISAPPEARANCE OF
ANOTHER TRAVELER

Berlin, the early days of October, 1839

JUST AS I WAS GOING to leave Moscow a strange
case was brought urgently to my attention and
forced me to postpone my departure.

I had ordered my post horses for seven o'clock
in the morning; to my great astonishment my
valet awakened me at four. I asked the cause of
this promptness and he replied that he had not
wanted to delay informing me of an event he had
just learned about and which seemed to him serious enough to oblige him to tell me as quickly as
possible.

A Frenchman, named Louis Pernet, who had
been in Moscow for a few days and was staying
at the Kopp Inn had been arrested in the middle
of the night (that very night). After all his papers
had been confiscated he was seized and taken to
the city prison and put in solitary confinement.

The poor prisoner had in Moscow at that time
no acquaintances other than a Frenchman named
R——. This M. R—— was staying in the same
inn as the prisoner.

As soon as I had dressed I went to see
M. R——. I found him up and he seemed disturbed. When I told him the reason for my very
early visit, he seemed embarrassed.

"It is true that I traveled with M. Pernet," he said, "but it was only by chance; we met at Archangel. I certainly am not one of his friends; I don't even know him."

"I know him even less," I replied, "but we are all three Frenchmen and should help each other in a country where our liberty, our lives, can be threatened at any instant by a power that one recognizes only by the blows it strikes."

"I can do nothing for him; I am under no obligation to him, and I advise you, sir, to be very circumspect in any step you undertake in his behalf as well as in what you say. You forget where we are. He is in prison; how can one get to him? It is impossible."

On leaving this very cautious traveling companion, I began to think the case more serious than I had judged at first, and I thought that to inform myself on the real situation of the prisoner I would have to see the French Consul. This second visit got me no farther than the first.

Although I had taken leave of everybody two days before, I decided to risk confiding in one of the Russians who had inspired me with the most confidence.

When he saw me enter his room, he already knew what had brought me. Without giving me time to explain, he said that by a strange chance he knew M. Pernet personally, that he believed him innocent, that the cause of this affair seemed to him inexplicable, but that he was sure only political considerations could have brought about such an imprisonment. He finished with these words:

"You are neither his relative nor his friend; you take only the interest in him that you think you should take in a fellow countryman, in a man you know to be in trouble: you have already acquitted yourself of this praiseworthy sentiment. Take my advice and leave."

"But if I left," I cried, "I would not have a moment's rest: I would be pursued by remorse in thinking that this poor man had no one but me to help him and that I had abandoned him without doing anything for him."

"Your presence in Petersburg, on the contrary, can become useful to M. Pernet. You will tell the French Ambassador what you know about the imprisonment."

Since it had been proven that I could do nothing here, I thought I would leave immediately. But the slowness of my guide, who undoubtedly had to make another report on my activities, delayed me the rest of the morning. I could not get the post horses back until four in the afternoon; at quarter past four I was on the road to Petersburg.

My diligence was in vain. I did not arrive in Petersburg until four days later. Barely down from my carriage, I hastened to see the Ambassador. He still knew nothing about the arrest of M. Pernet, and appeared surprised to learn it from me, especially when he knew I had been on the road almost four days.

The attention with which the Ambassador listened to me, the assurance he gave me that every-thing would be done to clarify this matter, his promise not to lose sight of it for a moment until he had unraveled the plot, the importance he seemed to attach to the smallest detail which in-volved the dignity of France and the security of our citizens put my conscience at rest and dissi-pated the phantoms of my imagination. The fate of M. Pernet was in the hands of his natural pro-tector.

But while I was rapidly and freely making my way toward France, my thoughts often went back to the dungeons of Moscow. If I had known what took place, I would have been even more agitated.

So that the reader will not be left in ignorance —as I was for six months—concerning the fate of the prisoner in Moscow, I am inserting here the facts which I did not learn until after my return to France concerning the imprisonment of M. Pernet and his release.

One day toward the end of the winter of 1840 I was told that a stranger was at my door and wished to speak to me. . . . On entering my room he said, "Sir, I learned your address only yesterday and today I hastened to see you; my name is Pernet and I have come to thank you, for I was told in Petersburg that I owe my liberty and, consequently, my life to you."

He told me he had been detained in the Mos-cow prison for three weeks, four days of which were spent in solitary confinement. You will see from his story how a prisoner is treated in that place. My imagination had not approached the reality.

The first two days he was left without food. No one questioned him; he was alone. During forty-eight hours he believed he was destined to die of starvation, ignored in his cell. The only noise he heard was resounding blows of the whip. Add to this the sounds of frightful sobbing and crying, the screams of the victims, the threats and imprecations of the executioners and you will have a faint idea of the moral treatment to which our unfortunate compatriot was subjected for four endless days, always without knowing for what reason.

After having thus penetrated, indeed in spite of himself, into the deep mystery of Russian prisons, he believed himself, with all too just cause, condemned to end his days there. He said to himself and not without reason: "If they had intended to release me, these people, who fear nothing so much as seeing their barbarity divulged, would not have put me here in the first place."

Finally, after four times twenty-four hours of torture, the horror of which, I believe, surpasses any effort we may make to imagine it, M. Pernet was taken out of this cell, always without explanation, and transferred to another part of the prison.

From there he wrote to M. de Barante, the French Ambassador, through General——, on whose friendship he thought he could count. This letter never reached its destination.

345

Three weeks passed in an ever-increasing anxiety for it seemed there was everything to fear and nothing to hope for.

At the end of this time, which had seemed an eternity to M. Pernet, he was released without further ado and without ever being able to find out the cause of his imprisonment.

The reiterated questions he addressed to the Director of the Moscow police clarified nothing. He was told that his ambassador had made representations in his behalf and he was simply ordered to leave Russia. He asked for and obtained permission to leave via Petersburg.

He wanted to thank the French Ambassador for the liberty he owed to him. He also wanted to obtain some enlightenment on the reasons for the treatment to which he had been subjected. M. de Barante tried in vain to dissuade him from his plan to seek an explanation from the Minister of the Imperial Police. The released prisoner asked for and was granted an audience. He told the Minister that he was not aware of any reason for the punishment he had suffered and that before leaving Russia he wished to know what his crime had been.

The Minister replied briefly that he would do well not to push his investigations further on this subject and dismissed him, repeating the order to leave the Empire without delay.

My insistent prodding finally elicited from M. Pernet that on his first trip to Russia he had been given in his passport the title of merchant and on his second that of lawyer. He added something more serious: before arriving at Petersburg, he had freely expressed his opinion against Russian despotism in front of several individuals whom he did not know. He assured me, in leaving, that he could not recall any other circumstances that could have motivated the treatment he had experienced in Moscow.

I AM FREE!

Berlin, the early days of October, 1839

NEVER WILL I FORGET what I felt while crossing the Niemen to enter Tilsit. At that moment more than ever I felt the innkeeper of Lübeck was right. A bird escaped from its cage, or coming out from under a vacuum bell would be less joyous. I can speak, I can write what I think, I am free! The first real letter I sent to Paris left from this frontier. It will produce a sensation in my small circle of friends who, up to now, without doubt have been the dupes of my official correspondence. Here is a copy of this letter: [See next chapter. Ed.]

THE RUSSIAN MIND CANNOT
ACHIEVE REAL ORDER

Tilsit, September 26, 1839

FINALLY I breathe! . . . I can write to you without the oratorical precautions demanded by the police: precautions nearly always insufficient, for there is as much touchiness of self-esteem as political caution in the espionage of the Russians. Russia is the dreariest land on earth inhabited by the handsomest men I have ever seen; a land where one is scarcely aware of the women cannot be gay.

At last, here I am outside and without the slightest accident! I have just covered two hundred and fifty leagues in four days, by roads often abominable, often magnificent, for the Russian mind—friendly as it is to uniformity—cannot achieve real order; the characteristics of this administration are: meddling, negligence, and corruption. One is revolted by the idea of becoming accustomed to all that but, nevertheless, one does become accustomed to it. A sincere man in that country would pass for mad.

A WORLD PRACTICALLY
UNKNOWN TO FOREIGNERS

Ems, October 22, 1839

HAVING LEFT Ems for Russia five months ago, I
return to this fashionable resort after a tour of
some thousands of leagues. The spa was distaste-
ful to me in the spring because of the inevitable
crowd of bathers and imbibers; at present, I find
it delightful as I am literally alone here, enjoying
the approach of a beautiful autumn, in the center
of mountains whose sadness I like, while collect-
ing my memoirs and seeking the rest which I need
after the rapid journey I have just made.

I have been to Russia; I wanted to see a country where the calmness of a power assured of its
strength reigns; but when I got there, I realized
that only silence and fear reign, and I drew a lesson from this spectacle entirely different from the
one I had come to ask from it. This is a world
practically unknown to foreigners: the Russians
who travel to escape it pay tribute to the fatherland from afar in artful praises; and most of the
travelers who have described it to us wished to
find there only what they went to look for. If one
defends his preconceptions against evidence,
what is the good of traveling? When one has decided to see nations as one wishes to see them,
then he has no need to leave his own country.

Ems, October 22, 1839

I am sending you the resumé of my journey, written since my return to Ems. You were present in my thoughts while I was doing this work; surely then it is permissible to address it to you.

RESUME OF THE JOURNEY

In RUSSIA, everything that meets your eye, everything that goes on around you is of a frightening regularity, and the first thought that comes to the mind of a traveler when he contemplates this symmetry is that such complete uniformity, such regularity, so contrary to the natural inclinations of man, could not have been achieved and cannot subsist without violence. Under such a régime man can know, and does know, from the first day of his life what he will see and what he will do to the last day of his life.

In Russia, the government dominates everything and gives life to nothing. In this vast Empire, the people, if they are not tranquil, are silent; death hovers over all heads and strikes them capriciously—this serves to create doubt of the supreme justice; there man has two coffins—the cradle and the tomb.

I do not believe suicide is common in Russia; there, man suffers too much to kill himself. What a strange creature is man! When terror dominates his life he does not seek death; he already knows what death is.

Furthermore, the number of men who kill themselves could be great in Russia without anyone knowing it; the knowledge of figures is a privilege of the Russian Police; I do not know whether exact figures reach the Czar himself; but

352

I know that no disaster is published under his reign without his having consented to this humiliating avowal of the superiority of Providence. The conceit of despotism is so great that it rivals the power of God. . . . A man with unlimited power can only be a crowned lie.

You understand that it is not with the Emperor Nicholas that I am concerned at the moment, but with the Emperor of Russia. One hears much of the customs that limit his power; I have been struck by the abuse and have seen nothing of the remedy.

I agree with true statesmen and practical minds for whom laws are less important than our rigorous logicians, our political philosophers believe them to be; for, in the last analysis, it is the manner in which laws are applied that decides the life of peoples. Yes, but the life of the Russian people is sadder than that of any other people of Europe; and when I say people, I am not speaking only of the peasants attached to the yoke, I am speaking of all those who make up the Empire.

A so-called strong government which pitilessly demands respect on all occasions must necessarily produce wretched men. Everything in a social order can serve the purposes of despotism, whether that social order be called a monarchy or a democracy. Wherever the operation of the political machine is rigorously exact, there is despotism.

In this country, different from all others, Nature herself has become the accomplice of the caprices of the man who has killed liberty in or-

353

der to deify unity. Nature too is everywhere the same: two types of trees, blighted and thinly scattered farther than the eye can reach in the boggy or sandy plains—the birch and the pine—make up the entire natural vegetation of northern Russia, that is to say, in the vicinity of Petersburg and the surrounding provinces which include a vast expanse of territory.

Where can one find refuge from the disadvantages of the social order in a climate where the open country can be enjoyed only three months out of the year? And what country! Add to this that for six months, the most rigorous of the winter, one dares to breathe the outdoor air only a couple of hours during the day, unless one is a Russian peasant. That is what God has created for man in these regions.

Now let us see what man has created for himself: without question one of the wonders of the world—St. Petersburg; Moscow is also a very picturesque city, but what can be said for the provinces?

The absence of soul betrays itself in everything: at every turn you feel that you are in the land of a people deprived of independence. From twenty to thirty leagues on all the roads only a single city awaits you; this is everywhere the same. Tyranny invents only the means of consolidating itself. The regiment and its circumscribed mind is the mold of this society.

Wavering for four centuries between Europe and Asia, Russia has not yet succeeded through its own efforts in making its mark in the history

354

of the human spirit because its national character has been effaced by borrowings.

Separated from the Occident by its adhesion to the Greek schism, Russia has come back after many centuries, with the inconsistency of a disillusioned self-esteem, to ask from the nations formed by Catholicism the civilization that she has been deprived of by an entirely political religion. This Byzantine religion, issued from a palace to help maintain order in a camp, does not satisfy the most sublime needs of the human soul; it helps the police deceive the nation—that is all. It has made these people unworthy of the degree of culture to which they aspire.

The independence of the Church is necessary to the flow of religious sap; for the development of the most noble faculty of peoples—the faculty to believe—depends on the dignity of the priesthood. The man charged with communicating divine revelations to man must enjoy a liberty unknown to any priest who has revolted against his spiritual chief. Thus the humiliation of the ministers of the cult is the first penalty of heresy; that is why one sees the priests despised by the people in all schismatic lands, in spite of the protection of the kings, or more accurately, because of this protection, which places them in dependence on the prince, even with respect to their divine mission.

In the depths of their hearts, peoples who understand liberty will never obey a dependent clergy.

While in the Occident the descendants of the

355

barbarians studied the ancients with an almost idolatrous veneration, they modified them in order to convert them to their own use. Who can recognize Virgil in Dante, Homer in Tasso, Justinian and the Roman laws in the codes of feudalism? Imitation of masters, entirely ignorant of modern ways, could polish minds in forming the language; it could not reduce them to servile reproduction. The impassioned respect that they professed for the past, far from stifling their genius, awakened it; but it is not thus that the Russians have used us.

Russia alone, belatedly civilized, has been deprived of a profound fermentation and of the benefit of a slow and natural cultural development, because of the impatience of her leaders. Russia has missed the ground work which forms great peoples and prepares a nation to prevail over, that is to say to enlighten, others.

The Russian nation will forever feel this absence of a proper course of life from which she was suffering at the time of her political awakening. Adolescence, that laborious age when the spirit of man assumes entire responsibility for his independence, has been lost to Russia. Her princes, and especially Peter the Great, counting time for nothing, made her pass violently from infancy to virility. Barely free of her foreign yoke, she thought everything that was not Mongolian domination was freedom; it was thus that in the joy of her inexperience she accepted servitude itself as a deliverance, because it was imposed on her by her legitimate sovereigns. This people, de-

356

based under conquest, felt happy enough, independent enough provided its tyrant was called by a Russian instead of a Tartar name.

The effect of such an illusion still endures; originality of spirit has flown from this soil whose children, broken to slavery, have, to this day, taken seriously only terror and ambition.

Many eras of memories are needed for the formation of a civilized people. . . .

Formerly, a certain refinement of taste characterized the Russians of the South, and, thanks to the relations maintained by the rulers of Kiev with Constantinople from ancient times and during the most barbaric centuries, the love of the arts reigned in this part of the Slav Empire. At the same time, the traditions of the Orient had preserved there the feeling of grandeur and had perpetuated a certain dexterity among the artists and the workers. But these advantages, fruits of former relations with peoples advanced in a civilization inherited from antiquity, were lost after the Mongolian invasion.

This crisis forced primitive Russia to forget its history: slavery produces degradation that excludes courtesy; courtesy has nothing of the servile since it is the expression of the highest and most delicate feelings. It is only when courtesy becomes a sort of currency with an entire people that one can say that this people is civilized; then the original crudeness, the brutal selfishness of human nature are effaced by the lessons each individual receives in his family from the time he is in the cradle. No matter where he is born, the human child is not merciful, and if, from the beginning of his life, he is not turned away from his cruel instincts he will never be really courteous. Courtesy is only the code of pity applied to the daily relations of society; this code teaches, above all, pity for the sufferings of self-esteem; also, it is the most universal, the most applicable, and the most practical remedy that has been found up to now for egoism.

Say what one will, all these refinements—the natural result of the work of time—are unknown to present-day Russians who remember Sarai [capital of the ruler of the Golden Horde, in Russia in the 13th century] much better than Byzantium and who, with few exceptions, are still only dressed up barbarians.

Peter the Great, with all the imprudence of uncultivated genius, with all the temerity of a man who is the more impatient because he is considered omnipotent, with the perseverance of a character of iron, set out to snatch quickly from Europe the fruits of a ready-made civilization instead of resigning himself to slowly cultivating the seed in his own land. This too much vaunted man has produced only an artificial work; it was astonishing; but the good that this barbarian genius did was passing, the evil is irreparable.

It would be necessary to stop and start over. Is such an effort possible? Can one take away the underpinnings of such a vast edifice? The too recent civilization of the Russian Empire, entirely artificial as it is, has already produced some real results that no human power would be able to annul. To me it seems impossible to direct the future of a people while counting the present for nothing. But the present, violently separated from the past, promises only misfortune. To avoid these misfortunes in Russia by forcing her to take into account her ancient history—which was simply the result of her primitive character—such will henceforth be the thankless task, more useful than brilliant, of the men called upon to govern this country.

Peter I and Catherine II have given the world a great and useful lesson, for which Russia has paid. They have shown us that despotism is never so redoubtable as when it pretends to do good; for then it believes its most revolting deeds are exculpated by its professed intentions and the evil that is given as a remedy has no bounds. Crime in the open triumphs for only a day; but false virtues lead the spirits of nations astray forever. Peoples, dazzled by the brilliant accessories of crime, by the grandeur of certain crimes that emergency has justified, believe in the end that there are two infamies and two morals, and that necessity—reason of State, as one formerly said —exonerates criminals of high birth provided they have been able to put their excesses in tune with the passions of the country.

Avowed tyranny frightens me little compared to oppression disguised as love for order. The strength of despotism is solely in the mask of the despot. Let the sovereign be constrained to lie no longer and the people is free; therefore, I have acknowledged no evil in this world other than falsehood. If you fear only violent and avowed arbitrariness, go to Russia and you will learn to dread, above all, hypocritical tyranny.

I cannot deny it; I bring back from my journey ideas which were not mine when I undertook it. Likewise, I would not exchange for anything in the world the pain that the experience has caused me. If I publish an account of my journey, it will be precisely because it has altered my opinions on several points. My opinions were known to all those who will read my account, but my disappointment is not; consequently, it is my duty to publish it.

I have been sustained in my resolution by an ever increasing disenchantment. Certainly, the cause of my disappointment had to be active and profound for disgust to overtake me in the midst of the most brilliant fêtes I have ever seen and in spite of the dazzling hospitality of the Russians. But I recognized, from the first glance, that in these demonstrations of interest that they lavish upon you there is more desire to seem obliging than there is to be genuinely cordial. . . . They occupy your every minute, they entertain you, they absorb you, they tyrannize you with attention, they ask how you spend your days, they question you with an insistence that belongs only to them, and with fête after fête they prevent your seeing their country. They have coined a phrase —"to engarland foreigners"—to express the result of this tactic they call obliging. Unfortunately, these assiduous attentions fell on a man who is always less amused than fatigued by fêtes.

360

But when they come to realize their direct approach has failed to produce the desired effect on the mind of the foreigner, they have recourse to roundabout means of discrediting his statements in the estimation of enlightened readers: they abuse him with a marvelous dexterity. Thus, in order to show him things under a false light, they lie about the bad as they had lied about the good as long as they believed they could count on a benevolent credulity. Often, in the same conversation, I have caught a person changing his tactics with regard to me two or three times. I do not flatter myself that I have always been able to discern the truth in spite of the artful efforts of people whose profession is disguising the truth; but it is already a great deal to know that one is being deceived; if I do not see the truth, I see that it is being hidden from me; and if I am not enlightened, at least I am armed.

When I was preparing to leave Petersburg, a Russian asked me, like all the Russians, what I would say about his country. "I have been too well received here to talk about it," I replied to him. Weapons to be used against me are made from this approbation in which I thought I had barely politely concealed an epigram. "Treated as you have been," they write me, "certainly, you cannot tell the truth; so, as you are capable of writing only the truth, you would do better to remain silent." Such is the opinion of a group of persons I am accustomed to heed. In any case, this opinion is not flattering to the Russians.

It is said that only the truth is shocking; this is

possible, but, in France at least, no one has the right or the power to silence one who has spoken the truth. My cries of indignation cannot be taken for the disguised expression of wounded vanity. If I had listened only to my amour-propre, it would have told me to be enchanted with everything: my heart was satisfied with nothing.

I have been allowed to penetrate into a prison; I have understood the silence of the terrified victims. And should I fear to reveal their martyrdom lest I be accused of ingratitude for the complaisance of the jailers in doing me the honors of the cell? Such caution would be far from a virtue. Therefore, I tell you explicitly that—after looking around carefully to see what was being concealed from me, listening attentively to hear what they did not wish to tell me, trying assiduously to evaluate the false in what was said to me—I do not believe I exaggerate when I assure you that the Russian Empire is the country where people are the most unhappy—because they suffer, simultaneously, the disadvantages of barbarism and the disadvantages of civilization.

The Russians, with their continual surveillance of themselves, seem to me the most pitiable people on earth. But, what is the purpose of all this trickery? What motive can we assign that would warrant so much pretense? What obligation, what recompense can make the faces of men support the fatigue of the mask for such a long time?

Would the play of so many batteries be destined only to defend a real and legitimate power?

362

Such a power has no need of them—truth defends itself. Do they wish to protect the miserable interest of vanity? Perhaps. However, to take so much trouble to achieve such a paltry result would be unworthy of the serious men who undertake this task. I attribute to them a more profound idea; a greater goal looms before me and explains to me their miracles of dissimulation and long-suffering.

An inordinate, a boundless ambition, the kind of ambition that can take root only in the soul of an oppressed people and be nourished only on the misery of an entire nation is astir in the hearts of the Russians. This essentially aggressive nation, greedy from want, lives in a state of submissiveness so degrading that it seems to be expiating in advance its hope of exercising tyranny over others. The anticipated glory and riches divert its thoughts from the shame it suffers. To cleanse himself of his impious sacrifice of all public and personal liberty, the kneeling slave dreams of world domination.

It is not the man they worship in Czar Nicholas, it is the ambitious ruler of a nation even more ambitious than he. The passions of the Russians are cut on the pattern of those of ancient peoples; everything in them recalls the Old Testament; their hopes, their tortures are great, like their Empire.

There, nothing has limits, neither sorrows nor rewards, neither sacrifices, nor hopes: their power can become enormous, but they will have bought it at the price Asiatic nations pay for the stability of their governments—the price of happiness.

Russia sees Europe as a prey which our dissensions will sooner or later deliver up to her; she foments anarchy among us in the hope of profiting by a corruption she promotes because it is favorable to her views. It is the history of Poland recommencing on a larger scale. For many years Paris read revolutionary papers, revolutionary in every sense, paid for by Russia. "Europe," they say in Petersburg, "is taking the line that Poland followed; she is enervating herself through vain liberalism while we remain powerful precisely because we are not free; let us be patient under the yoke, we will make others pay for our shame."

The plan that I reveal to you here may seem fantastic to heedless eyes; it will be recognized as true by any man who is familiar with the progress of European affairs and with cabinet secrets during the last twenty years.

Do you understand now the importance of an opinion, of a sarcastic phrase, of a letter, of a mockery, of a smile and, for even more reason, of a book in the eyes of this government facilitated by the credulity of its people and the complaisance of all foreigners? One word of truth hurled into Russia is like a spark landing in a keg of powder.

What does poverty, the pallor of the Emperor's soldiers, matter to the men who govern Russia? These living ghosts have the most beautiful uniforms in Europe; of what importance are the sackcloth smocks under which these gilded phantoms hide themselves inside their quarters? Provided they are poor and dirty only in secret and shine when they are on display, one asks nothing from them and gives them nothing. A draped misery—such is the wealth of the Russians; for them appearance is everything and appearance among them is more deceptive than among other peoples. Thus, whoever lifts a corner of the veil has forever ruined his reputation in Petersburg.

In Russia, whoever is not a dupe is considered a traitor. There, to laugh at bragging, to refute a lie, to contradict an expedient boast, *to justify obedience,* is an attempt against the security of the State and of the prince; it is to incur the fate of a revolutionary, of a conspirator, of an enemy of the established order, of a criminal guilty of high treason . . . of a Pole, and you know how cruel that fate is! It must be admitted that *a sensitivity* which manifests itself in such a manner is more dreadful than laughable—the minute supervision of such a government in harmony with the open vanity of such a people becomes frightful; it is no longer ridiculous.

One can and one must force oneself to every kind of precaution under a master who gives grace to no enemy, who does not overlook the slightest resistance, and who, therefore, considers vengeance a duty. This man, or rather this government personified, would take pardon for apostasy, clemency for self-neglect, humanity for lack of respect toward his majesty . . . what am I saying, toward his divinity! He is not a master to give up having himself worshiped.

Russian civilization is still so close to its source

that it resembles barbarism. Russia is no more than a conquering society; its strength is not in ideas, it is in war—that is to say, in ruse and in ferocity.

Consider, I beg you, that if the Russians succeeded in dominating the Occident, they would not govern it from their homeland in the manner of the ancient Mongolians: quite the contrary, they would hasten to leave their frozen plains and, without imitating their ancient masters the Tartars who oppressed their Slav subjects from a distance (the climate of Muscovy frightened even the Mongolians), the Muscovites would leave their country in droves the moment the roads to other lands were open to them.

Now they talk of moderation; they protest against the conquest of Constantinople, they fear, they say, anything that can enlarge an Empire where the distances are already a calamity; they dread even . . . judge the extent to which their caution goes! . . . they dread hot climates! Wait a bit and you will see what all these fears will end in.

And I should not point out so many lies, so many dangers, so many scourges? No, no, I would rather be mistaken and speak out than to have judged correctly and remain silent. If there is temerity in revealing what I have observed, it would be a crime to hide it.

To all that, the Russians will not give me an answer. They will only say: "Three months of travel, he has seen little."

Resumé of the Journey

It is true I saw little, but I sensed a great deal.

Or, if they do me the honor to refute me, they will deny the facts; the facts—the raw material of every report—which are usually counted for nothing in Petersburg where the past, the future, and the present are at the disposition of the master; for, again I repeat, the Russians themselves have nothing of their own but obedience and imitation; the direction of their minds, their judgment, their free will belongs to the sovereign. In Russia history forms part of the domain of the crown; it is the moral property of the prince, just as the people and the land are his material property; it is kept in the storeroom along with the imperial treasures and only that part of it which the ruler wishes to make known is displayed. The memory of what happened yesterday is the property of the Czar; he alters the annals of the country according to his own good pleasure and dispenses, each day, to his people the historic truths which accord with the fiction of the moment. Thus, Minin and Pojarski, heroes forgotten for two centuries, were exhumed all of a sudden and became fashionable at the time of Napoleon's invasion, for at that moment the government permitted patriotic fervor.

Yet, this exorbitant power is hurting itself; Russia will not submit to it forever: a spirit of revolt smolders in the army. I say like the Emperor Russians have traveled too much; the nation has become eager for enlightenment. The Customs has no power over thought; armies cannot extermi-

367

nate it; ramparts cannot stop it; it goes underground; ideas are in the air; they are everywhere, and ideas change the world.

The result of all the preceding is that the future, that brilliant future dreamed of by the Russians, does not depend on them. . . . If passions calm themselves in the West, if unity is established between governments and subjects, the avid hope of the conquering Slavs will become an idle fancy. Therein lies the danger of allowing them to interfere in our policy and in the counsels of our neighbors.

As a foreigner, especially as a foreign writer, I have been overwhelmed with protestations of courtesy by the Russians, but their kindness is limited to promises; no one has given me the facility for really looking into conditions. A crowd of mysteries remained impenetrable.

A year passed in Russia would have furthered my purpose little; the more the inhabitants assured me that one suffers little from the discomforts of the winter, the more I dreaded those discomforts. Furthermore, in this Empire of deep silence, of great empty spaces, of barren fields, of solitary cities, of cautious countenances whose lack of sincerity makes society itself seem empty, sadness overtook me: I fled before spleen as much as before cold. Needless to say, whoever wishes to spend the winter in Petersburg must resign himself to forgetting nature for six months to live imprisoned among men who have nothing of the natural.

I openly admit I have spent a terrible summer

in Russia because I succeeded in understanding only a very small part of what I saw. I had hoped to arrive at solutions; I bring you problems instead.

There is one mystery that I especially regret not having been able to fathom, that is the lack of influence of religion in Russia. In spite of the political enslavement of the Orthodox Church, should it not at least be able to conserve some of its moral authority over peoples? It has none! From what does the nullity of a church that everything appears to favor arise? That is the problem. Is it characteristic of the Orthodox religion to remain thus stationary while contenting itself with the exterior marks of respect? Is such a result inevitable everywhere that spiritual power falls into the absolute dependence of temporal power: I believe this is the case, but it is something I should have liked to be able to prove by dint of documents and factual data. Nevertheless, I shall sum up in a few words the result of the observations I have made on the relations of the Russian clergy with the faithful.

In Russia, I saw one Christian church, which no one attacks, everyone respects at least in appearance—a church that everything favors in the exercise of its spiritual authority; yet, this church has no power over hearts; it can only make hypocrites or superstitious beings.

In countries where religion is not respected, it is not responsible, but here, where all the prestige of an absolute power aids the priest in the accomplishment of his duties, where the doctrine is attacked neither by the written nor by the spoken word, where religious practices are, so to speak, imposed by the law of the State, where customs serve faith as they oppose it in France, one has the right to reproach the church for its sterility. This church is dead. However, to judge from what is happening in Poland, it can become a persecutor, whereas it has neither enough spiritual virtues nor enough great talents to conquer through the mind. In a word the Russian Church lacks the same thing that is lacking in everything in that country: liberty, without which the spirit of life disappears and the light goes out.

Western Europe is not aware of all the religious intolerance that enters into Russian policy. The cult of the reunited Greeks has just been abolished following long and secret persecutions: does Catholic Europe know that there are no more Uniates [Christians of an Eastern rite acknowledging the Pope's primacy] in Russia? Does it know even, dazzled as it is by the lights of its own philosophy, what the Uniates are?

Here is an incident which will show you the danger one runs in Russia in saying what he thinks of the Greek religion and its lack of moral influence.

Some years ago a man of parts, respected by everyone in Moscow, noble of birth and of character, but, unfortunately for him, devoured by love of truth—a dangerous passion anywhere but fatal in that country—dared to state that the Catholic religion is more conducive to the development of minds, to the progress of the arts than the

Byzantine-Russian religion; thus he thought as I do and dared to express himself—an unpardonable crime for a Russian. The life of the Catholic priest, he said in his book, a life entirely spiritual —or at least it should be—is a voluntary and daily sacrifice of the vulgar tendencies of human nature. This is the proof in action, incessantly renewed in the eyes of the incredulous world, of the superiority of mind over matter—a sacrifice endlessly renewed on the altar of faith to prove to impious eyes that man is not entirely subjected to physical force, and that he can receive from a superior power the means of escaping the laws of the material world. Then he adds: "Thanks to the reforms effected by time, the Catholic religion can no longer use its virility except to do good." In short, he maintained that the Slav race had need of Catholicism to achieve its great destiny because in this religion are found, at the same time, sustained enthusiasm, endlessly renewed devotion, perfect charity, and pure discernment. He supported his opinion with a large number of proofs and forced himself to show the advantages of an independent religion, that is to say a universal religion, over local religions—religions limited by policy; in brief, he professed a belief that I have never ceased to defend with all my strength.

This book, which escaped the attention of the censors—I do not know by what miracle or by what subterfuge—set Russia on fire. Petersburg and holy Moscow cried out with rage and alarm; at last the conscience of the faithful was so disturbed that from one end of the Empire to the

371

other punishment for this imprudent advocate of
the Mother of Christian Churches was demanded;
in the end there was not enough knout, not enough
Siberia, not enough galleys, not enough mines, not
enough fortresses, not enough solitudes in all the
Russias to reassure Moscow and its Byzantine
Orthodoxy against the ambition of Rome served
by the impious doctrine of this man, traitor to God
and to his country!

The sentence which would decide the fate of
such a great criminal was awaited with anxiety;
this sentence was slow in coming and people had
already despaired of the supreme penalty when
the Emperor, in his merciful impassiveness, declared that there was no basis for punishment, that
the man was not a criminal to be punished but a
madman to be locked up: he added that *the sick
man would be turned over to the care of doctors.*

This new form of torture was applied without
delay and in a fashion so severe that the supposed
fool was near justifying the derisory sentence of
the absolute chief of the Church and of the State.
This martyr of the truth was on the verge of losing the sanity which was denied him by a decision
from on high. Today, *at the end of three years*
of a treatment rigorously observed, a treatment as
degrading as it was cruel, the unfortunate theolo-
gian of broad horizons, only begins to enjoy a
little liberty. But is this not a miracle! . . . now
he doubts his own sanity and, on the faith of the
imperial word, he declares himself insane.

This is a very recent example of the way affairs

372

of conscience are treated in Russia today. I ask you one last time, has the traveler, fortunate or unfortunate enough to have collected such data, the right to allow it to remain unknown? In this kind of thing what you know positively throws light on what you suppose; and out of all this comes a conviction which you are obligated to share with the world if you can.

I have spoken without personal animosity but also without fear or restriction; for I have braved even the danger of boring my listeners.

It is necessary to have lived in this solitude without rest, in this prison without leisure, that is called Russia in order to be conscious of all the freedom one enjoys in the other countries of Europe, whatever form of government they may have adopted.

When your son is discontented in France, use my formula; say to him: "Go to Russia." It is a journey that would be beneficial to every foreigner; for whoever has really seen Russia will find himself content to live anywhere else. It is always good to know that a society exists where no happiness is possible because, by a law of his nature, man cannot be happy unless he is free. . . .